Captured at Arnhem

Captured at Arnhem

From Railwayman to Paratrooper

Norman Hicks

Pen & Sword
MILITARY

First published in Great Britain in 2013 by
Pen & Sword Military
an imprint of
Pen & Sword Books Ltd
47 Church Street
Barnsley
South Yorkshire S70 2AS

Copyright © Norman Hicks 2013

ISBN 978 1 78303 033 0

Typeset in Ehrhardt by
Mac Style, Driffield, East Yorkshire
Printed and bound in the UK by CPI Group (UK) Ltd, Croydon,
CRO 4YY

Pen & Sword Books Ltd incorporates the imprints of Pen & Sword
Archaeology, Atlas, Aviation, Battleground, Discovery, Family
History, History, Maritime, Military, Naval, Politics, Railways,
Select, Social History, Transport, True Crime, and Claymore Press,
Frontline Books, Leo Cooper, Praetorian Press, Remember When,
Seaforth Publishing and Wharncliffe.

For a complete list of Pen & Sword titles please contact
PEN & SWORD BOOKS LIMITED
47 Church Street, Barnsley, South Yorkshire, S70 2AS, England
E-mail: enquiries@pen-and-sword.co.uk
Website: www.pen-and-sword.co.uk

Contents

Preface

This book details my father's life from his earliest years to the end of steam at Royston Motive Power Depot in 1967. Sandwiched in between his work on the railway and consuming the bulk of this story are his experiences during the Second World War.

Tom Hicks started work on the London, Midland and Scottish Railway (LMS) as a calling up lad in 1934 and progressed through the grades to become a steam-engine driver. His work on the LMS was interrupted by military service during the war years of 1939–45 and was not resumed again until he was demobilised in 1946, from when he 'soldiered' on until retirement in 1982.

Tom's life as a soldier began in 1939 with his enlistment into the Royal Engineers (RE) and subsequent service on the Longmoor Military Railway until 1942. From Longmoor he was accepted as a volunteer into the newly formed 1st Parachute Squadron RE, a small 150-man unit attached to the 1st Parachute Brigade within which he served until 1945.

This story follows Tom's selection for parachute training, beginning with the rough and tumble of the airborne forces depot, followed by more rigorous pursuits as his training as a parachute soldier began in earnest. His war service is told as it was, simply and with humour and endurance that he maintained when the real soldiering began in North Africa, through the invasion of Sicily, the Battle of Arnhem and seven months as a prisoner of war in Germany, most of which was spent working underground in a lead mine.

Liberated by the Americans in April 1945, Tom was repatriated to Britain and returned to Longmoor to await demobilisation in 1946. After this he rejoined the LMS and Royston engine shed, where he worked as a driver until the end of steam in 1967. This is where the memoir ends, although he continued as a driver of diesel locomotives at Healey Mills until his retirement in 1982.

The wartime element of the book is based on numerous recollections and these have been placed in chronological order by referring to the historical accounts of the day and a wartime diary written by Tom during his time as a POW. Throughout these recollections humour is always to the fore, but there is also fortitude and pride. What cannot be doubted is that my father mostly enjoyed his railway and military life and hopefully this is conveyed through this book.

The book is not intended to be a military history, although factual details have been included to give context to the experiences described. Explanations of words and events within the text are given to provide the reader with more detail, particularly for those who may not be familiar with the times and terminology. A selection of contemporary photographs is also included to give a visual flavour of the era.

In the account of the war years military strengths and casualty figures are mentioned, and these figures have been taken from a number of wartime histories. Sometimes the numbers vary between sources and I would therefore use the term 'as far as can be ascertained' in relation to them, but I have included them in order to give a fuller impression of the events described.

Norman Hicks
April 2013

Acknowledgements

We would like to acknowledge the assistance of Peter Stainforth's *Wings of the Wind* (1952) in placing the relevant dates and the movement of the 1st Parachute Squadron RE in North Africa during 1942–3. Written in 1949 and published in 1952, this sensitive account provided us with many of the relevant dates and the atmosphere of those times. It was particularly helpful as an aide-memoire in structuring the questions put to Tom.

In 2004 an article featuring Tom's story was previously published in the *Yorkshire Post Magazine* as part of the sixtieth anniversary of the Battle of Arnhem commemoration. Extracts from the *Yorkshire Post Magazine* are used courtesy of Yorkshire Post Newspapers Ltd.

List of Abbreviations

BEF	British Expeditionary Force
CO	Commanding Officer
CSM	Company Sergeant Major
DZ	Drop Zone
LMS	London, Midland and Scottish Railway
LZ	Landing Zone
NAAFI	Navy Army Air Force Institute
PTI	Physical Training Instructor
RASC	Royal Army Service Corps
RE	Royal Engineers
RSM	Regimental Sergeant Major
RTU	Return to Unit
RV	Rendezvous
SNCO	Senior Non Commissioned Officer
USAAF	United States Army Air Force

Part One

Life on the Railway

Chapter 1

A Railway Family, Royston, 1932–9

My family arrived in Royston in 1932 from Stockingford on the outskirts of Nuneaton where my father was the running foreman at the LMS engine shed. Stockingford was a small country shed of only three roads, and it was so quiet that the engine crews were able to find time to tend an adjacent allotment between turns. We had only been in Stockingford for three years when it was announced that the shed was scheduled for closure, and my father was given the choice of moving to Coalville at Leicester or to the new shed at Royston in south Yorkshire.

We were a railway family which had its base in Widnes; here, before moving to Stockingford, my father had been a driver and then deputy foreman at Tanhouse Lane Engine Shed. At Widnes we lived at Ditton where my mother was the tenant licensee of the small Railway Arms pub, a situation that came about because my father was not allowed to own a business while working for the LMS. Sandwiched between terraced houses, the pub nestled up to the embankment of the main line to Liverpool. We were so close to the track that every passing train shook the windows and rattled the knobs on the brass bed that I shared with my younger brother Bob, momentarily drowning out the murmur of the drinkers downstairs.

My father's brothers were also engine drivers and both Bob and I were named after two of them. My namesake Uncle Tom was later killed by a train while walking through New Mills Tunnel on his way home to Gorton, and his funeral was held on the day that King Edward VIII abdicated in 1936.

After leaving Ditton our stay at Stockingford passed all too quickly and my memories are now dimmed by the passage of time. I recall that we lived in a terraced house at 5 Webb Street, where the most distinguishing feature of the street was a recreation ground at the bottom with swings that could be used free of charge, a facility that was unheard of in Ditton. The houses in Webb Street had pig sties at the bottom of the gardens and many of our neighbours kept pigs, although we didn't as my dad was on a good wage and so the sty became a place where we played.

Winter days were spent leaning against the wall at the end of the street where heat radiated through from a baker's oven on the other side, and summers were spent roaming freely if surreptitiously in the private wooded grounds of nearby Arbury Park.

Dad's new position at Royston shed was to be one of the two running foreman who were responsible to the shed superintendent, or shed-master. The running foremen were usually ex- engine drivers but the superintendent was more often than not from a LMS-sponsored college that produced its managers, and its graduates were known to us as premium men.

Not only was Royston a newly built engine shed but it was supported by a brand-new estate of 120 houses. Built on a broad street with front and rear gardens, it had a tree-lined square on which stood a hand-operated fire cart. The cart was manned by an on-call fire team of six volunteer railwaymen. The houses were spacious and equipped with the luxury of both an indoor, upstairs toilet and bathroom. The houses on the estate were financed and built to the specification of the LMS.

The new estate was named East End Crescent, reflecting its position as the last development on the east side of Royston. The houses were so modern that the local mining families would walk along the broad street to admire them in the evenings. The Crescent housed the influx of railwaymen that were required to staff the busy new shed, fulfilling the roles of the drivers and fireman, fitters, boiler-smiths, guards, signalmen, labourers, clerks and foremen.

East of the Crescent ran the busy four-track Midland main line which separated the new houses from the engine shed and its yard, while to the north Monckton colliery sat smoking on a hill among its chimneys and coke ovens, sending out gaseous flares as it looked down on the village and Royston's railway workings.

To reach the shed we had only to cross the road and turn left at Pools (Dalby's) farm followed by a short walk down the lane and under the bridge that carried the main line, with a journey time of a little over 10 minutes.

Chapter 2

Calling Up Lad – 'Knocker Up', November 1934

On our arrival in Royston we were forced into temporary digs on Midland Road until our furniture and possessions were found, as the container in which they were being carried had somehow got lost in transit! However, after a couple of weeks our belongings eventually turned up and were unloaded at the goods shed behind Royston station, from where they were duly carted round to the top end of East End Crescent for us to begin our new life at no. 92.

Once settled, I started attending the Catholic school in the nearby village of Cudworth ('Cudduth'). Each day I travelled to and from school by bus with other Catholic children, unless of course I was playing sport or detained and then I had to walk the 3 miles back across the fields to Royston. I left school in 1933 at the age of 14 and remember my first joyous feeling of liberation as I ran down the school steps for the last time, for my schooldays to me were a period of stuffy and austere confinement.

My first job was as a grocery delivery boy which entailed pedalling around the village with a heavy bike and basket. Then in November 1934, at the age of 15, I joined the LMS Railway. Starting at the bottom, my role on the railway had the grand title of calling up lad, or 'knocker up' as the job was known within the environs of the shed. The knocker up's responsibility was to call at the homes of the various train crews to wake them up prior to their shifts during the night.

I was one of the two knocker ups that were employed on a permanent basis working six nights a week. Knocker ups only worked in the hours of darkness as the day-shift crews bore their own responsibility for arriving at work on time. As I was 15 I had to work for two years in this job before I became eligible for promotion to the next grade, engine cleaner.

The minimum age that one could start work on the railway was 15 and my father being a foreman probably influenced my application. However, that was as far as the nepotism went, and from the start I was allotted more than my fair share of difficult and dirty jobs to dispel any notion of favouritism.

The foremen were respected figures around the shed and they dressed accordingly. The working attire of my father as an LMS foreman was that of a bowler hat, pinstriped trousers and a collar (white) and tie, which my mother must have found difficult to get clean.

My knocking up shift started at 2300hr and ran through the night until 0700hr the following morning. The job entailed visiting the houses of engine crews and sometimes a guard an hour before they were due to sign on for their shift during the night. On arrival at a house I would knock with a measured thump on the outside wall with a steel cotter pin, and I was not allowed to leave until the wake-up call was acknowledged. This took the form of a muffled shout through the curtains, and I would then deliver my message with a hefty adolescent bellow of, for example, 'Brown 0515 for Toton', stating the time and the job. I would then meticulously record the call in my book.

We had some awkward customers on some of these calls, who would on occasion report that they had not been knocked when in fact they had just gone back to sleep. These chaps were usually the ones who were partial to a night at the pub. When we had one of these disputed calls we were allowed to take a second man from the shed to act as a witness on their next call. This was routine procedure and acted as a stimulant for the suspected intoxicant to get out of bed. The engines still went out, though, even if a driver did not show, as Royston was a busy shed and there were always relief men on hand to cover most situations.

The duties of the two knocker ups were shared between home and away rounds. The home round was on East End Crescent and the away round was to houses as far as 1½ miles distant. The outlying round required a cycle which we had to provide for ourselves, while the home route was covered on foot. We sometimes had to knock three men to crew a train, the driver, his fireman and a guard. On many occasions one would live at the top of the street and the other ½ mile away at the bottom, both requiring the knock an hour before their shift was due to start. We couldn't be in two places at the same time and therefore one was bound to be called early or late, and some of these men would report us for not knocking on the dot. I was an exceptionally diligent knocker and wouldn't stop banging on the wall until my call was acknowledged, which often would come as an indignant 'orl rate … orl rate' and a positive shaking of the curtains.

We were out on our rounds in all weathers, on pitch-dark nights, in rain, snow, frosts and dense fog. Sometimes it was so windy or iced over that I had to hang onto fences to keep myself upright. On the away round we had to negotiate narrow muddy lanes and stiles with the only illumination provided by a weak carbide lamp and I was frequently pitched off.

My dad worked six-day shifts per week which alternated with that of the other shed running foreman, while the shed superintendent worked regular days. Dad's hours were on a two-week rota, afternoons from 1400hr to 2200hr one week followed by a week of nights starting at 2200hr until 0600hr. When he was working nights I used to go to work an hour earlier than my 2300hr start so that my mother could settle down and go to bed. We used to walk together side by side down Pools Lane and under the bridge to the shed with me pushing my bike, a steady but dark 10-minute journey.

After completing my two years as a knocker and having reached the age of 17, I gained my first promotion to that of an engine cleaner. I was to spend a year in this job before being allowed to ascend to the footplate on firing turns as a passed cleaner at 18, the minimum age that was allowed by the LMS.

Chapter 3

Engine Cleaner, August 1936

A full team of cleaners was required to clean two engines per shift. This entailed climbing over a filth-encrusted leviathan which in many cases stood over 10ft high and over 120ft long. Equipped with ladders and oily rags, we would set about removing all the muck, soot and ash before shining the outer casing up with a light engine oil. It was not just the casing that received our attention, we also had to clean down the motion, the wheels and the side rods. It was a cold and dirty job in winter, and made harder by the draughty and gloomy conditions of the dimly lit engine shed, and worse when carried out in the wind-chilled yard.

My promotion to cleaner did not start at Royston as there were no vacancies, so I was transferred to Normanton, which was the next LMS shed up the line. Normanton was about 15 miles away and depending on my shift I could either catch a train from Royston station or, if the trains did not coincide with my shift, I would have to cycle there. I could usually catch a train for one leg of the journey and would travel standing up with my bike in the guard's van among parcels and pigeon baskets.

Although now a cleaner at Normanton, I was occasionally required to carry out knocking up duties which was a bit of a nightmare at times, cycling around an unfamiliar town in the dead of night after a 15-mile ride to work. It was almost a year before a job became available at Royston and I was able to return to my home shed.

Back at Royston I joined a group of a dozen or so lads who when all were present worked in two teams. As cleaners we worked mostly on day shifts with the occasional night. Many of the lads were older than me as all new recruits on the railway had to start at the bottom as cleaners. The two years that I had served as a knocker up were counted in the time-served regime of seniority that the LMS rigidly adhered to for advancement. A 21-year-old that had served for a year as a cleaner would be two years my junior in seniority when I had completed my year's cleaning at 18. This system prevailed all the way up to the position of driver. There were no short cuts or accelerated promotion based on ability on the LMS.

The cleaners worked in teams of up to eight with the senior lad called 'the old hand', or as it is pronounced in Yorkshire, 't'old 'and'. His responsibilities were to obtain from the foreman the numbers of the engines that were required to be cleaned on his shift and to organise the work. He collected the light cleaning oil, the shoddy rags of waste cotton and the scrapers from the store and distributed them within his team. All jobs were decided by the tossing of the small metal 'pay checks' which were the numbered metal discs that were used for personal identification when drawing our pay. Tossed like a coin, the high numbers secured the pick of the area to be cleaned, which usually ranged from the cleaner top end to the filthier lower and included the motion for which the metal scrapers were required.

When the shed was particularly busy the cleaning team would be reduced to just a few lads as the over-18 seniors were taken away for firing duties. In these circumstances the remainder carried on as best they could. When full cleaning teams were available and the shed was slack we were often moved onto other jobs such as shovelling sand out of wagons into the sand hopper for drying, and then carrying the buckets of dried sand to the engines to be emptied into their sand boxes.* This was back-breaking work as the sand in the wagons was often wet and when dried the buckets had to be manhandled above head height before they could be emptied into the sand (brake) boxes. I made good use of our bath at no. 92 when I got home in those days.

Being young lads, we had plenty of laughs during our cleaning days. One particular prank springs to mind and was often played out on the senior drivers with the more grumpy demeanours. Before an engine leaves the shed one of the responsibilities of the driver is to oil the motion. He does this by removing the corks above the big ends on the side rods, some of which are high up beneath the engine. We would wait until the driver was well inside before creeping into the cab and rattling the reversing lever, a sure sign to the driver below that the engine was about to be moved. Alarmed, he would drop several feet into the pit below fearing that the motion was about to move and mince him. After the fall and the fright he would realise what had happened and would emerge from beneath the engine with a breathless growl of, 'I'll get you … you buggers …' but by this time we were gone.

Arthur Nicholson was a great one for practical jokes. All the drivers carried a purse in which to hold their small change, as railway overalls tended to spill coins. Arthur would remove the black thread from the cleaning rags and attach a long length to a purse, which was then placed on the ground by the wheels of an engine over an inspection pit, the thread played back under the engine. As a driver approached and spotted the purse, no doubt thinking of

---

* Steam locomotives used dried sand to assist braking and to reduce slipping on greasy and wet rails. The sand was stored in boxes that were situated on either side of the boiler on the running plate. The sand was ejected from the box down a pipe and under the wheels by a steam-assisted vacuum system controlled from the cab. 8F locomotives had six sand boxes which took around twelve to fourteen buckets to fill.

his good fortune, Arthur would pull the thread and the purse would disappear into the pit as he stooped to pick it up.

One day we were cleaning out the smoke box of an engine when Len Hutchinson went too far inside and the door was quickly closed behind him and locked. Our team then went off for our break chortling at Len's misfortune, but 10 minutes later Len came sauntering into the rest room as black as soot, nonchalantly ignoring our amazement as nobody had ever escaped before. 'Who let you out?' we chorused in unison. 'Nobody', he replied as cool as you like. Being a slim lad he had stood on the blast pipe and somehow had wriggled up and out of the engine's chimney.

The LMS did not give formal training to the men who aspired to be engine crews, and it was up to the individual to educate himself in the best way that he could. Promotion could not be achieved without sitting and passing both a theoretical and practical exam together with a medical. The examining of the would-be driver or fireman was carried out by locomotive inspectors and the medicals by an LMS company doctor who paid particular attention to eyesight, hearing and general physical fitness.

To prepare for exams the aspiring footplate men attended informal mutual improvement classes (MICs) which were run by qualified drivers and firemen. The classes were given and attended in the men's own time and without pay; as far as the LMS were concerned the MICs were unofficial. Some of these classes were held in the engine shed or local canteen, but many were also given in the backroom of a tutoring driver's own home. It was a tradition that had produced engine crews for as long as the oldest driver could remember, and it suited the railway company as they did not incur any cost. It was a worthwhile aspiration to become a driver – in 1936 a top-line driver's basic pay was on a par with that of a bank manager at £4 10s per week.

Boiler-smiths had a terrible job as they had to squirm into the firebox to inspect the tube plates and repair any leakages. Access was through a knee-high gap not much bigger than a slim man's torso. Working in the dark with a hand lamp was a hot, dirty and claustrophobic task. Due to the enclosed space, the lamps used by the boiler-smiths were fuelled by rape-seed oil as this did not give off any toxic fumes. But even these poor fellows were not immune to the mischievous cleaners who would set fire to an oily rag and place it in the damper beneath the engine where air was drawn into the firebox. As the black smoked drifted upwards the boiler-smith would come squirming out through the narrow door, red-faced and somewhat angry, but of course there would be nobody there.

The cleaners at Royston had a hideaway where they played cards in the dry water tank of an old engine tender. The dark rusty container was set up with a table, upturned buckets for seats and an oil lamp where they stole ½ hour away from the foreman's gaze, that was until a bundle of smouldering oily rags were thrown in and the water tank lid was slammed down. Shortly afterwards the heavy rusting lid was opened followed by five or six spluttering urchins gasping for air. Someone had repaid a previous prank in kind, but we never found out who did it, but it was odds on to be a boiler-smith or an agile old driver!

The environs of the shed in which we worked were a palette of every conceivable type of grime, from black through to white and all shades of grey. In the air we had the varying densities of smoke and soot that drifted within steam-carried droplets caking on grime. There was coal dust and cinders, grey ash and piles of white asbestos from boiler cladding, the latter being discarded and dumped waist high behind the shed. There were numerous spillages of oil and grease from all manner of applications, mixing with the small oily blue pools that had seeped from the axle boxes of engines. Yet among all this grime it seemed a perfectly natural and homely environment for us cleaners to work in, and to us the smell of the shed was not unpleasant and it provided a welcoming atmosphere as only those who have grown up on a steam railway would recognise.

Chapter 4

Passed Cleaner and Firing, August 1937

In 1937, on reaching my eighteenth birthday, I completed a very grimy year as an engine cleaner and was passed out by the locomotive inspector. I was now eligible for firing turns which is a job that requires much more than being able to shovel coal and a great deal of stamina. On entering the firing roster my seniority displaced another who had been firing for longer than me but had fewer years' service. This displacement was known as being 'nobbed', whereby someone with greater seniority comes in and pushes you back down the pecking order. It was a regular occurrence and happened from the top to the bottom of the system.

When I started firing there was no easy introduction at Royston such as rostering you onto a small engine for a short trip. My second turn was on a long run up to Pye Junction near Nottingham with a heavy train and a large engine. In anticipation of this I had been gathering information on the art of firing by talking to the passed fireman, assisting the shed-men and trying to remember the nuances and techniques that were required for the different types of engine. The drivers with whom I was rostered would often help by advising me on the state of the fire as we rolled along. Comments were passed such as, 'Keep it thin at the back … front or flat all over … don't pile coal on coal or you will lose heat' and other such tips and gradually I gained details about the classes of engines that we were firing at Royston.

At first the physical effort required to fire the engine was exhausting, shovelling tons of coal per shift with a steady swing in a bent-back stance day after day. Not all the drivers were accommodating and a poor driving technique could waste steam unnecessarily resulting in more effort from the fireman to raise it. One never shovelled coal with one's backside facing the driver on the LMS, it was considered bad etiquette and many of the old drivers would respond with a growled, 'Get yer arse out of my face'. The driver was the definitive master on the footplate. So we had to fire both left-handed and right-handed depending on which side of the engine the regulator and driver were positioned.

My dad was still the running foreman and was still following his policy of reverse nepotism, so if he was allocating the engines for a roster of mine, you could bet it wouldn't be a free steamer. When dad was on I always seemed to get a clapped out engine. Even the drivers for whom I was firing would grumble, 'If it won't for thee we would 'av 'ad a decent engine'!

I was fortunate in 1938 to get regular rostered firing turns due to my seniority, while the mutual improvement classes continued and I was able to pass my firing exams and shortly afterwards moved into a regular firing vacancy. My next step up would be to become a passed fireman, which is a fireman passed by examination for driving.

Chapter 5

The Working Day

From the 1930s to the 1950s the working week was a six-day roster of 8 hours per day followed by a rest day. Overtime was paid over the 8-hour shift and we had a paid annual holiday of one week. There was no paid sickness absence and men often struggled into work when they were clearly unwell.

Our shifts often overran the standard 8 hours by several hours due to fog, ice or the sheer volume of traffic blocking the train into a loop or siding. Overtime was paid for each hour over the standard 8 hours, which was increased by a night rate and time and a half on Sundays. Our wages were paid weekly in cash, which we collected in a packet at the shed on production of our numbered metal pay disc.

The shifts rotated am and pm. An am shift could start at 0005hr or 1155hr and any point in between. If your rest day was due on a Friday you might not finish work until 2355hr on the Thursday night and then be due back on an am shift at 0005hr on Saturday morning. The railway unions had agreed with the railway companies that a minimum of 12 hours must be allowed before a new shift commenced.

We also worked 'away and lodge' shifts whereby an 8-hour break was required before working a train back to the Royston area. These jobs were usually to Garston (Liverpool), Carnforth and Toton (Nottingham). The roster board would be written up as 'Garston and lodge'.

Chapter 6

Royston, Carlton Yards to Garston Docks, Liverpool

This roster took a heavy coal train of around forty fully laden 15 and 10-ton coal wagons from Carlton yards up through the Pennines to Garston Docks outside Liverpool. The scheduling was not a regular turn as it depended on the arrival in Liverpool of the steam-powered Elder-Fyffes banana boats from the West Indies, for which we were taking the coal.

During my first year of firing in 1937 the Garston turn often used to be a double-headed train of loose-coupled wagons, that is wagons that cannot be braked from the engine. These trains required both experience and judgement especially when travelling downgrade, the only way of slowing the train was by applying the engines brakes with the guard screwing down the brake in his van at the rear. The hundreds of tons in between would be pushing the engine and dragging the guard's van as the momentum was gradually decreased.

The engines rostered were either two ex-Lancashire and Yorkshire A class 0–6–0 engines or two 0–6–0 Fowler 4Fs, or either one of these with a 2–6–0 Crab. When single-headed it was a Derby 'Austin 7' 0–8–0 or if we were very unlucky an ex-LNWR 'Wessy' Super D 0–8–0.

The departure from Carlton was always around 0040hr, which required us to sign on at the shed at 2340hr. The journey could take up to 12 hours as delays were common. I was always dead beat when we arrived in Liverpool as I had shovelled several tons of coal into the firebox on the outward journey.

We had little protection from the elements on these older engines and the wind blew straight through the open cabs leaving us freezing above the waist and over warm below. On arrival in Liverpool we would draw to a halt alongside Edge Hill Shed where we were relieved by a local crew. These local men then took our train down to the docks at Garston to be unloaded. Following the unloading they then brought our engine back up to Edge Hill some 8 hours later for our return journey to Yorkshire.

The Garston and lodge turn required us to take an 8-hour break when we had reached Liverpool, and after signing off at Edge Hill Shed we went into digs or shift lodgings. The lodges were barrack-type buildings maintained by the LMS for transient crews and they were grim places, however I didn't mind as I dropped onto a bed as soon as I arrived. I would sleep solidly until shaken by the driver and guard for the return trip. They were usually quite refreshed and had found the time to have a nap, a drink as well as an amble around the town.

The LMS regulation that stipulated crews must have an 8-hour break also stated that they should also be back on the road within 10 hours, but for innumerable reasons these timings often went awry. We would find ourselves dragging our feet around the shops to kill as many as 5 hours over our mandatory 8.

Our return working could throw up a variety of trains which could be our own coal empties returning to Royston or fitted vans of bananas or cattle for Leeds. If it was a banana train we would have our engine replaced by a new Black 5 4–6–0, which were fitted with a train heating system to keep the vans warm to enable the bananas to continue ripening en route. The banana trains were fast freights and we would make good time on our way home.

The stock trains took Irish cattle from the ferry to the slaughter houses in Leeds. The passengers were ferocious-looking beasts with long horns and dung-matted coats and to us they appeared completely wild. They were accompanied by their drovers who stank as bad as the cattle. These men were dressed in ankle-length trench coats and long leather gaiters, both of which were liberally soiled with dried dung. If an animal went down inside the vans they would fearlessly wade in among the horns with a long pointed stick, prodding the animal until it was back on its feet. During the journey they would ride in the van with the guard, much to his consternation. The drovers were a hardy lot and would stretch out and go to sleep on the wooden lockers impervious to the hard boards and the shaking of the train. As we passed slowly through stations such as Huddersfield you could see the passengers on the platforms turning away because of the smell. The poor old guard of course suffered this all the way to Leeds as his van caught the draught from both the drovers and the train.

On occasions the weather and delays would be so bad on the run to Liverpool that we would be relieved at Stockport or Warrington, as our driving limits were in danger of being exceeded. When this happened we would relieve another crew taking coal empties back to our area or the fast Llandudno–Leeds passenger train. If we were unfortunate and had already worked for 6½ hours we would have to lodge at Stockport or Warrington. These overnight stops were awful as we were condemned to staying in exceedingly scruffy lodgings. At the end of these trips we eventually made it home on our own engine or by hitching a lift in another.

Chapter 7

The 'Barrow Babies' – Royston, Carlton Yards to Carnforth

This train used to transport coke from Carlton yards to the steelworks at Barrow-in-Furness, it was another turn through the Pennines and the Royston men used to take it up to Carnforth and lodge, returning the next day. The run up was by the way of Leeds, Skipton, Hellifield and then the left fork at Settle Junction to Giggleswick and on into Carnforth.

Once past Leeds the fireman wouldn't get much of a respite to admire the countryside as the engine was working upgrade and he would be hard at work. The 8F had a bunker holding 9 tons of coal and on a trans-Pennine trip to Liverpool or Carnforth I would estimate that I would shovel around 4 tons of it into the firebox, but what goes up must come down and the return trip was much easier.

The coke that we were taking was produced in the coke ovens of New Monckton and Manvers, from where it was brought into Carlton yards by the trippers. The train when assembled looked pretty impressive with a new 8F at the head of thirty or more bright-yellow, high-sided steel wagons specifically designed for coke.

Before leaving the ovens at the colliery the hot coke was doused with water to extinguish any remaining combustion in the hot cinder-like material. But this wasn't always completely effective because when we got going the draught often found hidden embers that began to burn. On more than one occasion when we looked back down the length of the train in a tunnel we would see the sides of a wagon glowing red in the darkness. We would then have to slow down to reduce the draught and proceed cautiously to stop at the next water column where we would thoroughly douse the offending wagon. We could lose quite a lot of time on these occasions as we would first have to notify the signalman, stop by his box, stand to be diverted into a siding or loop if a water column was not on our line and in some instances have to shunt the wagon out of the train before continuing on our way.

After passing Settle Junction the line passed close to Giggleswick public school where we used to look out for the lonely figure of the headmaster's son, who could often be seen in a chair on a balcony. It was said that the poor chap had suffered from polio, but wrapped in a blanket he always gave us a cheerful wave of his stick in response to a blast from our whistle. We were told that some of the Holbeck crews saw him so often that they sent him a present at Christmas.

On arrival at Carnforth we would be uncoupled from the wagons in the sidings and would then take our engine onto the shed for disposal. The wagons were taken on to the steelworks at Barrow by a local engine where they were emptied and returned for us the following day.

On entering Carnforth shed we would slip into the coaling road and refuel from the hopper ourselves rather than leave it to their shed men, which may seem a little unusual seeing as we took so much trouble to avoid it at Royston, but this was a dodge to secure good-quality coal for our trip home.

Carnforth's hopper had two shutes, one supplying quality coal for the express passenger engines and the other a lesser grade for the freight engines. Easing under the hopper with an almost empty tender we would fill our freight engine up with passenger coal and then ease forward and skim it over with freight coal. As the fireman, I would then climb up onto the tender to trim it off to cover our deceit. Duly camouflaged, we would be OK on leaving the shed the following morning if under the critical eye of their running foreman. He would not notice anything amiss. Our engine was then parked and would simmer through the night with the Carnforth shed men maintaining the fire.

We would lodge overnight at Mrs Hodgson's, a homely house providing rooms for LMS footplate men who were obliged to stay overnight before returning to their home depots. Early next morning we would pick up our engine and back it out of the shed and onto the returning 'Barrow Babies' in the siding. Our return run was light and easy, downgrade most of the way, steaming freely and coasting along on our good-quality 'express passenger' coal. The run was usually so good that even the fireman had time to sit back and enjoy the countryside.

Chapter 8

Firing Beyer-Garratts

The Beyer-Garratts were the largest freight locomotives on the LMS, and were in effect two engines being serviced by one boiler, tender and firebox. Used solely on heavy mineral workings, they presented a formidable task for a young fireman. There were two shovels on the Garratt, meant for a second fireman or for the driver to lend a hand. I never had a second fireman and it was rare that the driver would pick up a shovel.

The tender was so large that most of them were fitted with a revolving steam-operated coal bunker to bring the coal down to the footplate. The footplate and firebox were cavernous. My first turns on these engines were from Wellingborough and Toton where we took over iron-ore trains working to Chapeltown's Thorncliffe Steelworks, north of Sheffield.

On my first turns on the Garratt I was fortunate to have as my driver our next-door neighbour Vic Dennis. Vic was invaluable, seeming to know all the tricks of the engineman. One of my early turns found me firing for Vic on an engine without a revolving bunker. When the coal was depleted you could have used a wheelbarrow to bring it forward to within shovelling range of the firebox. Vic solved the problem by drawing up alongside a water column and showed me how to wash it down from the rear of the tender. It came down in an avalanche with water streaming everywhere, but it did the trick. It was a truly labour-saving innovation which I managed to use whenever we had a water stop on one of these unmodified engines.

The Garratt turn began by taking one of our smaller engines on a train out of Carlton sidings up to Toton where we would lodge overnight. The following morning we would relieve a Wellingborough crew on a Garratt at Trent Junction.

The huge 155-ton articulated Garratt would be simmering at Trent when we climbed aboard and my first job would be to build up the fire before we set off, for if we were underway before the fire was high you would never catch up. The dual engine would use more coal than you could put in. Once on the road the fireman had to work hard and fast to feed the enormous firebox.

Our journey north was by way of the Erewash Valley to Chesterfield, up the Dronfield bank and through Bradway Tunnel (1 mile 267yd long) before reaching Sheffield. Sometimes we could build up the fire and then ease off before entering the tunnel, this would lessen the effect of the dense clouds of sulphurous smoke that hit the roof and billowed back around the engine.

There are no lights in a tunnel and at times we would be almost down on our knees with rags over our mouths, such was the density of the smoke. This was further compounded when we met another train approaching on the opposite line.

In addition to being engulfed in the smoke, we had the deafening beat of our engine's exhaust as it barked at the roof, together with the high-pitched whoosh of the steam being ejected from the pistons, the clank of the side rods and the muffled thunder of the wagons behind. It was quite an experience for a young fireman. On reaching Thorncliffe Steelworks we would uncouple our train and travel light engine from Chapeltown down to Royston, a much easier ride.

During the late 1930s the rise and belligerence of Germany was becoming ever more prominent in the press, and as young lads we were watching developments with interest. By 1939 it became law for all young men to register for military training, but such was the media's call to arms that by this time many of us had already decided that we were going to enlist.

*

Recruiting for the Armed Forces

In 1938 the possibility of war with Germany was becoming increasingly probable and it was apparent that the British army was seriously under strength. To redress the balance the Secretary of State for War, Leslie Hore-Belisha, introduced the Military Training Act. The Act became law in April 1939 and required all men between the ages of 20 and 21 to register for six months' military training. In effect, the Act introduced conscription, but as the word conscription was unpopular with the British public following the First World War it was named the militia and so the young men who were called forward for training became known as the 'militiamen'. At the same time a list of reserved occupations was announced which detailed the industries and services that were essential to keep the country functioning in war time. The men employed in these occupations were exempt from conscription into the armed forces. Railway workers were on this reserved list. However, young men still had the right to volunteer for military training and at this time were allowed to leave their reserved occupations to join the armed forces if they chose to do so.

*

Chapter 9

Registering for Military Training, August 1939

The first registration for military training took place in April 1939 and as I was still only 19 years old I was ineligible to register. The registrations took place every six months so I had to wait for the second one in August 1939, by which time I had reached my 20th birthday. I went into Barnsley to register and attend a medical with a group of six other lads from Royston engine shed. On arrival at the register office we were requested to complete a form stating along with other details which of the three services we would prefer to do our six months' military training with. I requested the Navy, but the department of 'quota fillers' had other ideas and due to my railway experience I was destined for the RE. Little did I know that my anticipated six months' military training would turn out to be six years.

*

Conscription

When war was declared with Germany in September 1939 the army was still recruiting on a voluntary basis. This changed a month later when it was announced that all men between the ages of 18 and 41 that were not in essential occupations were liable for military service. Men between the ages of 20 and 23 that had not as yet registered to join the militia had now to register by law to be available to serve in the armed forces. The men that were currently undertaking or scheduled to undertake their six months of militia training were subsequently conscripted into the regular army for the duration of the war.

*

I was requested to report to Longmoor Military Railway (LMR) near Petersfield in Hampshire in November 1939. War had been declared on 17th September and as I contemplated the prospect of becoming a regular soldier in the RE, Royston prepared for hostilities. We had now entered the period that became known as the phoney war, with very little happening. Home Guard rosters were prepared and attempts were made to prevent the muck stacks of Monckton Pit glowing in the dark, so as not to become a beacon to enemy bombers.* Everyone seemed to be certain that the coal mines and railways around Royston were sure to be a target among the first waves of German bombers!

The newspapers published graphic accounts of the German bomber fleets attacking towns in Spain and it was the threat of aerial attacks that were being given prominence. Anderson shelter kits had been issued by the local council and they were erected in our back gardens to give us some protection from the anticipated bombing.** These small corrugated-iron shelters were intended to be partly buried in the ground and then covered with earth. However, our garden had a thick layer of clay at the surface which proved to be a challenge for the gang of installers to penetrate with their picks, spades and limited time. Subsequently our shelter was left on the clay, which collected water every time it rained and as a consequence the shelter was always damp and a foot deep in water most of the time. Nevertheless, when the first sirens were sounded there was a dutiful procession out of the house, often in nightwear and wellingtons. However, the lack of bombs and the depth of the water resulted in these nocturnal evacuations becoming increasingly infrequent.

The Local Defence Force, the precursor of the Home Guard, was being recruited and given basic military training in the village. Squads of men were drilling in civilian clothes with broom and pick-axe handles with all seriousness. Plans were being drawn up to post civilian guards at key points at railway sidings, signal boxes and engine sheds to guard against sabotage by fifth columnists.† Old soldiers had dug out their First World War medal ribbons and had sewn them onto the breast of their jackets, raising their perceived status in the heady atmosphere of 'let's be ready for them'.

Such was the enthusiasm and military naivety at this time that it often descended into farce and was to give us many a laugh in the years to come. One of our local doctors, Dr Henderson, a sporty young man who drove an Avon Speedster and was inclined to do his rounds on a horse, illustrated the fervour that gripped both the village and the country by setting up his own commando unit. Leading a group of like-minded young men and a few lads from the sheds, he organised cross-country runs and night patrols and even

---

*   The muck stacks were composed of soil, shale and poor-quality coal, and many smouldered and could be seen glowing at night. It was believed that these could be used by German bombers to pinpoint the coal mines. To prevent this water was pumped up to their summits to douse the fires.

**   Anderson shelters were free to men who were earning £5 or less per week, while those earning above this amount could purchase them for £7. By September 1939 over 2 million families had an Anderson shelter situated in their back gardens.

†   A group of people living within the population but working for the enemy.

had them swimming across the local spur of the Barnsley Canal with packs on their backs.

During my final weeks before reporting to Longmoor instructions came into the engine shed regarding blackouts and the precautions to be taken in the event of an air raid. These basically boiled down to 'get off the engine' and find a hole to shelter in, which we found quite comical as we pondered how we were to achieve this while bowling along at 60mph. Anti-glare tarpaulins were issued to be fitted over the engine's footplate between the cab and the tender, to lessen the chance of the glow from the firebox being spotted by enemy aircraft at night. The shed staff were issued with tin hats and we were all issued with gas masks as it was the local belief that Royston engine shed was a definite target.

An air-raid siren was mounted on the local police station and we had our first false alarm on the day that war was declared. I was on afternoons and approaching the shed to start my shift when the siren went off. As I entered the gloom alongside road number one I was met with the sight of all the shed staff sheltering in the inspection pits beneath the engines. Most were wearing tin helmets, and peeping out from beneath the buffer beam of one of the engines was my dad, helmet askew and his silver hair sticking out in tufts.

My driver and I were still laughing when later that day we had another false alarm on our return trip from Goole. We were leaving the town when an air-raid warning was sounded and as it was dusk we pulled the 'tarp' down over the cab to seal in the glow from the firebox, but were we glad to get it off again when the temperature began to rise! The tarpaulin may have kept in the glow from the firebox but it also retained the heat in the cab, and together with the tarry smell of the newly manufactured material it was quite a face-reddening experience. There were later reports of heat rashes and exhaustion affecting footplate men, but this was not to trouble me as I was shortly to be away in uniform.

Part Two

My Years as a Soldier, 1939–46

Chapter 10

Royal Engineer at Longmoor Camp, Hampshire, November 1939

A Brief Introduction to Longmoor Military Railway

The British army first started building railways overseas during the Crimean War in 1856. The need for railway troops was fully recognised during the military campaigns of the Sudan and Abyssinia in the nineteenth century. Initially, army engineers were supported by civilian personnel but in 1903 Longmoor Camp opened and the army began to develop its own railway capability as an integrated part of the RE. The initial concept for dedicated railway troops was for the building of military railways as a means of supplying an advancing army with ordnance, supplies and reinforcements.

In the First World War the additional purpose of operating and repairing damaged sections of existing overseas railways became the main objective, and this included the whole operation of locomotive driving, maintenance, signalling, track maintenance and engineering. In wartime it was realised that whole railway systems could be disrupted by shelling (1914–18) and later by bombing or sabotage by a retreating enemy. It was also assumed that the local civilian railway staff would be in short supply or reluctant to work in dangerous conditions. In these situations it was anticipated that locomotives, rolling stock, track, signalling and numerous other supporting components would have to be taken from Britain as replacements.

Prior to the Second World War the military railway units were operated on a volunteer territorial basis. They were formed into military companies that were self contained and able to run and maintain a section of railway where and when required. In addition the RE had developed railway survey companies with the skills required to survey and support the building of new railways and track configurations. Sappers were also trained in bridging skills.

In 1939 the LMR had five War Department locomotives and several on loan from private railway companies, and these were used for training purposes, scheduled freight and local passenger workings. Longmoor Camp had large storage areas supported by sidings which held the transportation stores that would be required to support the military's overseas operations. In addition, locomotives were stored and prepared for shipment overseas. Longmoor Camp had a massive input of stores in 1940 when equipment designated for the BEF (British Expeditionary Force) in France was diverted to it as a result of the Dunkirk evacuation.

Longmoor was to become a huge military complex as the war progressed and the following troop numbers for the 1939–45 period give an indication its size. At its peak the permanent staff increased to 7,000, and one-third of all RE was involved in transportation, approximately 59,000 men were trained at Longmoor, with a further 80,000 passing through as replacement drafts.

*

On my arrival at Longmoor the military railway was in the process of receiving men from all the pre-nationalised railway companies, the Southern, Great Western, London North Eastern and my own London, Midland and Scottish Railway. We were housed in a large, single-storey complex that was known within the camp as the 'spider block'. The name came about because of the numerous rooms that radiated off a central ablutions hub like the legs of a spider, and it became even more exotic when we were told that the building's official name was the New Martinique barracks.

Initially we didn't have uniforms and were not allowed to walk out on the main thoroughfares in case we met an officer. The reason for this was due to the regulation that men out of uniform were not allowed to salute. The military mindset was that it was considered contrary to good discipline to pass an officer without saluting, so we were kept out of the way to remove the chance of us meeting one.

My first impressions of Longmoor were that it was a cold and wet place and these feelings have remained, although I was to spend two summers there. Initially, I was put to work in the cookhouse where with others from my intake I spent my time peeling potatoes and scrubbing tins. However our boots* and uniforms were eventually issued and we were sorted into sections and began training on the military railway.

A further shock to our system was that we had to wash our own overalls in a big tank of water that was kept boiling in the engine-shed yard, where we stirred the clothing around with a wooden paddle. The overalls were constantly begrimed and the washing of them came to be quite a chore to me as my mother had previously washed mine at home.

Many of the young men did not have the footplate experience that I and the other Royston lads were recruited with, for I had two years' experience firing heavy freight engines and had passed my firing exams. Longmoor had only one of these engines, a new Stanier 8F 2–8–0, while my home shed at Royston had twenty or more.

---

* The black, standard-issue army boot had thirteen studs and an unlined collar and was designed for durability rather than comfort. The boots were known as 'ammo' boots, as in ammunition, because they were procured by the Munitions Board rather than the Army HQ at Horse Guards. Until they were broken in these boots caused great discomfort to the lads unused to wearing them, chaffing the ankles red raw.

Our instructors were initially the Regimental Sergeant Major (RSM) and the Company Sergeant Major (CSM). They were both army trained and their driving experience was mostly limited to the Longmoor track, except for occasional sorties as main-line observers. When the first 8F arrived the RSM wore dusty white gauntlets as he tentatively drove it around the Longmoor tracks. We were used to making the locomotives work hard and crack on, but the RSM would have had a fit if his engines had been worked like that. In those early days they were polished to a sheen by defaulters and stored safely under the cover of the shed at night.

The two senior instructors did not quite know what to make of us with our main-line experience and appeared to be a little wary of our history. We found, however, that they were theoretically very good and the Longmoor workshops and classrooms proved to be first class.

Once we had settled in and despite an initial cautiousness the Longmoor instructors were delighted to get trained railwaymen which was to make their jobs much easier. After an introductory period of square bashing (drill instruction) and rudimentary weapon training – I think I fired about five rounds with a Lee–Enfield rifle, we were set to work on the railway. I became Sapper T. Hicks,* service number 1898627 and although I did not know it, I was to be at Longmoor for twenty-six months. During this period I did very little soldiering with the exception of the odd parade and the occasional guard duty on the camp gate.

*

Shortage of Railwaymen

At this time the civilian national railway companies were losing so many men to the armed forces that they complained to the government. The problem being that their ability to run the national railway system was being severely compromised by men enlisting, and as a result of this the government classified railwaymen as essential workers and they were not allowed to join the armed forces. The windfall of trained railwaymen that the army had previously received now effectively dried up, making Longmoor's experienced railwaymen soldiers even more valuable as future drafts of men would now be inexperienced.

*

---

* A sapper is the RE equivalent of a private, the Americans call them combat engineers and the German's pionier. The original word sapper in the sense used by the French military was for one who excavated trenches to advance the besieging army's position under fire, which was referred to as sapping the enemy fortifications. The word was first used in the RE in 1856.

When war was declared in September 1939 I had already registered and my pending six months' military training had become permanent. However, when the shortage of civilian railwaymen became critical, I had the opportunity to apply to leave the army and return to Royston. I decided to stay, but some of our RE railwaymen did apply to be discharged and returned to civilian life with their original railway companies.

When I arrived at Longmoor the military railway had a complement of six steam locomotives for training and local camp rosters around Petersfield. It had access to the Southern's main line at Liss and a terminus at Bordon with an operating length of about 12 miles. There were workshops capable of carrying out major repairs and classrooms for instruction in all manner of railway work, mechanical, track-laying, signalling and even a paint shop.

Locomotives were often deliberately derailed to be re-railed in training exercises using steam cranes or block and tackle. We also used a portable V-shaped rail to put the locomotive back onto the track. These Vs were placed behind or in front of the loco's driving wheels, the loco was then put into motion and it would often re-rail itself. The training was to simulate the difficulties that could arise in places such as the wilds of Persia or Iraq where steam cranes were in short supply. Once they were filming a wartime serial and had meticulously planned for a spectacular crash, but after all the preparation when the locomotive was derailed it managed to stay on its wheels and bury itself in the mud. The sappers then went to work digging it out and re-railing it.

As well as drama we also had episodes of humour, such as the time the painters were painting the steel cross over bridge at Longmoor Downs. The bridge carried the military railway's main line over the shed yard before descending down into the station. In order to paint the upper span the painters had to put a trestle on either side of the bridge suspended by ropes, one balancing the other. Somehow they had managed to loop a rope over the upper track and then just like a Chaplin comedy a locomotive came across and cut the rope while they were painting – they fell down in a heap and were covered in green paint which caused no end of mirth around the camp.

At Longmoor I was classed initially as a trainee fireman second class and then progressed by examination to locomotive driver second class, each promotion being rewarded with a pay rise. There were very few drivers classified as first class as these positions were held by the regular army personnel such as the RSM and CSM. The reason being that the first-class qualification included bulldozer driving, an anomaly that seemed strange in a railway company but someone at sometime had considered it to be part of the job.

I recall that winter of 1939 was cold, so cold that we used to stop during rifle drill to pound our hands on the back of the lad in front to keep warm as we could hardly hold our rifles. The billet was also freezing, being heated by two inefficient coal-fired stoves positioned at either end amd which struggled to keep us warm.* We were not allowed to light the stoves until 1700 hours because like many other things during the war the coal was rationed. I was on shift work and it was difficult to sleep in those cold thirty-man-room billets after working all night. If it wasn't the cold keeping you awake it was the comings and goings of the day men with their clattering boots and unconcerned verbosity, we were even woken by the orderly officer demanding to know why we were still in bed!

We, the locomotive footplate crews, were eventually moved out into Nissen huts at Weavers Down.** We were then more or less left to our own devices, and the night-shift men were able to sleep during the day and the orderly officer in general gave us a wide berth. As a result of this, our hut took on a definite non-military appearance. We soon solved the rationing problem by throwing coal off the locomotive's footplate as we passed by on the nearby line, collecting it later and storing it under our beds. Now in our warm, cosy huts we decorated the walls with numerous illustrations of locomotive valve gear, which we drew during our frequent discussions on our previous company experience, usually arguing over the superiority of our own particular locomotives!

As well as working on the locomotives we were also required to undertake occasional stints on the coaling stage, the raised roofed platform where coal was manually transferred from wagons into the locomotive tenders. It was a filthy job, and the swirling black dust that was raised up got beneath our clothes and stung our eyes red. We were using compressed coal dust in the form of small balls or Cardiff embossed briquettes to fire the locomotives. The briquettes were easily shattered creating more dust, and back in Royston where the round ones were regularly used they were known by the rather rude sobriquet of 'niggers' knackers'.† The briquettes were not popular with the footplate men, especially the round ones which were easily shaken out of the locomotive tender and then rolled around underfoot. It was essential on a moving locomotive to maintain balance and so this situation could become particularly hazardous when swinging a firing shovel. The round briquettes also had the disadvantage of creating plenty of ash which had to be removed from the smoke box at the end of a shift, a task that fell to us if a civilian shed man (labourer) was not available.

---

*   The definition of billet is quarters for soldiers in a private house, but the word is also used by soldiers to describe any building where they are based for a period of time, be it a hut, barrack block or mansion.

**   A Nissen hut is a prefabricated, curved, corrugated-steel hut, designed by Major P.N. Nissen, RE in 1916.

†   A term used without malice but one that would not be acceptable today. Such descriptions were not considered to be untoward in the 1930s when racism was not generally recognised as an issue.

One of the jobs that I disliked the most at Longmoor was the training of new men in shunting operations, whereby a train of thirty wagons would have to be split up and reassembled in a large siding. It was a necessary skill, but boring and laborious. The job entailed constantly shuffling backwards and forwards on a small locomotive, and during these shifts I dreamed and longed for an open road and distant horizons.

We went through a difficult period at Longmoor following the evacuation of British forces from Dunkirk (during May and June 1940) as the country expected to be invaded and all leave was cancelled. It was anticipated that if the Germans landed the south coast would be evacuated of civilians and all the rail routes would be operated by the railway troops of the RE. In preparation for this some of the lads were seconded to the Southern and Great Western railways on road learning and locomotive familiarisation duties.*

By this time we had all been issued with a personal weapon that remained close at hand, even on the footplate, and mine was a five-shot Canadian .303 Ross rifle that had been manufactured during the First World War. Ammunition was kept in a personnel locker by the bed and the rifle was propped against the wall, the only concession to safety being that we had to remove the bolt when we were in the billet or when it had to be left unattended. We were constantly made aware and were reminded that we must be ready to fight at a moment's notice.

The leave embargo lasted for several months until the threat of invasion receded, and during this period there were many anonymous graffiti messages daubed around the walls of the camp demanding leave. The married and betrothed who were new to military service felt particularly aggrieved. Little did they know what lay ahead of them as many were to be posted out to the Middle East and would not return until 1946.

When the leave embargo was eventually lifted and my turn came to go home, I was required to take my personal weapon with me. The threat of invasion had not entirely disappeared and we had orders to report to the nearest military unit with our rifles if it occurred. So I arrived home, 20 years old and swaggering up the garden path like Davy Crockett with my Canadian Ross rifle. My dad took one horrified look at it and locked it in the coal house for the rest of my stay.

A good proportion of our off-duty hours were spent in the Navy Army Air Force Institute (NAAFI), the canteen-come-leisure facility that every sizable military camp had for ranks under Senior Non Commissioned Officer (SNCO). The Longmoor NAAFI was grim with a mainstay of tea, bread, jam and rissoles of dubious composition. We preferred the Church of England

---

* All locomotive drivers are required to spend months learning routes, gradients, speed restrictions and signalling before taking trains over routes that are unfamiliar to them.

Club which offered the luxury of fish and chips for 6*d*, but we were often so skint that we couldn't even afford a cup of tea by the end of the week. We always looked forward to our weekly pay parade when we were paid in cash.

Although a serving soldier, I was still entitled to my LMS rail passes and privilege tickets that gave me free and reduced fare rail travel. This enabled me to give (unofficially) my free passes to my Scots pal for his long journey home to Stirling while I used the privilege tickets for the cheaper journeys to Royston. The only snag was that we needed the Railway Transport Officer in Stirling to stamp my leave pass as proof that I had made the supposed journey up to Scotland. To get around this I persuaded Jack Thewsey, a railwayman in Royston who was also a part-time printer, to copy a Railway Transport Officer stamp off an old pass and my pass was duly endorsed. The counterfeit worked a treat, but poor old Jack later told me that every time he saw a police constable walking down Cross Lane he thought that his number was up and that they were coming for him!

On the morning of 14 August 1940, my 21st birthday, I was on parade at Longmoor with a squad of other lads. Looking up we could see a large formation of aircraft in a V formation with their underbellies glinting silver in the blue sky. We thought they were our aircraft until they started peeling off, then we were dismissed on the run and dashed for the shelters. We were about to experience our first air raid. One of the buildings hit was the camp post office in which a birthday cake baked for me by my mother and younger sister Freda was waiting to be collected. When I eventually received the cake in its box I found it to be riddled with shards of broken glass, but a Parker pen and a Rolls razor from my father came out unscathed. This was our first taste of the war. Further insights were provided from the top of the shed water tower, from where we viewed the red glow over London as it suffered the Blitz in September 1940.

I was studying hard and taking my training seriously and was already instructing new lads and newly commissioned RE officers in the techniques of firing a locomotive. The lads were OK but some of the officers were unused to the hard labour of shovelling. However, one young officer I had on the footplate for a short period was the son of Sir William Stanier, the locomotive designer, and he proved to be the exception to the rule and wasn't too bad at all.

In retrospect I realise I was too keen, and my mates who were not in a permanent staff position such as myself started to be posted overseas. I wanted to go with them and share their experiences but I was kept behind on instruction duties, and as often as not on the dreaded shunter. It was not what I had joined up for and it was with no little envy that I watched as my mates were posted out to the Middle East with 190 Operating Railway Company.

Now anxious to move on, I was ready to leave Longmoor and applied to transfer from my staff position to 189 Operating Company, which was also on the move. But I was refused. I did not want to spend the war at Longmoor and I believed more than ever that I was now missing out on the chance of a lifetime of travel and adventure.

The Commandos were requesting volunteers at the time so I thought this is the job for me, I hadn't joined the army to be a railwayman, and I submitted an application. Unfortunately, Captain Wainwright, Officer Commanding

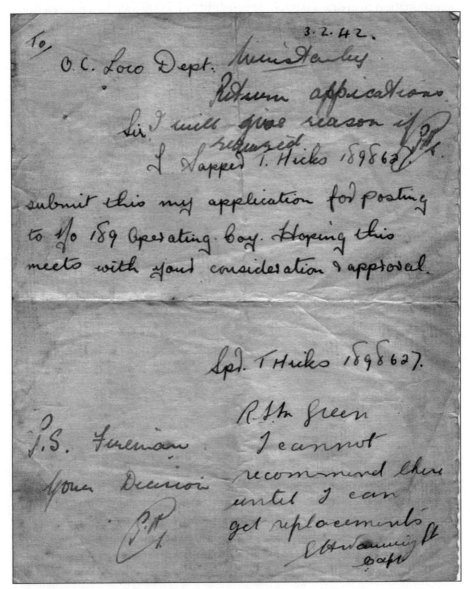

Application to transfer to 189 Railway Operating Company, dated 3 February 1942. It was refused, 'not recommended until I can get replacements'.

Loco Depot and known to us as 'Daddy Wainwright' on account of his shock of grey hair, didn't agree. He patiently explained that the Company needed experienced men and also his difficulty in obtaining replacements, and the outcome was that my application was rejected. I submitted another request shortly afterwards when further volunteers were requested but again the Captain turned me down.

Winston Churchill, however, had already come to my rescue as his determination to create a parachute capability of 5,000 men had filtered down to my unit. The request for volunteers came from the top and had the specific order that units could not block applications.

Chapter 11

The Paratroops

Origins and Development of Parachute Troops

In the early 1930s the Russians began training parachute troops. By 1935 they had thirty battalions which they demonstrated to the military representatives of foreign armed forces the same year. Among the visitors were Reich Marshall Goering of Germany and General Wavell of Britain. On his return to Germany Goering immediately started the formation and training of German parachute troops who were to become the 1st Fallschirmager.

Britain was slow to follow Russia and Germany and General Wavell was unable to raise any enthusiasm at home for the concept of airborne soldiers. In May 1940, following the success of German operations with parachute troops in Norway, Belgium and Holland, the British Prime Minister Winston Churchill issued instructions the following month for the War Office to develop the formation of 5,000 parachute troops. At this time the Air Ministry which had the responsibility for the training of parachutists was more concerned with the development of bomber and fighter aircraft. The army was occupied with home defence and was in the middle of a post-Dunkirk re-building process. Subsequently, both the RAF and army did not give Churchill's instruction a high priority.

Many senior officers could not see a parachute force developing further than having the capability of a small raiding unit. Churchill had not been taken seriously. As a consequence of these reservations and unknown to Churchill, volunteers were only requested from 2 Commando to undertake parachute training. These volunteers were renamed No. 11 Special Air Service Battalion and based at Knutsford, Cheshire. The base was chosen because of its proximity to the RAF Central Landing School at Ringway aerodrome situated on the outskirts of Manchester.

The training situation was difficult from the start as the Air Ministry did not give its full support, facilities were limited and parachutes were old and in short supply, as were suitable aircraft. The Whitley Mark 3 bombers that were supplied for parachute training by the RAF were few in number (six), unsuitable for parachutists and in poor repair, and as result all had to be modified. The instructors were mostly RAF personnel and were few in number. In addition, the Air Ministry and the Army High Command were involved in a bureaucratic confrontation over responsibilities, and this lack of commitment delayed the implementation of Churchill's June instruction to create the force of 5,000. In fact, by December 1940 only 500 had been trained and volunteers had ceased to be requested in contravention of Churchill's instruction.

In May 1941 Germany completed the rout of Yugoslavia and Greece and then launched a massive airborne assault on Crete spearheading the attack with paratroops. On 27 May 1941 British troops were forced to abandon the island with massive losses. The same day Churchill was appalled to learn that his instruction to form a paratroop capability had only resulted in a force of 500. Various histories record the degree of his reaction from shocked to extreme anger. As a result, three days later the Chiefs of Staff announced that Britain would form a parachute brigade of around 2,200 men.

With Winston Churchill driving the issue forward the recruitment of volunteers for a full parachute brigade gathered pace. No. 11 Special Air Service Battalion comprised the first 500 and became the 1st Battalion in September 1941 when it moved from Knutsford to Hardwick Hall. The pressure was now on to recruit and train the brigade as quickly as possible. The 2nd and 3rd Battalions were to be composed of the men who responded to the requests for volunteers after August 1941.

In addition to the recruitment of the parachute infantry, the 1st Air Troop of the RE was formed to support the 1st Parachute Battalion after the experiences of the Tragino raid,* which were expanded into Tom's future unit, the 1st Parachute Squadron RE.

In August 1941 a memorandum was sent to all home army commands requesting volunteers to apply for the proposed parachute brigade. The request stated that units would not be able to block applications. It had been decided that three battalions would form the brigade with a wartime establishment of 696 men and 36 officers per battalion. The battalions were to be supported by parachute engineers and field ambulance. However, due to recruitment difficulties, injuries in training, wastage and the later casualties in the field these establishments were rarely if ever maintained. Sir Basil Liddell Hart stated in his *History of the Second World War* (1989 edn) that a parachute battalion during 1942 numbered about 538 men of all ranks.

In September 1941 Ringway near Manchester was chosen as the Airborne Forces Establishment and parachute courses were run here. Hardwick Hall near Chesterfield was selected as the basic training and reception centre and became the headquarters of the 1st Parachute Brigade and Airborne Forces Depot. It was at Hardwick where the volunteers were formed into the 2nd and 3rd Battalions, the 1st Parachute Squadron RE and 16th Parachute Field Ambulance. Hardwick Hall started receiving the first of these volunteers in September 1941 to commence physical fitness and resilience tests. When the volunteers had successfully completed preliminary training and had been formed into battalions, they were then taken in company strength (approximately 120) to Ringway to make their qualifying parachute jumps.

The 1st Parachute Squadron RE (sappers) comprised 150 men who were divided into A, B and C troops together with a small HQ company. The squadron was commanded by a major with a captain in command of each troop supported by several lieutenants.

---

* See Appendix 3.

The memorandum of August 1941 requesting volunteers stipulated that all men must be A1 physically fit and endorsed as such by their unit medical officer. They must be between 20 and 32 years of age, have satisfactory eyesight (must not wear glasses) and have a body weight not exceeding 196lb. It was further specified that volunteers must be of good character. To establish this it was requested that on attending Hardwick volunteers were to arrive with their disciplinary record and good-conduct report. It was stressed that the units sending volunteers must not see this as an opportunity to offload unsuitable and underperforming soldiers.

In the event this was largely ignored, and units sent men without good-conduct records and with dubious histories. As a result, 50 per cent of volunteers were returned to their units (RTU) before training commenced. Such was the rejection rate that Lieutenant Colonel John Frost recalled that there were serious concerns as to whether two battalions could be made up to strength.*

A further inducement to volunteer was the extra pay. A parachute soldier was to receive an additional 2s per day, with 4s for officers which would commence after the completion of eight parachute jumps. This was later readjusted to 2s for officers in order to give parity for all ranks.

Not every army unit was timely in bringing the request for volunteers to the attention of their soldiers. The first that Tom became aware of it was in February 1942, some six months after the order was issued, when REs were required. Tom applied and was summoned to the Guards Depot in Birdcage Walk, London where a panel was interviewing RE personnel to form the 1st Parachute Squadron, which would comprise 150 men.

The overall objective was that the 1st Parachute Brigade would be part of the 1st Airborne Division which included paratroops and glider-borne infantry with supporting weapons. The Division was to be commanded by General 'Boy' Browning and was expected to be ready for action by the summer of 1942. A glider-pilot regiment was also being formed concurrently with the parachute brigade.

In April 1942 Hardwick Hall was established as the Airborne Forces Depot with the Parachute Regiment being officially formed on 1 August 1942. The distinctive red beret, which is actually maroon, was chosen for the new Airborne Division together with the divisional patch of claret and Cambridge blue, the horse-racing colours of its commander, General Browning.

*

I submitted an application to join the parachute engineers and once more the captain tried to dissuade me, explaining once again that the LMR needed trained men. He stated further that I would be promoted within a few months. I knew I had it cushy, I had my own room, the food was good

---

* John Frost, *A Drop Too Many* (1992), p. 27.

and I would earn extra pay on promotion, however my mind was made up and I wanted the adventure and requested that my application be approved. My application was testily stamped and I waited to be called for selection.

A few weeks later I was summoned to the Guards depot at Birdcage Walk in London where around twenty other lads and myself were given a talk on the proposed formation of the parachute brigade, the training involved, the expectations and the estimation of a 70 per cent casualty rate. I thought they were trying to scare us off or rattle the faint-hearted. Following our briefing, we were told to disappear for a couple of hours, have lunch and to return if we were still interested. It was further explained that if any of us had reservations we could return to our units without recrimination or reproach.

A few hours later I returned to Birdcage Walk with half a dozen others, our names and numbers were recorded and we were instructed to return to our units to await further contact. Within a week I was summoned to Aldershot to undergo a medical and shortly afterwards my movement papers came through, and I was required to report to Hardwick Hall near Chesterfield to begin the next stage in the selection process to become a parachute engineer. It was early March 1942 and I was then 22 years of age.

One of the interviewing officers at Birdcage walk was a Captain Douglas Murray who was later to become my squadron commander as a major in the 1st Parachute Squadron RE in North Africa.

Chapter 12

Paratroop Training at Hardwick Hall, March 1942

I arrived at Chesterfield railway station and with others was taken by truck to Hardwick Hall to be billeted in hastily erected Nissen huts within the grounds. The following morning we were reminded that we were volunteer soldiers and began the intensive physical selection process which was to be the first stage of our training. There were lads from many regiments present, guardsmen, artillerymen, Scots wearing tartan trews and glengarry hats with their large regimental badges, signallers, medical corps and last but not least the sappers such as myself from the RE.

The selection began with a programme of punishing physical fitness exercises which included running and set gymnasium work, all under the uncompromising scrutiny of the Physical Training Instructors (PTIs) who were pretty heartless. On one occasion a lad fell off the parallel bars hitting his head on the floor with a crack, he was out cold. Several lads moved to his assistance but were halted with a shout of 'leave him', and the PTI then pointedly stepped over his prostrate body as if he wasn't there. Fortunately, he did come round later, albeit groggily. The emphasis on high levels of physical fitness was to become part of our way of life from there on.

Parachute training was still in its infancy at this time. The 1st Battalion's training had started at Ringway and from there they had moved across to Hardwick. When I arrived the 1st Battalion had already been moved down to Bulford (Wiltshire) to make way for the formation of the 2nd and 3rd Battalions, the remaining troops of engineers and field ambulance.

The Hardwick training was innovative, and it seemed to us to be developing on the hoof to toughen us up and simulate the hard knocks that we were about to receive. It appeared that new ideas were dreamed up overnight and if the latest one didn't work, shoulders were shrugged and our pragmatic instructors thought of something else.

During this period those among us who couldn't take the knocks or maintain the required level of stamina were weeded out, as were those with a poor attitude and disciplinary record. The spectre of an RTU whereby the volunteer was returned to his original unit as unsuitable was a real concern to us. It was a rejection that those of us who were striving to be part of the new paratroop force were desperate to avoid.

An air-sickness test was contrived by using a long suspended swing upon which lads would be made to lay down and the contraption was then put in motion. I somehow never undertook this test and was fortunate not to suffer from air sickness, but some lads did and were rejected because of it. The test, however, proved to be ineffective as some of those that had passed later found that they had air sickness to contend with as well as jumping from the aircraft, sometimes into situations where they were also required to fight.

Once accepted for parachute training, I was placed in C Troop of the 1st Parachute Squadron RE which was the last of the three troops to be formed within the squadron. The three troops of the squadron were to be attached in a supporting role to the three parachute battalions but remained as independent entities with their own commanding officers (COs) and a small HQ company.

Chapter 13

1st Parachute Squadron Royal Engineers

Formation

The 1st Parachute Squadron RE evolved from a RE Air Troop, a much smaller body of men who were recruited as volunteers from RE Field Companies in 1941. With the formation of the 1st Parachute Brigade it was recognised that each parachute battalion should be supported by a specialist troop of parachute engineers.

The 1st Parachute Squadron began forming its first troop in early 1941 when A Troop was created from the nucleus of the original Air Troop, and this was followed by B and finally C Troop, which was completed in April 1942.

The squadron totalled approximately 150 sappers divided between the 3 troops plus a small HQ company. Each troop had four sticks of men that included an officer and a troop sergeant.* It was unusual for all the men to be fit due to the nature of the calling and the HQ company would usually jump among the sticks of ten. Similar to the parachute battalions, the squadron's complement of NCOs was higher than that of a normal infantry unit.

A, B and C Troops were respectively attached in support of the 1st, 2nd and 3rd Parachute Battalions. However, men were occasionally borrowed by another troop or battalion if there was a shortage of sappers for a particular task, and on occasions the squadron deployed together, but mostly the troops supported their designated battalion.

*

Upon being accepted we were placed into a battalion or troop and were issued with lanyards, the colour of which distinguished your unit within the brigade. The lanyards were made of plaited parachute cord and were worn looped over the left shoulder under the battledress epaulette and then tucked into the adjacent breast pocket. The 1st Battalion wore green, the 2nd yellow, the 3rd red, the field ambulance maroon and blue and the engineers royal blue. The issue of the lanyards was the first recognisable step in belonging and they were proudly worn as the colours of our team. But these were early days for us and we still had a great deal of training to come before the ultimate challenge of jumping from an aircraft.

---

* A group of ten men was known as a stick.

We trained to simulate falling from a variety of contrived situations, and at one point we were driven around a rough field on a flat-bed lorry and were required to fall off backwards while it was still moving. Inevitably, we sustained injuries. When the orthopaedic ward at the local hospital in Chesterfield started getting a regular supply of Hardwick lads, eyebrows were raised and this particular exercise was discontinued.

The roundabout was another piece of equipment that was guaranteed to raise a few bruises, as the name implies it was a roundabout with looped trailing ropes replacing the comfort of a seat. The contraption was driven around and we trotted alongside holding the loop until our feet left the ground as the speed increased. Some of us flew high and some of us flew low, and when your number was called you had to let go and deal with the unceremonious landing. Following the fairground theme, we also spent time swinging from huge scaffolding supported in a parachute harness. Swinging high as if on a trapeze, we practised body control exercises to give us a foretaste of what to expect from an undulating parachute.

Now that we were suitably conditioned to receiving a daily ration of bruises we moved on to the next stage of our training in preparation for our first parachute landing. One morning we were introduced to a raised mobile platform which stood about 10ft feet above the ground. The platform was supported by four legs mounted on wheels with a raised hole cut into the centre through which we were required to drop.

On top it had room for an instructor and up to ten lads, which was our first introduction to a stick, and the whole contraption was pushed along by another group of lads below. On the word 'go' we were required to drop through the hole onto the ground in quick succession. Through practice the exit was speeded up into a sequence of drop, touchdown and roll. The key was to roll away as quickly as possible when hitting the ground to avoid being squashed by the next man coming down – fortunately for us we had been issued with rubber soled boots on acceptance for training.

The drop through the hole on the platform was made from a sitting position and required a quick scramble to get through with the requisite speed to satisfy the instructors, who as always were looking for perfection. The platform was designed to simulate the method that would be used when we eventually dropped from an aircraft, which in our case would be Whitley and Albermarle bombers.

The modified Whitleys and Albermarles had circular holes cut into the floor pans through which we left the aircraft. The hole in the Whitley was more of a straight tube of approximately 3ft depth. The hole was not very wide and it was not possible to jump through it in a standing position. To access these holes we had to approach in a sitting position that entailed a lot of synchronised shuffling. When launching yourself through the tube a rigid position of attention had to be maintained to facilitate the smooth exit of the upper body, any slight bend risked hitting your head on the rim. It was to be even more of a risk when we later had a parachute pack on our backs.

The Albermarles were worse than the Whitleys for gaining access to the hole as these aircraft had a stepped floor pan that required a degree of bunny hopping as well as shuffling. I was later to make two training jumps from an Albermarle onto Salisbury Plain after we had moved down to Bulford.

At Hardwick there was also a large shed within which sections of aircraft fuselage were mounted on high wooden legs above a neatly raked sandpit. It was used for the last phase of our training prior to being transferred to Ringway, and sometimes we moved into here on inclement days if we were lucky, but such was the pressure on the facilities that often as not we would be outside. In all of the 'drop through the hole' simulations at Hardwick we were training without a parachute pack on our backs, and the only exception to this was the practical instruction in the quick release of an open parachute in windy conditions.

The parachute harness had a quick-release box positioned over our lower chest into which all the connecting webs were locked, and on landing we had to release these quickly to discard the parachute to become an effective soldier. If it was windy, the parachute would drag you along the ground and the stronger the wind the faster you were pulled along. By hitting the box with the heel of the hand a quick release was activated unlocking the webbing, then by immediately raising your arms above your head the webbing and parachute were disengaged and blown away … in theory.

We practised quick ground release in the wind and had a merry old time. The practice went like this, on a suitably windy day we were strapped in a parachute and laid down on our backs, two men then held your ankles and the parachute was released and allowed to billow out (deploy). The wind filled the deployed parachute and as it strained to blow away your ankles were released and away you went along the ground. Hitting the box was another problem. Some of us were flipped over onto our stomachs and the quick-release box filled with earth and grass preventing release and then you were dragged across fields, into hedges and ditches collecting all sorts of bruises and muck along the way.

Alongside these more creative training ideas were the relentless gymnasium work outs, floor exercises and sit-ups using the log and parallel bars. During the weeks at Hardwick our strength, suppleness and stamina increased as we were put through physical training virtually every day.

When allowed an evening out, many of us headed to the bright lights of Chesterfield for the dance halls and pubs; a stolen bicycle was the usual method of return for those that missed the last bus or liberty truck back to camp. Ample evidence of this practice was later obtained when the lake at Hardwick Hall was drained revealing a pile of rusty bikes at the bottom, but by the time this came to light we were long gone.

Another amusement at Hardwick was the Scots. We had a generous sprinkling of Scottish lads throughout our squadron and the battalions. C Company in the 2nd Battalion was completely made up of Scots and was generally referred to as 'jock' company. Being from a variety of Scottish regiments, they would banter among one another when the English were scarce, but the brigade would have been poorer without them and the Scottish contingent in C Troop were all good lads.

Hardwick Hall suited me very well as it was much nearer to Barnsley than my previous camp at Longmoor and I was able to get home on leave to Royston. I recall my first weekend pass from Hardwick. I was at home and taking a bath when my Dad popped his head round the door for a chat, taking one look at me he called downstairs to my mother, 'Annie, come up here and see our Tom.' When she arrived she burst into tears as I was black and blue from the knocks I'd received in training. Mum was quite upset, 'I never thought I'd see one of my sons in such a state as this' she sobbed as I tried to assure her that it would soon wear off. It didn't seem out of the ordinary to me as we were all mottled with the various hues of green, black and blue at Hardwick.

Many men dropped out during the initial training at Hardwick Hall, some due to the lumps and bumps received and others who did not consider it worth the extra daily pay, an inducement that was to be earned by a parachute soldier on completion of his training.

Following nine weeks at Hardwick we were ready and I along with several hundred other lads was looking forward to our move up to Ringway for the next stage in our training.

Chapter 14

First Parachute Jumps at Ringway, April 1942

Conditions

Ringway Central Landing School, now the site of Manchester International Airport, had been re-named the Airborne Forces Establishment in 1942 and was under the command of the Air Ministry. The training and facilities had been improved since Churchill's intervention but there were still limitations stemming from the RAF's initial disinterest. New Nissen huts had been built to accommodate 250 trainees and the small number of RAF parachute instructors had been boosted by the addition of several army instructors from the 1st Battalion which had formerly been based at nearby Knutsford.

Aircraft and parachutes were still in short supply and a wet day could make parachutes unserviceable. The parachute shortage was being overcome with the introduction of the new X-type parachute which allowed parachutists a degree of directional control by pulling on the rigging lines. Nevertheless, courses were delayed for days due to the need to dry wet parachutes.

Training apparatus was still evolving when the 2nd and 3rd Battalions were taken to Ringway for a period of fourteen days to complete their qualifying jumps. The equipment at Ringway was ahead of Hardwick in both variety and innovation and had picked up the name of 'Kilkenny's Circus' after the RAF Flight Lieutenant John Callistus Kilkenny who was responsible for its development. Kilkenny was the Chief Parachute Instructor at Ringway from 1941–5.

The overall shortage of aircraft, instructors, equipment and accommodation resulted in the numbers being limited to courses of 250, and men were therefore sent from Hardwick in company strength (120 men) rather than by battalion. Further stretching resources and in addition to the parachute training were the men and women of the Special Operations Executive who were being trained for their solitary missions in occupied Europe.

*

In April we were taken from Hardwick to Ringway where together with the rest of my course we were billeted in the Nissen huts adjacent to the airfield. It was here that our real parachute training began in earnest. We were physically very fit, accustomed to hard knocks and were keen to start parachuting. Much of the training was carried out within the confines of aircraft hangars, within which there was a variety of apparatus designed to enable us to simulate leaving an aircraft quickly and landing in a parachute harness. The instructors on my course were mostly RAF SNCOs as the army did not have sufficient parachute training instructors at the time.

Theoretical instruction preceded the fitting of parachutes, and we were introduced to the parachutes' construction, principals of deployment and watched demonstrations from the ground. We were also shown the WAAF parachute packers at work, carefully folding the long lengths of silk and cord on long tables. But it wasn't so much the girls that caught my eye but the sign above their heads which read, 'Remember a man's life depends on every parachute – you pack'.

We trained on giant slides from which we would exit at speed to perfect our feet and knee landing position. Dropping from a height of 20ft was practised by jumping in harness from a tower attached to a rope, the rope in turn was attached to a fan which controlled the speed as you fell. Feet, knees and roll came into play as you hit the ground. The hangars echoed with the shouts of our PTIs yelling, 'Feet and knees together!' To further strengthen our arms and backs we spent hours on giant swings, 'tramming' hard to gain and maintain height.

It was constantly drummed into us that when parachuting from an aircraft the quicker the disembarkation the more effective we would be, the troops fall closer together making for faster regrouping and defence on the ground. To this end we continued to practise fast exits. The training apparatus that we used for aircraft exits at Ringway was similar to that which we had trained on at Hardwick, with a long platform standing 10ft above the ground with the hole in the centre. The difference now was that we were training in sticks of ten all the time. The ten men were lined up in a sitting position with five men on either side of the hole, on the command to move the row quickly shuffled forward with the lead man dropping through the hole followed by the rest in rapid order. There could be no hesitation. On hitting the floor you had to react as at Hardwick with an instant sideways role or the next man in would land on top of you. If you were slow you were 'bawled out' because at this stage you were expected to be better. This was practised relentlessly until our exits were fluid.

The round exit hole was designed to simulate the hole in the floor of a Whitley or Albermarle bomber which were the first aircraft that were used for parachute training. Both these aircraft had been modified to carry paratroops and both were unsuitable. Later the Douglas Dakota C47 was introduced and we were then able to jump from a standing position through an open door in the side of the aircraft.

To give us the experience of landing with an open canopy we were introduced to a large tower from which we did a couple of controlled descents. On this apparatus the parachute was held open by a frame. After climbing the tower we were strapped into the harness and lowered by a cable at the estimated speed of a falling parachute. Although time was limited on this apparatus due to the numbers of men passing through, I was able to experience two descents.

Our training moved on and we learned to fit and adjust our parachute harnesses in earnest, with emphasis placed on tightening the straps as much as possible to prevent them working loose. To achieve the required degree of tightness we had to assist one another, often by putting a knee into the back or the stomach of the person you were helping to compress the clothing beneath the webs, procedures that were to become a serious ritual before all of our future jumps.

When the time came for our first parachute jump it was to be from one of the barrage balloons that were tethered in the grounds of Tatton Park, a short distance from Ringway. These balloons were played out from the ground by a winch to a height of 800ft, and suspended below was a basket that held four would-be parachutists plus the instructor. The balloon's basket had a centrally placed round hole in the floor with a raised steel bar above it. The method of exit was to sit with your feet dangling through the hole with the static line connecting the parachute to the bar, then upon command you launched yourself through. The static line pulled open the parachute as you fell. There were no safety harnesses and we only had one parachute.*

The risk of injury or of later being killed or wounded did not particularly concern us. The general feeling among those of us who had made it so far was that if it happens, it happens, we can't do much about it so why worry and the risks were stoically accepted.

Our parachutes were the X-type statichute that were opened automatically by a static line attached to the bar in the balloon (hook-up cable in an aircraft). These were an improvement on the rip-cord type, which had to be pulled manually or 'ripped' to activate opening.** The new statichute also had the advantage that it could be manoeuvred in a limited way by pulling on the rigging lines.

At Ringway there often appeared to be a shortage of parachutes and getting us through our course was quite a feat of organisation by the parachute packers and training staff. Rain in particular was a problem because if the parachutes were caught in a shower with the canopies open, they needed to be dried before repacking could take place, I recall seeing a large hangar that was filled with rows of suspended parachutes drying off.

---

* The Russians had reserve parachutes as early as 1931, while US paratroops had reserves from their inception. Several reasons were given for not providing British paratroops with a reserve parachute: cost, the small apertures in the floor of the bombers through which they had originally to jump and the fact that the low height from which they jumped would not allow sufficient time for a reserve parachute to deploy fully.

** These parachutes were used by aircrew for 'baling out'. Those used by aircrew were smaller than those used by parachute troops as they were not required to carry weapons and ammunition.

The night before our first static jump we were staying inside an aircraft hangar at Ringway. Many of us were nervous and we spent the night exchanging banter and singing the songs of the paratroops, many of which related to mishaps. One song in particular related to the roman candle and was sung to the rousing tune of 'John Brown's Body', the first verse stating:

'Is everybody happy?' said the Sergeant, looking up.
Our hero feebly answered, 'Yes' and then they hooked him up.
He jumped into the slip stream and he twisted twenty times,
and he ain't going to jump no more'

The final verse was:

'There was blood upon the lift webs, there was blood upon his 'chute,
Blood that came a' trickling from his paratrooper's boots,
and there he lay like jelly in the welter of his gore,
and he ain't going to jump no more.'

Few of us were able to sleep in the knowledge that refusal to jump from either the basket or an aircraft at any time during training resulted in an immediate RTU. It was also understood that once the eight qualifying jumps had been completed and our wings had been awarded, any refusal to jump would become a court-martial offence. By now we had few illusions about the dangers.

The following morning we were taken down to Tatton and introduced to two huge barrage balloons that were tethered about 15ft above the ground. Below the balloons were the baskets attached by limp cords and the balloon was attached to a motorised winch.

Our turn had come. Four of us with parachutes and the instructor climbed into the basket and the winch was played out. We were off, the balloon swaying nauseatingly as it climbed slowly up to 800ft.* It was deathly quiet up there and the pervading silence seemed to increase our collective nervousness.

Our instructor was an RAF SNCO named Sergeant Billy Baker who was an ex-Bertram Mills circus trapeze artist. He sauntered fearlessly around the swaying basket with much show. When the basket came to a stop at 800ft we were huddled in the four corners pale-faced and trying not to turn green.

Billy Baker looked at us and began to give us his final instructions, first he said, 'Here are your numbers' and pointing at each of us in turn he counted

---

* The height of 800ft was the starting height which gave plenty of time for the novice to get sorted out in the air. Having competed training, the usual practice and operational jump was 600ft, which in some instances of pilot error came down dangerously close to 400ft.

out 'One, two, three and four' and then he stressed that when he said 'Go' we jumped. 'Remember,' he continued, 'do not lean forward or you will hit your nose on the rim in front of you ... do not lean back or your parachute will catch the back of the hole and throw you forward ... sit on the rim with your legs dangling in the hole and go straight out on command'. He slowly continued and he had our rapt attention, 'It's daylight and you're static ... you're not in an aircraft bouncing around ... if you hurt yourself it's your own fault because you have been told what to do'. He then relaxed and started to crack jokes which must have been for his own amusement as none of us found them at all funny. We just kept to our corners nervously licking our lips.

Sergeant Baker then gave a quick glance over the side to check that the Aldis lamp was winking the all clear on the ground.* He said, 'OK, No. 1 take up your position.' I was the No. 1 so into the hole I went, legs dangling, static line clipped to the bar and with hardly time for a wriggle or a tremble he gave the command, 'Go'.

We had practised jumping so many times from all manner of apparatus that on the command 'Go' I went, no hesitation, and I couldn't have stopped myself if I'd tried because I had become so conditioned. I must have dropped a 100ft before I felt the tug of my static line pulling the cover off my parachute which then opened with a rush, wonderfully restraining my descent.

Looking around with all nervousness forgotten I thought, 'This is not so bad ... I'm halfway down already'. But my reverie was short lived as I was brought to my senses by an officer shouting up to me from down below with a megaphone, 'Good exit No. 1, keep your feet together' and he talked me down. Knees together and bent, touchdown and a roll through the hip and the shoulder and I was safely on the ground.

The other three followed me down and no sooner had the last one landed when the winch started winding down the balloon. As it descended we were quickly assisted into another parachute and up we went again for our second jump. With our two static jumps completed we were curtly told, 'Back down to the airfield tomorrow for your aircraft jump, same height 800ft' and so the following day we were taken out onto the airfield where we were introduced to the Whitley for the first time. We had already seen it from a distance and heard the fearsome racket that it made on take-off, but now that we were close up it looked ugly and ominous in its jet-black paint.

---

* Aldis signal lamps were employed in optical communication using Morse code, and were operated by opening and closing the lens shutters. They were invented by A.C.W. Aldis and pioneered in the late nineteenth century.

Armstrong Whitworth Whitley Bomber

The Armstrong Whitworth Whitley bomber was a twin-engine aircraft introduced in 1937. Initially used on bombing raids over Germany, it was capable of carrying a 4,000lb bomb. In 1941 many were made redundant due to the aircraft's slow air speed, its vulnerability to faster German night fighters and the introduction of faster four-engine bombers. These redundant Whitleys were converted to tow Horsa troop-carrying gliders and drop paratroops.

*

Before we made our first jump, we were taken up for an air-experience flight. Once airborne, the hatch was pulled back and we were shown the hole through which we would be required to jump later that day, it was similar to the one in the balloon basket but deeper. The term jump is often used but in fact it was a drop through the hole in the floor, and we didn't start jumping until we moved onto the Dakota aircraft later in the year. The short flight was our first experience of the noise, vibration and the aircraft's bounce in the turbulence. When the hatch in the floor was opened we heard the high-pitched whistle from down the funnel-like tube and a cold blast of air. For most of us it was the first time that we had ever flown in an aircraft.

Jumping from a Whitley bomber is a different kettle of fish to jumping from a balloon, as inside they are long, narrow, windowless and dark with no room to stand up straight. The floor on which we had to sit was hard decking as the Whitley didn't have any seats. We sat alternately opposite one another down the sides of the aircraft with our legs out straight, five before and five aft of the hatch that covered the hole. We all disliked the Whitley.

Parachute static lines were hooked to a cable that ran at shoulder height along the roof of the fuselage, and once hooked up we were numbered off, one, two, three, etc., the number of men jumping from an aircraft was referred to as a stick.* On jumping, the static line remains attached inside the aircraft, at the end of its tether it pulls the flap of the descending parachutist's pack allowing his parachute to open. After the paratroops have left the aircraft the static lines and covers trailing along outside the fuselage are winched back inside.

---

* Initially, a stick comprised ten men which included a sergeant. This number was dictated by the paratroop-carrying capacity of the Whitley. Later, the size of the stick increased with the change to the larger Dakota C47 which would usually carry eighteen. The minimum ratio of ten men to a sergeant usually remained the same, and the reason for this was to increase the odds in favour of an SNCO landing with the troops on the ground. Officers were also included within the stick.

Our first jump from the Whitley went without a hitch. On approaching the Drop Zone (DZ) the hinged doors of the hole were folded back and the first man positioned himself on the rim with his legs in the hole, the next man sat directly opposite with his legs askance ready to swing his legs into the hole to follow. The green light came on and we were out. As practised many times in simulated training, the approach to the hole was made alternately on our backsides from either side of the aircraft.

The whistle and cold blast of air from the hole was ignored as all concentration was on getting out fast. As you dropped out of the hole the strength of the slipstream threw you almost horizontal until clear of the aircraft and then you started to drop. Our first experiences were disorientating. We were dropping alternately, with five of us facing the direction of the aircraft's flight as we came out and face down, while the other five were facing the rear and on their backs. Later, when we were laden down with kit the slip stream had less of an effect than jumping solely with a parachute.

As we went through our drop sequence the Whitley continued to drone in circles above Tatton Park until we were all out. At the time it seemed to happen very quickly, but when viewed retrospectively and in the light of our future jumps we were clumsy and slow.

From the start of our jumps from an aircraft we had an imaginary container release included in the jump sequence. The containers were the large cigar-shaped pods that were later to carry our weapons and equipment. The Whitley carried two that were mounted in the bomb bay, where they hung waiting to be released in the middle of our stick of ten. They descended like us with their own individual parachutes. It was as if they were additional unseen paratroops jumping from a different part of the aircraft, and as such a pause had to be made to fit them into our jump sequence. To accommodate their release, a pause of 2 seconds was required to prevent the sixth man in the stick colliding with them outside of the aircraft.

We began jumping in what were termed 'slow pairs', that is two men jumping one after the other shouting their number as they swung into the hole. The third man would shout, 'Container … container' creating the 2-second pause in our exit, the sequence then continued with another two men jumping. This was followed by the same procedure in 'quick pairs' and then in slow and quick 'fives' and finally with ten men achieving the stick. By this time the 'Container … container' shout was the mid-stick responsibility of the sixth man.

We were reminded many times both before and after our first Whitley jump, that the same care was required when leaving the Whitley as was needed when leaving the hole in the balloon's basket. Leaning forward or backwards could result in your head hitting the rim of the hole. Facial injuries were common and lads walking around with a dressing across the bridge of their nose weren't unusual; these accidents were known as 'ringing the bell'. Although we disliked the Whitley, it was far more preferable to jumping from a balloon.

When we jumped in our first stick of ten it was considered to be a milestone in our training, we were beginning to click, on our 'backsides' we had moved down the aircraft's floor in a smooth if cumbersome shuffle and out down the hole. On landing all seemed satisfied, so much so that we were told that we would all be back down at the airfield the following evening for a night jump, which was to be our last at Ringway.

Although we were gaining confidence, there was always a shadow of apprehension when jumping, but the belief we had gained in our equipment and training steadied our nerves. The night jump went without a hitch, although eerie, and my eyes were sticking out like chapel hat pegs as I strained to pick up light on the ground. The ground comes up pretty fast and hard in the dark and you need to be pretty nifty with your footwork to roll through your body to avoid injury. Serious injuries were not common but jarred spines, twisted ankles, knees and bruising were a fairly regular and accepted occurrence.

The Ringway qualification course had lasted for two weeks and ended with the successful completion of eight jumps, two from the balloon and six from an aircraft which included the final night jump. We were then presented with our parachute wings in an aircraft hangar by the RAF Station Commander.

We were also issued with our airborne divisional badge, the pale-blue Bellerophon astride a winged Pegasus on a maroon background, together with the crescent-shaped shoulder flash which in my case was embroidered with 'Royal Engineer Parachute'. We were very proud of our insignia and displayed them at every opportunity, sitting on a bus or train we managed to sit with our shoulders firmly up to the window displaying them for all to see. We were recognised as paratroops among the country's throng of khaki – we were different and very proud to be members of the 1st Parachute Brigade.*

This pride was the beginning of our perceived elitism and we believed that we were disliked by many other regiments because of it, but this perception had a positive effect and far from giving us a complex bonded us together even further. We were up for any special forces' operation and believed we could do it, we were almost always disappointed when planned operations were cancelled, as many were.**

---

*   The 1st Parachute Brigade was initially to comprise four battalions, but the 4th Battalion was recruited and trained after the 2nd and 3rd Battalions became the nucleus of the 2nd Parachute Brigade. The strength of the 1st Brigade and subsequent parachute brigades were also to be kept at three battalions.

** Between 5 December 1941 and the end of May 1942 the 2nd and 3rd Battalions, the 1st Parachute Squadron RE and 16 Parachute Field Ambulance qualified as parachute troops completing the formation of the 1st Parachute Brigade. It had taken eighteen months for the first brigade of Winston Churchill's requested parachute-troop capability to be completed.

The Structure of the British Army

During 1939–45 Britain had a number of armies, for example, the 1st Army and 8th Army were fighting in North Africa in 1942.

- An **army** comprised several **corps**.

- A **corps** comprised several **divisions**.

- A **division** was usually the smallest unit capable of independent operations and was made up of between 10,000 and 30,000 men. A typical division would consist of: 3 infantry brigades, mechanised armour and support units, e.g., combat engineers and reconnaissance and medical troops. The 1st Airborne Division numbered a little over 10,000 men. In place of armour it had light artillery support.

- A **brigade** was a unit of between 2 and 5 **battalions**.

- A **battalion** consisted of between 500 and 1,500 men. Parachute battalions were smaller than infantry battalions, having approximately 670 men at full strength. Parachute brigades were also smaller than infantry brigades, having only 3 battalions. A parachute battalion had 3 **companies**.

- Each **company** had around 200 soldiers.

- Each **company** was subdivided into 3 to 5 **platoons**.

- A **squadron** was a company sized unit in the RE, Royal Corps of Signals, Royal Army Medical Corps, Corps of Transport and the SAS to name but a few. Squadrons were divided into **troops**. The 1st Parachute Squadron RE was a company sized unit of 150 men comprising A, B and C Troops and was part of the 1st Parachute Brigade.

Chapter 15

Training at Bulford Camp, April 1942

From Ringwood we were taken down to Bulford on Salisbury Plain to continue our infantry and specialist training. At this point although our squadron had been formed, we were under strength and men were still coming in to us throughout May.

Our standard operational dress was army serge khaki trousers, modified for paratroops by having chamois-leather-lined pockets to prevent the contents breaking through, battledress, gaiters and standard-issue hobnailed boots.* A green camouflage parachute smock (Denison) with a broad fork tail was worn over the battledress top. The tail on the smock came down from the back, between the legs and up to fasten at the front and was designed to prevent the smock ballooning when descending from the aircraft.

Over the smock was a Bren gun ammunition harness that held four pouches of ammunition and a webbing belt around the waist to which were attached more pouches holding hand and phosphorous grenades. A double-edged Sykes Fairburn fighting knife was slipped into the chamois-lined pocket on the outside of the right trouser leg.

Headgear comprised a metal reinforced protective helmet which had replaced the rubber-rimmed type that we had used in training. Around the neck we wore a face veil, which was in effect an olive-green scarf made of a netted scrim material designed to camouflage the face when draped. Other items carried were an entrenching tool, water bottle, shell dressing and a toggle rope, after training the latter was discarded or 'lost', being considered of little use.

In the early days it was only the officers and SNCOs that jumped with a weapon, usually a Sten gun. The other weapons, as previously mentioned, were carried in containers. The Sten guns were lightweight machine carbines which were considered to be pretty unreliable and we preferred the heavier, two-man-operated Bren. The Bren guns were also dropped together with their ammunition in our containers. When we jumped on operations the officers and SNCOs were always well spaced within the stick to reduce the odds of a leader being lost on landing. Casualties and separations were common and

---

* We were initially issued with rubber-soled boots during training, but these were withdrawn from us on leaving Ringway.

for this reason parachute units always had a higher number of NCOs than infantry units.

At Bulford we continued with our airborne training and in particular the use of containers. At Ringway we had worked up to a stick of ten with an imaginary container, but now our future jumps would be with real containers. The containers were to be an essential part of our equipment and were used on all exercises and operations to carry our weapons, ammunition, explosives and a host of other items that were required to do a job. When dropped it was essential that they landed among us, if they were lost the success of the operation and possibly our lives would be compromised. To guard against damage on impact the containers had a shock absorber built into the base together with a small number of blue lights to help us to locate them at night.*

We were still jumping from Whitleys and our training jumps were mostly onto Salisbury Plain having taken off from either RAF Netheravon or Boscombe Down. The emphasis of our training was now on a smooth and fast exit and the timing of container release. The container-release procedure centred between the fifth and sixth man. As the fifth man went out a switch was thrown by the RAF crewman releasing the two containers from the bomb bay, where they hung beneath and forward of our exit hole. When our stick jumped the sixth man paused as he called the well-practised phrase, 'Container ... container' allowing the containers to hurtle past below, and he then went out followed by the remaining four men.

Timing was crucial in the middle of the stick, if you went too soon you were in danger of being hit by a container as it was released. A collision ran the real risk of a fatality. There had been a near miss several weeks before we left Ringway, when a lad had been hit by a container on leaving the aircraft and had broken his legs. When we arrived, the incident was being used to emphasise the element of timing when jumping as the sixth man. The watch words were, 'Do not go too soon ... do not go too slow and hold up the remainder of the stick'.

To avoid trees and obstructions we put into practice the theory that we had been taught about how to manoeuvre the 'chute by pulling on the web straps. Some movement was achieved but with limited success as we were now jumping from 600ft and occasionally, more by accident than design, as low as 400ft. The lower heights left little time to control the direction of the parachute.

---

* The containers' parachutes were later coloured so that each unit could identify their own. The sappers would usually have blue, Field Ambulance red and an infantry company yellow. The coloured lights in the container's base plate were the same colour as the parachute for night identification. The reason for this was to prevent troops having to run from one container to another trying to locate their individual weapons and equipment.

We had also gained the quickness of thought to observe the performance of the parachute and could influence its deployment by mid-air kicks to straighten out the rigging lines. This kicking out would sometimes increase in tempo to approaching panic in the case of a thrown line or a roman candle, the latter being the more serious of the two. The thrown line happens when a rigging line or lines snag over the canopy preventing its full deployment, while the roman candle is where the turbulence on exit spins the parachutist twisting his rigging lines into a spiral. The severity of the spin can twist the rigging lines all the way up to the canopy preventing it opening. Both conditions result in an ever-increasing speed of descent. Although incidents of a full roman candle were rare, lesser twists were not uncommon especially when jumping without the weight of our kit which made us more vulnerable to the buffet of the slip stream.

We were very lightly armed during these training jumps with most of us carrying only the Sykes Fairburn knife. When jumping the knife's primary function was to cut free rigging lines if they became entangled in trees or scrub. I never found myself in a situation whereby I needed to fight someone with the knife and never came down in a tree, but it was always reassuring to have it to hand, especially for opening ration tins when we were without a tin opener!

Finally, before jumping we were usually issued with our parachutes an hour or so before boarding to enable our harnesses to be adjusted and tightened. The parachute was secured to the harness by D bolts on our shoulders. Once adjusted, we took the whole assembly off and chalked our names on the side of the pack, and this way we would not be caught out by having to refit if we were delayed for any period of time, as we often were.

My specialty was that of an airborne engineer and as such I retained the title of my rank as a sapper. Our sapper squadron now began infantry training in earnest, sometimes we worked on our own and at other times we worked in support of the battalions. Our weapons work was based on the use of various machine guns, hand grenades, mortars and on occasion flame throwers. Later, we were to study and learn how to use enemy weapons which we were to use whenever we could get hold of them.

As our squadron was drawn from the broad skill base of the RE field companies there were always men to help our training along, so as a squadron we were not starting from scratch. Officers and men worked together as we began the theory and practice of bridge building and demolition, and we also learned that it was our responsibility to remove the demolition charges from enemy-held bridges. We were taught how to lay and clear mines and how to formulate conventional explosives for specific jobs.

We were introduced to the use of plastic explosives and shown how to cut steel rails, bridge girders and how to blow the tracks off tanks. We visited the GWR railway works at Swindon where we were shown where to place explosives on steam engines, which I had a good idea of, but we then went on to a power station and the critical disabling points were demonstrated. We never seemed to be still.

Our training was fast moving and compressed into five or six weeks in the rush to get us ready. The lads that had volunteered from the RE field companies were way ahead of me as it was more of a conversion course for them. The two of us that had transferred from the RE railway company were at a disadvantage as we had had no previous field experience and were expected to catch up as we went along.

The explosives that we were working with were TNT, gun cotton, ammonal powder and the plastic explosives 808 and PHE. Both plastics could be moulded into shape and we practised the amount and shape that were best suited to different types of jobs, always inventive and employing lateral thinking, we used the putty-coloured PHE for heating our dixies when making tea.* A small piece of PHE when lit burned like oxyacetylene and generated enough heat to bring the water to boil in little over a minute. The plastic 808, however, gave off fumes which could give us a tremendous headache so we avoided inhaling the stuff as much as possible. The explosives were accompanied by a variety of detonators and fuses with which we practised and experimented to achieve the best results.

In addition to the various types of hand grenades that were used in our infantry training we were also introduced to the Gammon bomb, which was an innovation by one of our officers. Used for attacking light-skinned vehicles, it was basically an elasticated bag filled with plastic explosive with a detonator in the collar. It was designed to be thrown from close range and was both cheap and effective. On impact it exploded and shredded any metal sending out slivers of shrapnel. The story within the battalions was that Captain R.J. Gammon (1st Battalion) devised his bomb by using the elasticated leg of a pair of NAAFI ladies' knickers. I don't know how true this was, but it fitted well with the spirit of improvisation that prevailed at the time.

As we settled in at Bulford the characters in the squadron began to emerge and our CO Major Dorman was one of them. The Major was one of those chaps who had a facial expression that appeared to be set in a permanent smile, but unfortunately it wasn't. Many of the lads were initially caught out on his approach by returning his 'grin' only to be taken aback as his 'rictus' disappeared with a sharp, 'What are you smiling at?' Major Dorman kept us very busy.

We were never idle as our physical build-up continued with exercise and route marches. We toiled for hours up and down Beacon Hill at Bulford with our Everest carriers loaded with sandbags. The Everest carrier was a shelved

---

* Folding alloy mess tins that were used to prepare and re-heat food and eat from.

open rucksack similar to the ones used by the Sherpa porters in Nepal. Our adaptation became the standard for the squadron, enabling us to carry much heavier weights than the packs that were originally issued.

From Bulford we were taken south to Southampton for a short period where we were to undertake training in street fighting. Areas of the city had been evacuated leaving sections of the closely packed terraced streets deserted. These were cordoned off and we 'fought' from house to house and street to street. Adjoining walls were kicked and blasted out, as were the attics, as we practised the technique of 'mouse holing', which is creating holes through the walls of one house into the next. We made a bit of a mess in Southampton.

We were taken to Cornwall to undertake cliff climbing and across to Minehead and Porlock in Devon where we went on route marches carrying and pulling weights. By this time we were so fit that we were overtaking the local bus as it laboured up Porlock hill. Beating the bus became a bit of a challenge for us. We would be stripped to the waist as we pulled our loaded airborne trolleys at pace with as many as six lads harnessed by toggle ropes.*

The endurance levels expected of parachute troops was that a battalion must be able to cover 30 miles on foot in 24 hours. This mileage had to be sustainable over several days. A smaller body of men in platoon strength was expected to be able to cover 50 miles in 24 hours carrying full packs and weapons.** 1st Parachute Squadron RE carried additional weights to the battalion rifle platoons and these were loaded onto our Everest carriers; other heavier kit was placed on our trolleys and pulled along.

All three battalions were sent individually to Exmoor where they spent two weeks on manoeuvres supported by a troop from our squadron. When our time arrived we supported the 3rd Battalion around Withypool where we lived under canvas and endured miserable weather during most of our stay. Our tents were the old army bell tents with raised wooden floorboards under which we could hear rats scuttling about at night, probably trying to keep dry, while above the rain rattled down on the sagging canvas. Some nights we stayed out under our capes living rough on the moor as situations and exercises were created to improve our endurance. At the end of the exercise we were made to walk back to Bulford using the run–walk gait of the parachute troops.

The 1st Battalion had previously covered the distance of 110 miles from Exford to Bulford in under three-and-a-half days. The standard had been set and we dared not be beaten or we would never hear the last of it. Our officers

---

*   The airborne trolley was similar to a two-wheeled barrow consisting of a rigid tubular steel frame, folded canvas body and wheels with pneumatic tyres. These were despatched from the aircraft with a small parachute in the same way that containers were despatched. They were used to carry equipment, weapons, explosives and wounded.

**   Weights carried were often in the region of 112lb (1cwt).

were raring to go. As an inducement for matching the pace of the 1st Battalion we were told that we would be allowed a period of leave when we arrived back at camp. This was followed by the caveat that our leave started now so that every day taken on the march would be a day's less leave. The standard set by the 1st Battalion was also to be our target, three-and-a-half days.

We ran, walked and slept at the roadside eating hard rations as we went. Those who needed toileting had to do so al fresco. Such was the pace that in the early hours as we were resting we were roused with the call, 'Come on lads, let's do a couple more hours' and up we would get to start moving again. We came in on time and were allowed out on leave, but on our return we found that our kit had been packed away wet and had gone mouldy, so one of the first tasks was to sort it all out.

Our battalion commander, Lieutenant Colonel Gerald Lathbury, and John Frost (later to command the 2nd Battalion) ran alongside us, as did all our officers which further fostered our *esprit de corps*.

Returning from leave during that summer of 1942 we had an unusual and pleasant exercise. The squadron was sent out from Bulford to 'survey', in the loosest sense of the word, possible enemy glider and parachute landing grounds in the south of England. We were despatched in pairs into the countryside, without any money other than our own and a list of map references. The objective was to inspect and mark on the map possible obstacles to an enemy airborne landing. The supposition was that a flat area on the map could be discounted if large trees, marshes and other uncharted obstacles were present. The weather was beautiful with sunshine and clear blue skies as Len Hook and I made our way from one map reference to another. We travelled around the countryside by walking where we pleased and hitching lifts on the plentiful army transport that traversed the lanes of southern England.

At night we approached farms where we sought the permission of farmers to sleep in a barn, and we were often offered an evening meal as well as a hayloft. A request for a glass of water at a country cottage would sometimes be accompanied by a slice of pie. Occasionally, we passed an army unit and would approach the sergeant cook with a humble, 'Any chance of a spare bite, Sarge?', and one delighted us with, 'Sure, sit down lads', and then with an aside to those within earshot, 'Real soldiers these lads' which delighted Len and I but did little for the paratroop fan club.

Every few days we would meet up with our officers and other members of the squadron at a previously determined village to present our information and receive further briefings. It really was a pleasant few weeks, but all good things come to an end and it wasn't long before we were once again back at Bulford.

As the summer progressed our training jumps were restricted due to the fear that the number of injuries we sustained was reducing our unit strength. To compensate a variation of exercises was being introduced to keep us both mentally focused and physically fit; we were taught to be observant and to improvise. One such exercise entailed being sent out in small groups on what were termed store reconnaissance forays, to list and record any items that could be used in the field. On our return we would discuss the items found and exchange our ideas with other groups, for instance railway yards had stocks of timber and steel rails that could be used for bridging, as could empty oil drums in transport depots. We were being kept alert and on the move and had little time for idleness.

Within our squadron of engineers we had a multitude of skills that had been learned both in the army and civilian life, with every trade seemingly represented. We had metalworkers, plumbers, builders, electricians and numerous others. Whatever problems we encountered someone among us would have the experience to be able to work out a solution or improvisation. There was a real confidence within the squadron that we could achieve whatever we were asked to do.

Chapter 16

On Exercise and How 'Smudger' Got His Own Back, August 1942

O ne exercise followed another as we were taken around the country to train on different types of terrain. Twice we went up to the North Yorkshire Moors, once in battalion strength and once as a squadron. Due to the shortage of aircraft, most of our journeys were made by road and we spent many hours sprawled on our kit in the back of slow-moving trucks.

Our second trip north started from Skegness in Lincolnshire, once again by truck. On arrival, the squadron was broken up into small parties and we had to walk across country into North Yorkshire on a map-reading exercise. We carried our supplies and slept rough. My hazy memories are of Corporal (later Sergeant) 'Smudger' Smith's phobia of sleeping with rats in a barn. I recall their green eyes being reflected in the beams of moonlight that slanted in through the gaps in the walls. We all had a hoot when one dropped into Smudger's lap, he yelled and the rat shrieked, both frightening the other. We fished in a river with hand grenades and had a dangerous experience when stumbling out of a harbour-side pub during Whitby's blackout.

Our next exercise was in late August when we flew up to Scotland with the 3rd Battalion, the plan being to arrive on a night drop and then to live rough in the hills for two weeks. The area to which we were headed was to be in and around New Cumnock in Ayrshire. The aircraft was our usual Whitley, a black, ugly aircraft that made such a racket on take-off that we always wondered if it would fly, but it did, bouncing us around like peas in a drum as it fought to get off the ground. On this particular exercise the flight had been extended to take us out over the Irish Sea, skimming Northern Ireland before approaching the coast of Ayrshire as if on an invasion.

It was dark, noisy and bitterly cold in the Whitley as we began our circuitous flight to towards Scotland. We were sprawled upon the vibrating floor of the aircraft in our usual stick of ten, five forward and five to the rear of the covered hatch. We were already kitted up for the exercise and were fully rigged in our webbing and parachutes, our weapons and small packs stowed in the two containers beneath in the bomb bay.

About ½ hour into the flight the RAF crewman brought in a huge flask of scalding cocoa and it was passed around gratefully. One of our lot laced it with rum and it was as welcome and warming as one could have hoped, but we were soon to be in trouble.

Several of us needed to pass water and before long with the increasing cold we all needed to go. Above the roar of the engines that drowned out all conversation, Smudger Smith attracted the crewman's attention. By signals and mime he managed to convey the problem. The crewman nodded and with a thumbs up he ducked out of sight and returned with a rubber bottle. The bottle was passed around amidst lots of scuffling and muttered curses as we released our kit and struggled with flies and draws to attend the call of nature. It was not something that we had trained for in that dark confined space.

Eventually, with smiles all round the bottle was returned to Smudger, who indicated to the RAF crewman that the bottle was full. By further signs and gestures Smudger was directed to a piece of equipment that appeared to be a flare-despatching chute situated in the gloom at the far corner of the aircraft – this was the disposal solution. There were several valves above and below the 'chute' and tip it in went the crewman's signals, but something went awry as Smudger operated the control in the wrong sequence. There was a whoosh and we all got our own back with the force of the contents of the bottle hitting Smudger full in the face. He was drenched, and turning to us he shouted at the top of his voice, 'Bloodeeee hell … it's a good job it had some rum in it!' This unfortunate story was to give us many a laugh in the difficult days that lay ahead.

We dropped in the dark at around midnight and when down on the ground went in search of our containers, but we were only able to locate the container that carried our weapons. The other carrying our small packs and personal kit had gone, so we were without razors, soap, underwear, shirts and other small comforts that you take when you are on exercise. I remember on our return to Bulford queuing at the quartermaster's store to get replacement kit, and we each had a list as long as your arm. The stores' sergeant was playing steam at the exaggerated claims, wheedling in disbelief that all the items requested would fit into a paratrooper's small pack.

In Ayrshire we marched, bridged and underwent general infantry training, with some nights spent in tents and others out in the open. At the end of the two weeks we entrained at Ayr for the long journey south to Bulford.

Shortly after leaving Scotland the train slowed as it entered Carlisle Citadel station and someone from among us threw a dummy explosive onto the platform, and a terrific bang echoed throughout the station startling both civilians and servicemen. Howls of laughter went up from our carriages. When the train stopped the 3rd Battalion RSM J.C. Lord had us all out in lines on the platform. I recall him shouting, 'Step forward the man who did that', but of course nobody moved an inch. He then went into a harangue of what he was going to do to us when we arrived back at Bulford, but I don't remember what did happen other than we went back into training and were issued with the red beret for the first time. Up to this time we had been wearing the standard-issue khaki forage cap with our original unit badges; we continued to wear these badges after the issue of the red beret. Later, the three battalions were issued with the chrome-plated winged badge synonymous with the parachute regiment, while the sappers continued to wear the brass RE badge. All airborne forces were now distinctive through wearing the maroon (red) beret which drew many a 'hoot' from the troops outside our brigade. Initially, it was usually a wolf whistle but this was soon forgotten as the red beret became the mark of an elite unit.

Regimental status was given to the three battalions of parachute troops in August 1942. The original pre-regiment men were from then on referred to as the 'Batt Boys' (as in battalion) by the men who had joined the regiment after this status had been conferred.

It was also in the late summer of 1942 that we were introduced to our new aircraft, the Douglas Dakota C47. We were taken to RAF Netheravon where we carried out our first Dakota jump in a standing position from the port-side door, rather than the accustomed backside scramble to the hole in the floor of a Whitley. It was faster and easier, especially when encumbered with full kit. One of our officers was later to write, 'We were now able to leave the aircraft like gentlemen', and it was true! The Dakota also had the further advantage over the Whitley in that it was able to carry up to eighteen paratroopers against the Whitley's ten.

We immediately liked the Dakota. It had more room than the Whitley with the interiors being taller and wider. The Perspex-type windows that were spaced along the fuselage let in light and allowed us to look out so we no longer had to sit in the dark. There was also a touch of 'luxury' with metal bench seats running along the sides of the fuselage and a chemical toilet – there was to be no more passing round the bottle!

Unlike the Whitley, our two containers were slung outside and beneath the aircraft further down towards the tail, which lessened the chance of us colliding with one when we jumped. The suspended containers were now to be released before the paratroopers by a trigger from within the aircraft, removing the need for our well-rehearsed 'Container ... container' pause in a moving stick.

The procedure for jumping from the Dakota was for the preliminary warning to be given approximately 20 minutes from the DZ. We then stood up and hooked our static lines to the mid-line anchor cable. Each man checked his own line and then the line of the man in front. He then returned to his own line, which he held in his left hand away from his body. His right hand was placed firmly on the right shoulder of the man in front. Then 5 minutes before the jump the red light would be switched on by the aircraft's navigator, and on seeing this the stick would bunch up into a tight line.

Standing in the open doorway the first man in the stick was unable to see the green light and relied on the second man to give him his signal to jump. When the green light came on the second man gave the first a firm slap on the back while simultaneously pulling the container release trigger. The containers were away as the first man jumped, followed in rapid succession by the rest of the stick. As the 15ft static line snapped taught the parachute was pulled out of its bag and the canopy began to open, with full deployment being achieved within the first 100ft of the drop. It took as little as 20 seconds to reach the ground when we were jumping from around 600ft in full kit.

My first jump from a Dakota was in mid-October onto Salisbury Plain after taking off from RAF Netheravon. This was around a week to ten days after we had suffered four fatalities in the first group that had jumped from the new plane. On 9 October 1942 two of the lads 'chutes had failed to open and a further two had died when a rigging line had become entangled on the fixed tail wheel of the aircraft, and caught in suspension the next lad out had collided with him. On those first Dakota jumps there were several near misses with lads coming perilously close to both the rear wheel and the tail plane.

There seemed to be great urgency to familiarise us with the Dakota and following a hurried investigation two problems were found, the first concerning the two parachutes that failed to deploy. In this case it was discovered that the parachute's static line which was attached to an anchor cable inside the aircraft had become detached at the moment of jumping. The procedure was that we clipped our static lines onto the anchor cable and held the static line in our left hand. As we approached the port-side door at the rear of the aircraft, the static-line clip followed along the anchor cable and was then thrown to our left immediately before jumping to get it out of the way. Unfortunately, in this instance the running clip had snagged against the seating causing it to open at the moment they left the aircraft, resulting in the static line becoming detached and the parachutes not opening. Our parachutes did not have a rip-cord option. Following these fatalities the clips on the end of our static lines were modified with a split pin to prevent them from opening.

The second problem was that the standard static line that we had used in the Whitley was much shorter than that required for jumping from a Dakota. This lack of length resulted in the parachute being pulled out of its bag before the tail wheel had been cleared, which snagged the rigging lines. The problems were sorted out by lengthening our static lines and taping the tail wheel and door hinges. Due to the rush to get us converted, these problems were resolved by trial and error, but when jumping with only one parachute there was not much room for error.

I had by now been allocated the role of Bren gunner in the lead position of No. 1. The squadron was an independent unit and as such was able to provide its own defence when we were out engineering. We were also expected to fight as infantry as and when required. Each of the squadron's three troops had four Bren-gun teams, which equated to one team per stick. I didn't mind the job, our Squadron had plenty of men with explosives experience and as I had not had time to learn all the complexities of preparing explosive mixtures the Bren gave me a definite purpose.

*

Jumping from a Dakota

The Dakotas belonged to a United States Army Air Force (USAAF) troop-carrying group and were crewed by Americans. The Americans had only recently entered the war and were flying the aircraft with men who were mostly ex-airline personnel who had little or no experience of carrying airborne troops. In addition to this, many had not been in the forces for very long.

At this time the US technique of dropping paratroops was still being developed. The current method was to position the aircraft in a nose-down position to place the tail plane higher than the exit door and therefore lifting the tail wheel above the jumping paratroops. To achieve this, the pilot climbed from 600ft to 800ft and then went into a shallow dive at which time the green light came on and the paratroops jumped. The aim was to jump from 600ft but sometimes the last man could be as low as 500ft or less. There were occasions when the pilot dived too steeply with the first man jumping high at 600ft and the men behind him in the stick at a lower height of 400ft, which resulted in the last men out landing with a thump before the first men!

*

There were two men in a Bren-gun team. The No. 1 was responsible for the weapon and fired, maintained, carried and packed it in the containers (1942–3). Later, we were to jump from the aircraft with it in a valise (1944). The No. 2 was responsible for replacing the magazines in action, carrying the spare barrel and protecting the No. 1 with his Sten gun when he was clearing blockages, which occasionally happened when the barrel became hot. Lucky Luckhurst was my No. 2 and we both carried spare magazines, and I also carried a shaving brush which I dedicated to keeping the dust off, so mindful was I to keep it in tip-top condition. The Bren originally had a 5ft telescopic tripod for positioning the gun when firing at elevated targets, which the No. 2 also carried. The tripod was later discarded as we considered it to be of little benefit when balanced against carrying its additional weight.

As we approached the end of October 1942 several operations had been planned and cancelled and by now we were used to the anti–climax of a stand down. But shortly after we had completed our first Dakota jumps we heard a party taking place in the officers' mess. We realised that something was afoot as they didn't usually break into song like this, and sure enough the

The Bren 'light machine gun'. Its name was taken from **Brno**, the Czeckoslovakian city where its design originated, and **Enfield**, the location of the British Small Arms Factory. A gas-operated weapon, the Bren used the same .303 ammunition as the standard British Lee–Enfield infantry rifle. The firing rate was between 480 and 540 rounds per minute depending on the model. The Bren was a magazine-fed machine gun and had a slower rate of fire than the belt-fed guns. This slower rate of fire had the advantage of keeping the barrel cooler and lessened the tendency to jam. Its effective range was 600yd.

next morning we were assembled and informed that we were going on an operation.

There was a further surprise when it became known that only the 3rd Battalion with its engineer and medical support would be going. We had expected that any operation would be in brigade strength alongside the other two battalions, but it didn't dim our enthusiasm and we were delighted to get these orders. There was now a great debate as to where we could be going and the general consensus was that it would be a drop into occupied France. We were keen to go anywhere – we were extremely fit and confident in our ability, we could not wait to get into action and our officers were of the same mind. There was a real buzz among us.

Our small force of 450 was made up of our own C Troop RE, the medical detachment from 16 Field Ambulance, the two 3rd Battalion companies with its mortar platoon and HQ Company. We were taken to Netheravon and isolated. Looking out across the airfield we could see Dakotas lined up alongside the runway and billeted nearby were their USAAF air and ground crews. We still didn't know where we were going and there was an air of mystery, and the only information we had was that an operation was imminent and we were the selected few. We had left the rest of the brigade at Bulford to be confined on this airfield in what appeared to be great secrecy.

We were to be there for almost two weeks and during this period none of us were allowed out. This had happened to us before and we accepted these confinements and saw to our own amusements. However, a few of the US crews did not take to it at all and several of the more truculent individuals had to be physically restrained from leaving the camp.

During our stay our equipment was checked and weighed to be distributed throughout the aircraft. We now knew that we would be carrying extra fuel and there were to be limitations as to the amount of equipment that we could take with us. Parachutes had been issued and the harnesses had been individually adjusted and chalked. Adding to the suspense, we were ordered to remove all insignia from our uniforms and put away our distinctive red berets lest we should advertise that we were on the move.

From our airfield confinement we were then taken by lorry down to Hurn near Bournemouth, where once again we found our aircraft waiting. The weather then closed in with a blanket of fog and several days of inactivity followed and nothing happening. We now knew that we were not going to France as we had been issued with a card listing words and phrases in Arabic, but exactly where was still a mystery.

From lolling around there was a sudden burst of activity as we were abruptly told that the operation was cancelled and that we were to pack up for the journey back to Bulford, another anti-climax! We loaded up and were taken by lorry to a nearby railway station where a special train was drawn up and waiting. Our journey began ostensibly back to Bulford via Salisbury and we entrained in darkened carriages that had all the blinds down tight.

Sometime into the journey our suspicions were aroused when the train pulled into a large station that we identified as Bristol Temple Meads. We had smelled a rat, as this was not the route to Salisbury, and from now on every opportunity was taken to squint behind the blinds to determine our progress. It had taken us quite a while to pick up on the deception, partly because all the station and signal-box name boards had been removed, and being soldiers we had tended to doze off after having made ourselves comfortable in the warmth of the enclosed carriages.* But we were alert now, and after Bristol a blacked out Exeter was identified and then the unmistakable run along the sea wall through Dawlish and over the Tamar. Our journey finally terminated in Cornwall at a blacked out Newquay station which appeared to be devoid of any railway staff. From here we were transported by a combination of RAF trucks and buses to the nearby airfield of RAF St Eval.**

---

*   At the beginning of the Second World War when an invasion was expected all the signs giving place names and directions on the both railways and roads were removed. An emergency measure to confuse invading forces, it was also intended to make it difficult for the movement of enemy agents, and anyone asking directions was to be treated as suspicious.

**   St Eval airfield no longer exists as an airfield but was located close to RAF St Mawgan, which is the airfield that replaced it.

Preparations

Due to the shortage of aircraft, the whole of the 3rd Battalion could not be taken on the pending operation. The three company commanders were to cut cards to decide which of the three rifle companies would be left behind. A Company drew the unlucky hand and as a result remained behind with the brigade. In all some 450 men were to go. They were B and C Companies, a mortar platoon, C Troop of the 1st Parachute Squadron RE, elements from the 3rd Battalion HQ company and a contingent of 16 Parachute Field Ambulance. The 3rd Battalion CO for the operation was now Lieutenant Colonel Geoffrey Pine-Coffin, who had replaced Lieutenant Colonel Gerald Lathbury when he had moved on to a staff job. The RE Squadron commander was Major Stephen Dorman, with the C Troop commander Captain Tony Hewitt. The paratroops were still not aware of what their objective would be, but they had in fact been placed at the immediate disposal of Lieutenant General Anderson commanding the British 1st Army that had landed in French North Africa (Algeria) at the start of Operation Torch one week earlier.

*

On arrival at St Eval all our Dakotas were again lined up alongside the runway having been flown down ahead of us from Hurn. We had been told the operation was off and that we were going back to Bulford earlier that same morning, but we already knew that the Bulford information was incorrect as we were now in Cornwall. Looking at one another we were wondering what was to happen now.* We were soon to find out as we were taken into a large aircraft hangar to be met by the sight of all our previously adjusted parachutes, still packed and ready with our names chalked upon them.

Once inside the hangar we were ushered over to where there was a large covered map on the wall, and standing beside it was the commander of the airborne forces, General 'Boy' Browning. We were all ears. General Browning welcomed us and once we had gathered round proceeded to explain why we had been brought to St Eval in such strict secrecy. The map was uncovered and he revealed that our destination was to be somewhere in North Africa, but he declined to tell us exactly where. General Browning's briefing informed us that we would probably encounter both Germans and Italians. He went on to enlighten us on the unpredictability of the French troops that we might also meet, his insinuation being that we might have to fight them as well.

---

* The fog had lifted at Hurn on 8 November but the forecast was for it to return that evening and remain all day on the 9th, but in the west of Cornwall it was expected to stay clear. The Dakotas were therefore 'scrambled' and moved in haste to St Eval through a weather window without embarking the paratroops. The troops had to follow by train unaware that the operation was still on.

His words intimated that we were not exactly popular with the French at the moment due to the fact that we had just sunk their fleet.* General Browning finished his address with a pep talk and then invited us to enjoy the meal that had been prepared, he wished us good luck and we were dismissed. We then tucked into a huge meal of steak and chips and all the trimmings, which went down very well after our journey. We were fed like fighting cocks and were well sustained for the flight to come.

*

The Position of France in November 1942

France at this time was a divided nation. Northern France was occupied by the German army, while southern France was a self-governing area collaborating with Germany in an arrangement to prevent total German occupation. The collaborating area was administered from the French city of Vichy and the whole region was referred to as Vichy France.

The French colonial territories of Tunisia, Algeria and Morocco in North Africa were still technically governed by Vichy and it had as many as 120,000 French and colonial troops garrisoned throughout the region.

French territory was now to be invaded by both the Allies and the Germans. The question was would these French troops in North Africa oppose the Allied landings. The Germans expected them to do so, but the loyalty of the various French commanders was split. Anticipating the worst, the invading Americans and British were prepared to fight both the Axis powers and the French if necessary.**

Behind the scenes frantic negotiations were taking place between the Allies and the colonial French in North Africa to prevent a confrontation with the invading Allied forces. It was obvious to the Germans that the Vichy French did not have total control of their colonial forces and that Vichy had now become an unreliable ally. During the negotiations the Germans occupied Vichy as they realised that there was every likelihood that the colonial French would not fight the British and Americans.

The scene was rapidly changing and as a result of the negotiations the colonial French leadership signed an armistice agreeing not to fight the Allies, but there were still many doubts. Not all French commanders were believed to be in agreement.

Meanwhile, having occupied Vichy, the Germans began pouring troops into the area around Tunis and Bizerta to support the Afrika Korps which had been pushed back across North Africa to the southern Tunisian border by the British 8th Army.

---

*   These were not comprehensive battles, but actions against the Vichy French fleet at Casablanca and Oran the previous day, 8 November. French troops initially opposed the landing of the Allied troops during Operation Torch.

** The Axis powers comprised Germany and Italy.

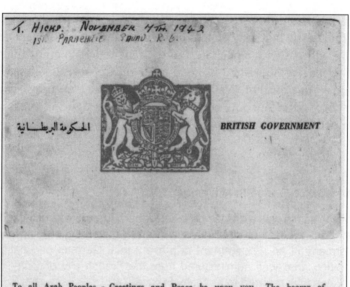

To all Arab Peoples - Greetings and Peace be upon you. The bearer of
this letter is an Officer of the British Government and a friend of all Arabs.
Treat him well, guard him from harm, give him food and drink, help him
to return to the nearest British soldiers or American soldiers and you will be
liberally rewarded. Peace and the Mercy of God upon you.

The British High Command in the East

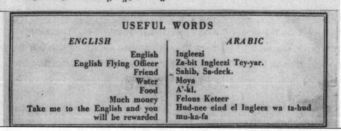

USEFUL WORDS

ENGLISH	ARABIC
English	Ingleezi
English Flying Officer	Za-bit Ingleezi Tey-yar.
Friend	Sahib, Sa-deck.
Water	Moya
Food	A'-kl.
Much money	Felous Keteer
Take me to the English and you will be rewarded	Hud-nee eind el Ingleez wa ta-bud mu-ka-fa

This small, pocket-sized booklet was intended to help communication with the local Arabs in
the event that paratroops were separated from the main force.

The front and back of this Banque De L'Algerie 5 franc note is signed by several officers and men of 1st Parachute Squadron RE in Tunisia in 1942. Front: Lucky (Luckhurst), Tony (Jones), Ramsay Pratt (killed in Sicily), Chin Massey, R. Macdonald, Stan Paulson and Tom Hicks; back: Captain Livesey MC, Captain George MC, Ginger Holland, George Costadinos and Archie Cooke.

After our meal things began to gather a pace. We were issued with notes of the local currency which were to be used should we find ourselves isolated after jumping. It all appeared very civilised, but little did we know that the local Arabs were hostile and would have taken our money, clothes, boots and slit our throats if they found any of us alone, unarmed or injured.

We felt privileged to have been selected for the operation and the other battalions had been openly envious of our perceived good fortune, which had only encouraged us to raise our banter and to burnish our new found 'warrior' status. Temporarily, we were top dogs. Most of us had never been out of Britain before and although we had all heard of Africa, it wouldn't have made much of an impression on us if we had been told that our destination was to be Algeria and Tunisia, as to most of us they were just names on a map.

*

Journey by Sea

While the 3rd Battalion and C Troop RE were preparing to leave for North Africa, the rest of the brigade, comprising the 1st and 2nd Battalions, A Company of the 3rd Battalion, A and B Troops of 1st Parachute Squadron RE and the main body of 16 Parachute Field Ambulance, had been taken by train to Greenock on 29 October 1942 on the Clyde for transit by sea to Algiers. In Greenock they were joined by an RAF parachute-packing section (all male) which was to accompany them on the voyage to repack and service the brigade parachutes at Maison Blanche. The convoy set sail on 30 October 1942. The reason given for why the rest of the brigade was being taken out by sea was once again due to the lack of aircraft. Less than 400 men from the 3rd Battalion, together with sappers and field ambulance which took the total force to around 450, were being flown out on the Bone operation. This small force was allocated thirty-three Dakotas, twenty-nine of which were to make it to the DZ and drop the paratroops.

Chapter 17

Away at Last, 9 November 1942

North Africa, 1942

A fortnight after the British 8th Army had begun its attack on the German Afrika Korps at El Alamein, Operation Torch began on 8 November in the west. A total of 35,000 US troops landed near Casablanca in Morocco, 39,000 at Oran and 23,000 British and 10,000 US at Algiers.

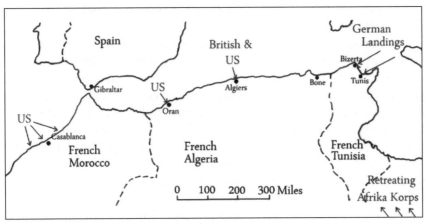

US and British landings, November 1942.

The objective of Operation Torch was to cut the German Afrika Korps from its supply line and to defeat the German and Italian forces in North Africa as a prelude to an invasion of Europe. The Germans and Italians were now to be caught between the British 8th Army advancing from the east through Libya and the Americans and British landing in Morocco and Algeria from the West. The German objective was now to hold Tunisia to buy time against the inevitable invasion of Europe that would follow the fall of North Africa.

*

It was dark when our aircraft started to take off from St Eval at 2330hr on the first stage of the flight to Gibraltar, which was expected to take around 7 hours. The Dakotas took off in ones and twos setting out over the Channel and across the Atlantic approaches towards Portugal. I remember looking down at the cold, dark waves with the spume lit by moonlight and thinking, 'By hell ... I wouldn't like to come down in this'.

In our Dakota there were less than our usual eighteen due to the additional fuel that we had on board. The large, padded tanks for this were inside the aircraft near the front bulkhead. In addition to ourselves were the aircrew, which were USAAF with an RAF navigator, the USAAF crew comprising the pilot and co-pilot, wireless op' and jump master. The jump master was responsible for opening and despatching us from the large door in the side of the aircraft. During the flight he wandered around keeping us informed of our progress and supplying us with coffee.

The extra fuel tanks were viewed with suspicion by some who no doubt envisaged an inferno should they be hit by flak,* but some of the smaller lads such as myself had no such reservations and climbed up on top and settled down. We found that their exterior padding was quite comfortable when compared with the vibrating metal bench seats or the floor and we managed to get some sleep. However, there was no doubt that if we encountered any sort of flak or an enemy fighter we would have been off them like rabbits.

As we approached the coast of Portugal we had to divert further out to sea to avoid the possibility of being caught by German night fighters, which we were told were routinely patrolling out from the French coast. The US crew chief briefed us in advance of these manoeuvres shortly before our aircraft began to vary its height and direction. Dawn had broken as we approached Gibraltar and my first sighting was of a large, lion-shaped rock rising out of the sea. As we got in closer the rock was clearly defined with both the coasts of Portugal and Spain on either side. When we eventually came in to land it was daylight on a beautiful Mediterranean day. It was my first time on foreign soil.

Our aircraft had arrived in Gibraltar without mishap but the aircraft that my pal Sammy Dobbie was in developed an engine malfunction and started to lose altitude. In order to maintain height, the pilot had requested that as much equipment as possible was thrown out of the door. Earlier in the flight the newly married Sammy had taken off his battledress top, in the pocket of which he had a picture of his wife. We had a laugh as the story was told about the jump master rapidly throwing out anything he could get his hands on with Sammy on his hands and knees franticly hunting for his battledress to retrieve his precious photograph, which he managed to do.

Once on the ground we were taken to a large barracks where we were once again isolated, before being moved into an aircraft hangar where we spent the rest of the day leisurely checking our kit and resting. Tensions were often relieved by humour in C Troop, they never really had time to build up before some wit had us all laughing. I recall Chin Massey who had been an apprentice

---

* Military slang for anti-aircraft shellfire.

stonemason retrieving a small chisel from his pack. Slowly waving it around he asked, 'Does anyone want their name carved on a stone before we go … I'll make a nice neat job?' He was to do this several times before operations and it became one of our rituals.

*

The British Paratroop Drop at Bone, Algeria

The Allies began landing in Morocco and Algeria on 8 November 1942 with the start of Operation Torch. The task of the British paratroops would be to drop ahead of the main army to secure the colonial French airfields to prevent them being used by the Germans as forward positions. Bone was to be the first target.

This was the situation as the 450 paratroops prepared to fly out of RAF St Eval en route to Gibraltar on the first leg of their journey to Algeria. At this time they were still unaware of the job that they were required to do.

To extend their range for the flight to Gibraltar, the Dakotas had been modified to carry extra fuel. This was achieved by fitting large padded metal tanks inside the aircraft which were positioned adjacent to the front bulkhead. Aviation fuel was to be transferred in flight from these internal auxiliaries to the wing tanks by a manual pump. The Dakota had a normal payload of 5,000kg which had been reduced for this operation to 3,000kg due to the weight of the additional fuel. This in turn had decreased the number of troops and equipment that could be carried.

The Dakotas were part of the 60th Carrier Group of the USAAF and were crewed by Americans with the exception of the navigators who were from the RAF. The inclusion of an RAF navigator was a result of the fact that the USAAF did not have enough navigators for the huge numbers of aircraft that they had sent over to Britain since entering the war in December 1941.

Many of these USAAF crews had transferred directly into the military from commercial airlines where direction finding was achieved by the pilot flying along radio beams, and so conventional navigation and navigators had not been required on these routes. On arriving in Europe where radio-beam technology was unavailable navigation had to be achieved by map and compass, so the shortfall was filled by RAF navigators. It was not uncommon for flights of aircraft to take off with only one navigator in the lead aircraft, with the rest following closely or running the risk of getting lost. The perception that Americans could not navigate was unfounded because in reality they simply did not have the resources.

*

Later that evening everything changed. We were roused from our leisure to repack the aircraft quickly and prepare for an early departure. We took off from Gibraltar with a sense of urgency at 0430hr on 11 November 1942, bound for Maison Blanche airfield, which was 16 miles from Algiers.* On arrival we were once again assembled in an aircraft hangar and given a briefing as to our final destination and the object of the operation.**

A large map was unveiled revealing our objective as an airfield near the port of Bone in Algeria,† which was about 300 miles along the coast from Maison Blanche and 150 miles from Tunis. Our small force was to drop and take the airfield in a daylight operation. We were briefed that we could expect opposition from both German and Italian troops who were thought to be on or near the airfield, and possibly the French who could also be in the vicinity.

The briefing further explained that no intelligence was available concerning the type of weapons that the enemy might have on the ground and that it was possible that they could have anti-aircraft guns or artillery. To guard against this it had been decided that our lead aircraft would overfly the airfield first, and if it was found that it was already occupied we would drop a mile away and then proceed to attack it on foot. In summary, the only intelligence we seemed to have was of Bone's geographical location.

The general belief was that we had the element of surprise on our side and that we were going to fly in low, sneak up, drop out and get at them. There was a real feeling of confidence and we were eager to get started.

---

*   When the paratroop force landed at Maison Blanche their numbers had already been reduced from the 450 men that had boarded the 33 aircraft at RAF St Eval. Of the 33 Dakotas, 2 developed engine trouble at St Eval before take-off, 1 crashed into the sea on leaving Gibraltar and a fourth was damaged by Allied flak when it strayed over Algiers on its approach to Maison Blanche. Only 29 aircraft took off on the last leg of the operation with a force that was now reduced to around 390 men.

**   The previous day on arrival in Gibraltar Lieutenant Colonel Pine-Coffin had attended a briefing, the upshot of which was that the movement of German troops into Tunis had once again injected urgency into the operation. The paratroopers were required to move quickly to forestall the Germans occupying the French airfields from which they would be able to attack the main Allied army.

†   Bone is now called Annaba.

Chapter 18

Maison Blanche to Bone, 12 November 1942

On Maison Blanche airfield we unloaded our parachutes and containers from inside the aircraft, the release triggers were once again checked and the containers were secured in their carriers beneath the aircraft. We then waited.*

We eventually took off from Maison Blanche early the following morning, 12 November 1942, at 0430hr, the same time that we had left Gibraltar the previous day. To avoid detection by patrolling enemy fighters, our aircraft skimmed low across the unfamiliar landscape of coast and hills. We were headed east into a lightening sky.

As we approached the DZ on Bone airfield we had our warning to hook up, and we were all ready and anticipating the call. We stood and hooked our static lines onto the anchor cable and made ready to jump on what was to be our first operation. Ahead of us and now in full kit, the jump master looked

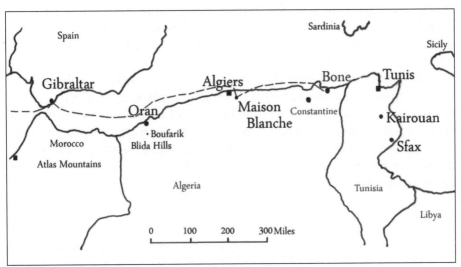

The 3rd Battalion's route into Bone, November 1942.

---

* It had been decided that despite the urgency a daylight approach would be the safest given the fact that the US crews lacked experience in night-time navigation and the dropping of paratroops.

a formidable sight dressed in his armoured waistcoat and steel helmet as he stood on the flak-protection steel plate by the door.

Quiet and purposeful and not a little anxious, our bravado had been overtaken by the moment ahead as we watched the red light. All words were lost in the roar of the engines and the whistle of the air as it ripped past the open door. When the green light came on my stick moved forward without hesitation. We jumped at a height of just above 400ft, which was quite low. Looking down as my parachute deployed I could clearly see the airfield below and it was deserted, all there was to see was the frame of a burnt-out wooden shed with a glider inside.

I hit the ground hard and fast as it was baked hard, and unfastening my 'chute I quickly joined the others to locate our containers and weapons. This was followed by a rapid deployment into defensive positions to safeguard our own vulnerability and secure the airfield

We were disappointed as we were prepared and had expected to fight but the place was empty. It was a beautiful day and around us the birds were singing. However, we had sustained casualties, and one man was killed when his parachute failed to open. Within our troop our most serious casualty was a head injury sustained by C Troop commander Captain Tony Hewitt, who was to remain unconscious for four days. Another injury, which demonstrated the unreliability of the Sten gun,* was sustained by a troop sergeant when he accidentally shot himself in the leg. Both he and Tony Hewitt were taken to a nearby French convent for treatment. Our other casualties were a collection of the usual landing injuries, which seemed to have increased due the hardness of the ground and the low height from which we had been dropped.

Shortly after we had landed our patrols were sent down into the town of Bone to meet 6 Commando, which was coming in by sea. We dug slit-trench defences around the airfield and camouflaged our positions with netting. The next day a large Italian seaplane flew low and lazily over us and was a sitting duck to shoot down, but we remained beneath our camouflage nets and let it pass, not wanting to reveal our presence. Of course, the Germans already knew we were there as they had seen us landing.

---

* Sten guns were cheap and sometimes unreliable weapons, occasionally jamming, and if dropped with the safety catch off, the jolt could activate the spring, load a bullet and fire it. The safety catch could also be inadvertently moved from on to off when scrambling around. The 1st Battalion also had four men wounded by the accidental discharge of a Sten three days later on their drop near Souk-el-Arba. Even two years later incidents were still happening, which were typified when Brigadier Lathbury's Sten discharged just missing the foot of Major General Urquhart at Arnhem (see Major General C.B. Urquhart, DSO, *Arnhem* (1958), p. 62).

Opposition to the Allies

In the dash by the British and Germans to occupy the French airfields in Algeria and Tunisia the 3rd Battalion only just pipped the Germans to occupying Bone airfield. It was later learned that a German parachute force was approaching in a fleet of Junker 52s to drop in the same place just as the 3rd were landing. Seeing the British already on the ground, the German force turned back.

The French were not in the immediate vicinity of Bone and did not take any steps to oppose the landing of the British paratroops. However, at Casablanca and Oran there was French resistance to the Americans and British.

The recently signed armistice with the colonial French eventually held and following the German occupation of Vichy France, the French colonial forces began to co-operate with the Allies. Within months they had moved from an unsteady stand-off to joining in the North African war against the Germans.

*

Following our drop, 6 Commando sailed into Bone harbour on a destroyer in a quick in and out job. We were surprised to see that the commandos were dressed in US helmets and oddments of uniform, looking to all intents and purposes like a US unit. The reason for the subterfuge was because the French were still unpredictable and it was considered that they would be less likely to fire on US troops than British. However, in the event the French were not around and once they were ashore the commandos removed the US uniforms in favour of their own.

In addition to landing 6 Commando, the destroyers also dropped off a number of crates onto the quayside containing Oerlikon anti-aircraft cannon, and when I say dropped I mean dropped. The ships were in such a hurry to get out to sea again from their stationary position on the quayside that the crates were almost thrown over the rail, and it seemed that they were moving away before the crates had stopped bouncing. The guns were in sections and were thickly packed in grease. We carted the crates up onto the airfield where with much grimacing and cursing and set about the filthy job of cleaning them up with petrol and rags, before assembling them with the aid of an instruction manual.

We were told that the Oerlikons were intended for us to defend the airfield, although we had never used them before. Once they had been assembled, our Lieutenant 'Ropey' Cox threw a challenge to Chin Massey, saying, 'You're a Bren gunner, Chin … climb aboard and have a go'.* Oerlikons are large

---

* Lieutenant Cox was warmly known as 'Ropey' within the troop because in our opinion he always managed to be on the untidy side of smart.

guns that are adjusted and loaded by the turning of wheels, and the gunner standing behind the single barrel is held in position by shoulder straps. We loaded the gun and the hapless Chin duly opened it up, and so powerful was the recoil that it took Chin off his feet and the gun swung round firing off rapid, haphazard bursts in several directions. I think he could have shot half the battalion if we had been a little less fortunate!

We stopped on the airfield for five days and encountered little trouble other than several ineffective dive-bombing attacks from German Stukas. They didn't bother us much on the airfield as they were mostly concentrating on the vicinity of Bone town and harbour. A lone Spitfire landed on the last day of our stay and the pilot came across and had a chat with us, it was all pretty casual.

There was also another situation for which we had not been briefed. We were to learn that the local Arabs were hell-bent on stealing our discarded parachutes and any other kit that was lying around loose. In future, when on exercise and at rest we had to take the precaution of placing guards on any of our kit that was portable.

On our last day on the airfield, 6 Commando took over our positions and we moved up to Bone railway station to wait for a train to take us back to Maison Blanche in Algeria. Back in Algiers, the rest of our brigade was now disembarking after its voyage down from Greenock.

Our last night in Bone was spent uncomfortably on the hard platforms of the railway station. We were all lying around and, just like the others, I had taken off my boots after having had them on for five days. At dawn a few of us were called forward to carry out a job and I put my boots back on. One of them felt a bit odd, just as if my sock had rumpled into the arch of my foot, but I stamped around for a while until I had a moment to take it off. Stamping some more, I caught a smirk and then one or two of my pals began to laugh, and I knew I was missing something. When I eventually took off my boot I found that my sock was OK but the frog that I shook out was quite flat.

Practical jokes, taking the p*** with the capacity to laugh at one another's misfortune even in the direst situations had brought us closer together since our formation at Hardwick. This was especially so among the three troops in our squadron where we were always on the lookout to get one over on the other.

Needless to say, our unopposed drop on Bone didn't go unnoticed and became known as the NAAFI drop by the other two troops in our squadron. They were initially envious when we were selected for the operation as we were all keen to get into action, and we had been strutting around 6in taller than the rest of the brigade. Unfortunately, we had been letting them know it, but now much to their delight our lack of opposition provided them with an opportunity to wind us up, and wind us up they did. From then on every time the Bone operation was mentioned somebody would pipe up with, 'Oh, you mean the NAAFI drop', implying that our operation had been so easy that the NAAFI wagon should have been waiting on Bone airfield with tea and biscuits.*

---

* Ribaldry apart, strategically the drop was considered a success as it denied the Germans the use of both a forward airfield and the port of Bone in the scramble for positions in North Africa.

Chapter 19

Returning to Algiers from Bone

It was only 300 miles by air but it took us five days to get back to Algiers on the train that was brought in to collect us from the railway station at Bone. This train was made up of covered vans and carriages, the former for us and the two carriages at the front for the officers. On the side of the vans I noticed a stencil in French stating '10 cheval [(horses]/40 hommes [men]'. You can imagine the derision that this raised among the lads when it rolled in, but all turned out well as the carriages became stinking hot in the sun. Our vans remained cool and airy as the draught flowed freely through the large sliding doors, and although the planked floor of the vans were uncomfortable, they were far more preferable to the enclosed carriages.

During the journey the doors remained open and we were able to sit on the edge with our legs hanging out. The smaller lads like me were light enough to fashion hammocks from our blankets which we slung from the upper window bars – this is the life we thought. We were quite happy swaying to the rhythm of the train with our boots off and feet cool watching the unfamiliar country passing by.

The railway system was still functioning in both Tunisia and Algeria and seemed to maintain a degree of normality despite the uncertainty of the war. I noticed that both the station masters and locomotive drivers were French and the firemen were mostly Arab. On its route our train made numerous halts at wayside stations. It was an unhurried journey as these stops were often accompanied by the leisurely process of taking on water and an occasional top-up of coal. As we travelled further away from the front line, we were often held up for hours in loops to allow other trains to pass by on the single-line system.

When the train did stop we would disembark in a khaki swarm, jumping down onto the track side to brew tea and heat soup in our burners. To fuel the burners we pinched the neat white fencing around the French stations as kindling, leaving small piles of smoking ash when we left, which we did rather rapidly at times as the French driver gave us little notice. We also encountered the local Arabs in large numbers who seemed to materialise from nowhere to sell eggs and fruit. Wandering among us, we soon learned to our cost that they would steal anything that they could lay their hands on.

A crow from the engine's whistle and the groan of the couplings was often the only warning we were given that we were on the move again. As the train shunted forward, we had hastily to scramble back on board with the locals running alongside to complete a transaction. As it picked up speed, anyone caught short would jump onto the last few vans and then have to negotiate the swaying roof tops to return to their 'seats'.

On arrival back in Algeria we went into billets at Maison Caree which was near Maison Blanche airfield, and here we found that the rest of the brigade had arrived. The 1st Battalion had both arrived and left on the operation to Beja, flying from Maison Blanche and dropping at Souk-el-Arba on 16 November 1942. Fortunately, we had arrived too late to help manhandle the brigade stores from the docks, which, due to the absence of stevedores, was undertaken by the lads of our squadron that had come over by sea.*

As ordinary soldiers we were not always aware of our particular position on the map of North Africa. In addition, we had little knowledge of the strategies that were unfolding around us and simply followed where we were led. It was often said within our tightly knit unit that 'our war was in front of us' and that was all we had to deal with, and for most of us that was enough.

With no further parachute operations planned we were now to be moved into the front line to be used when and where required. Being lightly armed and mobile, we were used to plug gaps in the line, often being moved at short notice. As sappers, we were to be attached to the fighting patrols that were sent out to probe for weaknesses in the enemy's front. We were to live rough in the open for a lot of the time and my memories of the Tunisian hills in December were of being constantly wet and cold.

*

Allies Versus Axis Powers in North Africa

The British 1st Army (which included the US 2nd Corps under British command) was now preparing to advance through the North African hills and down onto the plain towards Bizerta and Tunis. Getting their superior numbers of tanks and artillery through the hills was now seen as the key to defeating the Germans in North Africa.

As the Allies landed, the Germans were rushing troops into Tunisia to block all the routes onto the plain which they achieved by dominating the high ground above the valleys. In the south, Rommel's Afrika Korps had retreated in front of Montgomery's 8th Army and was now on the Tunisian border.

While both sides were building up their forces, the Allies took the decision to use parachute troops to capture or destroy relevant French airfields. These operations were intended to prevent occupation by the Germans and additional loss of life, which would be inevitable if the airfields were occupied by the enemy in front of the 1st Army's advance.

---

* Normally port operations were carried out by a RE Dock Company (based at Stranraer) which was trained specifically to handle this work.

Following the 3rd Battalion's Bone operation, the next to go out was the 1st Battalion (supported by A Troop of 1st Pararachute Squadron RE), which flew out shortly after its arrival by sea. It left Maison Blanche and dropped at a road junction near Beja in Tunisia, where it was in action at Mateur and Sidi N'Sir.

The third operation, on 29 November 1942, was taken by the 2nd Battalion (supported by B Troop 1st Parachute Squadron RE), which flew out to attack the airfields around Depienne. The objective, unlike the 3rd Battalion's at Bone, was to take and destroy rather than hold the airfields ahead of the 1st Army, again to deny the Germans the advantage of using them. On this occasion, the plan was for the 1st Army to move the front line forward and link up with 2nd Battalion 60 miles ahead of them.

Unfortunately, the 1st Army plan was ill-conceived and torrential rain bogged down the tanks and artillery so they could not be moved forward, and as a consequence the advance had to be cancelled. This left the 2nd Battalion isolated some 60 miles in front of the Allied lines with no hope of support. The battalion was left to make its own way back on foot through the hills to the 1st Army's lines at Medjez-el-Bab. During the forced march from Oudna to Medjez the men were attacked by the enemy and became separated in the harsh terrain. A total of 16 officers and 250 men out of an approximate battalion strength of a little over 500 were killed, captured or wounded.* The CO of the 2nd Battalion was Lieutenant Colonel John Frost.

Following these operations, where the three parachute battalions acted independently, they now rejoined the 1st Army as a brigade to be used as infantry, and they fought in this capacity for the remainder of their time in North Africa.

As 1943 progressed the overall German position in Tunisia became desperate. Both the Germans and Italians were being pressed by the British 8th Army from the south and the Allied 1st Army from the west. They were completely surrounded and outnumbered in troops, aircraft, artillery and tanks. The front line stretched from the north to the east coast, arcing from Enfidaville in the east through the mountains and in front of the towns of Bou Arada and Medjez-el-Bab and the Tamera gorge in the north.

Rommel had been recalled to Germany and his retreating Afrika Korps had linked up with the German and Italian troops in Tunisia. General Von Arnin was now in command of the remaining North African Axis forces, numbering 300,000 men, the officers of which were under orders from Hitler to fight to the last man in the defence of Tunisia.

The German high command believed that if Tunisia could be held until the winter of 1943 the Allies would not be able to invade Europe until the following spring. Their reasoning was that the winter weather along the coast of Europe was unsuitable for successful beach landings by assault craft. Hitler was convinced that the time that was being bought by fighting on in Tunisia would enable Germany to recover from its reverses and develop the new weapons that would be its salvation.

---

* Figures taken from Ministry of Information, *By Air to Battle* (1945), p. 44.

At this time the German troops in North Africa were still not beaten and remained a potent fighting force – they were tenacious and desperately clinging to the hills through which the Allied armies had to pass. To relieve the pressure on their gradually reducing perimeter the Germans began to counter attack the Allied line.

The positions of the Allied armies surrounding the remaining German and Italian forces in northern Tunisia, April 1943.

Chapter 20

Boufarik, Algeria to Beja, Tunisia, 12 November 1942

Four weeks after arriving back at Maison Blanche from Bone we were on the move again. The 3rd Battalion, Brigade HQ, elements of 16 Field Ambulance and us, C Troop RE, were taken back into Tunisia. Following another five-day journey by train, we arrived at Souk-el-Khemis on 17 December 1942 and were trucked straight up to Beja, where we were based in several farm buildings on the road to Djebel Abiod.

The 1st and 2nd Battalions were already in the area. The 1st had dropped at Souk-el-Arba and advanced through Beja to Medjez-el-Bab, while the 2nd were still recovering from their losses and the 60-mile forced march back from Oudna.

The squadron's introduction to the area began with aggressive patrolling and harassment through small scale-attacks,* which were started almost immediately to establish the strength of the enemy positions. During this period our Squadron Commander Major Dorman was killed in an ambush while reconnoitring an enemy tank position.** He was replaced by Doug Murray, now promoted to major, who had been on my original selection panel at Birdcage Walk.

One of the more dangerous tasks that we undertook from the start in Tunisia was the laying of various types of mines. This work was carried out as a troop or in smaller numbers, the latter when we accompanied our parachute infantry patrols. On these patrols two or more sappers would carry the mines and the patrol would give us cover while we laid them. It was essential that the mines and detonators were kept apart and great care was taken to ensure that if tripped we could not fall on them.

---

*   These attacks were made on enemy troop concentrations for both their nuisance value and to tie down enemy troops. They were welcomed by both officers and men who were keen to get into action. The 1st Battalion with A Troop was already engaged in this activity by the time the 3rd Battalion and C Troop arrived at Beja.

** As a captain, Stephen Dorman was the original commander of the 1st Air Troop on its inception in 1941. When the Air Troop was expanded into the 1st Parachute Squadron RE in 1942 he became its first CO.

Our main task in the Beja area was to mine the small roads and tracks to disable any enemy vehicles and tanks that might be probing our way. The distances that we had to cover were large, the terrain was rough and we were very thinly spread out. If we encountered enemy troops, we switched from sappers to an infantry role and as such I carried my heavy Bren up and down dale in all weathers.

If laying mines was a soul-destroying job, disabling the mines of the enemy was worse. We had to search for the mines on our hands and knees using a short bayonet as a probe. Once found and lifted, we placed the mines outside a white tracing tape that we used as a demarcation between the cleared and un-cleared areas. One German mine in particular could be tricky and was known to us as the 'Tellermine', approximately 4in thick and the size of a dinner plate with an arming slot in the centre. The slot could be turned with a coin to deactivate it. Occasionally, the Germans would lay them in the deactivated position, and then we ran the risk of turning them on to live when we were clearing them, which tended to make us take particular care in these painstaking tasks.

The mines that we laid were mark IVs and Vs, which were similar to the German mines but thicker. One of ours that could be particularly deadly was the Hawkins anti-tank grenade. The Hawkins was oval in shape and approximately 8in by 4in and very sensitive to handle; its mechanism had a small, brittle glass tube carrying a copper wire and if the wire was broken the mine would detonate.

The dangers of the Hawkins were stamped into our minds when a tragic incident took place involving men from our A Troop. It happened on the night of 23 December when a detachment from A Troop was out supporting the 1st Battalion. The men were tasked with blocking a road to prevent German tanks escaping from the 1st Battalion's attack on their harbour. The detachment was moving in single file in the dark with pre-primed Hawkins in sandbags on their backs. It is not known precisely what happened, whether it was enemy action or a stumble that caused the detonation, but as a result a sympathetic explosion took place as the shock waves from the first detonated the others with tragic consequences – all nineteen men on the detachment were killed. Our squadron only had a strength of around 150 and to lose so many men at once was a shock.

The carrying of pre-primed mines was unusual. We were never trained to carry them in a live condition and it can only be presumed that on this occasion they were pre-primed to save time. After this I never came across the practice again, although the incident was used in future training as a classic example of why pre-priming was a bad idea.

We would also booby-trap our vacated positions and any tracks that we considered the Germans would use in the future. During our 'leisure' time we would give considerable thought to new and innovative ways of making the lives of the enemy as uncomfortable as possible, which usually involved explosives. The most common method of laying explosive traps was centred around the hand grenade and S-mines, both of which were light and portable and could be carried easily when out on patrol.

Hand grenades with their pins removed were hidden in vacated slit trenches, bivouacs and across tracks and were nearly always secured by some form of trip wire. A simple form of this anti-personnel weapon was to stretch a wire along the ground tight between two pegs with the hand grenade or grenades positioned beneath the wire which would hold down the spring lever in place of the withdrawn pin. The wire and grenades were then camouflaged. When the wire was tripped, the lever sprang out detonating the grenade. The skill was in the positioning of the trip wire and its camouflage.

Another example of our innovations was the blanket trick. We would leave behind apparently abandoned blankets with a grenade beneath, with a flat stone hidden among folds of the blankets to retain the spring lever, which was waiting to be released when the blanket was moved. Who could resist an extra blanket in the cold hills of Tunisia?

S-mines were also used. These mines were a little smaller than a jam jar and were packed with ball bearings and buried in the earth leaving only three small prongs above the surface, which when trodden on would spring 3ft into the air before detonating. The Germans also took part in this unsporting activity and we always tried to keep alert to their potential traps. As with the laying and clearing of mines, the setting of booby traps had to be carried out carefully and with great concentration, as slips could be fatal. When positions were taken from the Germans it was usually our task to check them out before the battalions moved in.

The Germans were far better equipped than us in most areas relating to infantry, particularly in their weaponry. We considered their Schmeiser sub-machine gun to be far superior to our Sten. We used captured weapons whenever we could get hold of them, especially Schmeisers as they used the 9mm ammunition that was interchangeable with our own. When we first handled the German weapons we were amazed at how well engineered they were and many of the lads thereafter referred to our Sten as a piece of scrap, although it was to prove its worth at close quarters. Similarly, the German Spandau heavy machine gun was superior to our Bren, firing twice as many rounds at 1,000 per minute.

Soon after our arrival in Beja we were put on standby as assault engineers to clear any mines and booby traps ahead of a proposed main army drive towards Tunis, but like so many other operations that we were briefed to undertake it was cancelled.

Operation Cancelled

The reason for the cancellation was due to the appalling weather. It had rained in torrents for over a week, bogging down the 1st Army transport and armour in mud. Further progress towards Tunis and Bizerta was impossible, and with the Allies stuck in the mud the Germans and Italians took the opportunity of reinforcing their positions. General Anderson, the Allied 1st Army Commander, was to be hard pressed to hold the positions that had been gained. A further question for General Anderson was how best to deploy the specialist 1st Parachute Brigade, which had been used as infantry since its initial parachute operations.

*

General 'Boy' Browning visited our brigade just before Christmas and offered to take any mail that we had on the flight home with him. Those of us who were available and not on patrol dashed off to scribble a line or two, and he must have had quite a few sacks to take away.

We spent Christmas Day 1942 in Beja. The town was a bit of a shambles having been badly damaged by bombing, but nevertheless it didn't stop us having Christmas dinner served to us in a school building by our officers, as was the tradition. The Christmas period was a bit of a mishmash as we couldn't sit down as a squadron as many of our men were still out on patrols, but every effort was made to get men in from the hills for a bit of a rest at some point.

On Boxing Day the first of our lads from C Troop was killed. George Hepple was out with us laying Hawkins anti-tank mines when he was involved in an accident.* It was a particularly poignant moment for us being just after Christmas.

*

The Red Devils and 'Waho Mohammet'

It was at about this time that the brigade started to be referred to by the Germans as 'Die Roten Teuful', or 'Red Devils'. There are several stories explaining how this soubriquet came about. One was that a German officer was taken prisoner and among his papers was an un-posted personal letter to his wife in which he had written that the Die Roten Teuful would give them no peace. Later German prisoners were captured with written tactics on how best to fight Die Roten Teuful. The former reference appeared in the forces' newspaper, the *Union Jack*.

---

* Sapper George Hepple was aged just 26 and was buried in Medjez-el-Bab war cemetery (5.D.9.).

It is often presumed by many that the name Red Devil refers to the distinctive red beret worn by the Airborne Brigade. However, the most probable explanation is that the troops were regularly plastered in red mud from living rough in the rain-soaked hills of Tunisia. Whatever the origin, the name was proudly accepted and is regarded as a battle honour.

It was also around this time that the 'Waho Mohammet' communication call and battle cry came into being. It started with the 2nd Battalion and was quickly adopted by the rest of the brigade. The call was copied from the local Arabs who seemed to shout the call as an opening to their conversations between distant hilltops. It was to be used as a battle cry, recognition and location call by the brigade for the rest of the war.

Chapter 21

Back to Boufarik

Shortly after Christmas in early January 1943 the squadron left Beja for Souk-el-Khemis where we entrained with the 1st Battalion and 16 Field Ambulance. The rumour that was going around was that we were returning to Boufarik for a rest period, but we didn't hold our breath – the lead-up to many of our operations started with the subterfuge of being withdrawn from the line for a 'rest period'. However, after our recent deployment and discomfort in the hills the rail journey was not turning out to be too unpleasant an experience.

*

Withdrawal and Brigade Movements

The reason for the battalion's withdrawal was in fact to begin training for a parachute operation to capture the coastal town of Sfax in conjunction with an American Armoured Division. The object of the operation was to prevent Rommel's retreating Afrika Korps joining forces with the German forces in Tunisia. The Americans, however, encountered fierce fighting around Gafsa and the operation never materialised.

The 3rd Battalion had left the Beja area several days earlier to carry out an attack on two hill features with the Buffs in the northern sector. The 3rd was to take Green Hill and the Buffs an adjacent feature named Baldy which overlooked the main road to Bizerta. In appalling weather Green Hill was taken but the Buffs failed to drive the Germans off Baldy, from which they launched counter attacks on the 3rd, now holding Green Hill. The outcome was that the 3rd had to abandon the hill due to a shortage of ammunition, and they were then withdrawn and followed the 1st Battalion back to Boufarik by road and by rail four days later.

The severely depleted 2nd Battalion remained in the Beja area to await the arrival of almost 200 replacements. It then moved on to Sidi N'Sir and to Bou Arada, where it rejoined the rest of the brigade on 24 January.

*

We left Souk-el-Khemis on another train of covered vans on a journey that took about three days, winding up through the mountains before descending down to Algiers on the coast. Sometimes our train had three locomotives, one at either end and one in the middle. I noticed that the locomotives on the network were mostly a mixture of French and German with an occasional US Baldwin, and all appeared to be very old.

We were now experienced van travellers and made good use of the numerous stops, washing and shaving in mountain streams, trading with the local Arabs and generally enjoying the scenery and inactivity. At nights we either hung in our homemade hammocks or sprawled as best we could on the van floor. But we all hung onto our boots. Negotiating the sprawl of bodies to answer a call of nature at the doorway was a tentative journey in a swaying van, so much so that any receptacle close at hand seemed to be fair game so long as it wasn't your own. I was OK as my aerial position in my blanket-come-hammock was assured with my boots tied together and hooked onto a nail. Not so for those down below, and I can still hear the cries of outrage as someone found that his boot had been peed in during the night. Howls of laughter would greet each expletive, but lessons were learned and some lads began sleeping with their arms firmly locked over their boots.

Our cooking was carried out on the move and looking out down the train there were numerous 'biscuit-tin' braziers hanging outside the vans, with lads brewing tea and warming up compo as we rolled along. Halts were still frequent as trains passing up to the front took priority. One day we halted outside a small town alongside an engine shed where a couple of locomotives were simmering in the yard. Always interested and in need of hot water, I sauntered up and climbed aboard the footplate of one of them. On the footplate there is a narrow-bore armoured tube called a 'fizzle pipe', which is used as an ancillary aid for washing off the footplate and dousing down the coal in the tender to allay the dust. When operated it emits scalding water from the boiler and it is very useful for making tea. Filling my can, I wandered back among my mates who were waiting for their burners to heat up over a newly kindled fire. Noticing that I had already brewed up, they wanted to know the secret, so back we went to the engine and I showed them the 'fizzle pipe', and how to inject replacement water into the boiler from the tender. Well, soon there was a queue. The injector must have been applied liberally and too much water was being injected and the locomotive began blowing off steam from its safety valve, followed by water and steam and made an enormous din. The French drivers came running down the yard remonstrating in true Gallic fashion while our lads bailed out of the cab, misinterpreting the commotion as a sign that the locomotive's boiler was about to blow up!

Despite the discomfort, the journey was enjoyable as we were at rest and making the most of it. I found both the changing scenery and the railway system interesting. Some gradients were traversed via switchbacks on the hillsides with the train moving backwards and forwards along a length of track to gain height. There were also pretty French stations marred only by the gaps in their fencing.

On arrival in Algiers we were moved 30 miles inland to Boufarik where we went into camp on one of the many farms in a flat agricultural area. We were now told that the real reason for our return from Beja was to begin training for a parachute operation, but like so many others it had been cancelled and we were free to relax. After our time around Beja we found Boufarik to be a very pleasant place. It was situated on a flat plain with mountains behind and was very green, with our farm being surrounded by citrus groves, grapes and wild flowers.

After a few days of lounging around we were once again active and had taken up chariot racing around a circle of palms. The chariots were our airborne trolleys with which we competed in teams of three. Our horses were two lads pulling and one lad as charioteer in the back with a whip, we had great fun hurtling around our 'stadium' with numerous spills. We were so enthusiastic that we were battered to bits and it came as a relief when at the end of the week we started training again. However, by our standards it was almost relaxing as we undertook route marches in the nearby Blida Hills which were supplemented with light physical fitness sessions.

During this period the squadron received its first batch of replacements, and among those who came into C Troop was Tony Jones who was to become one of my lifelong mates. Another new chap was Redding. We were very soldiery and proud of our status and Sapper Redding was quite an anomaly and destined to give our newly promoted Squadron Commander Doug Murray quite a few headaches. Redding apart, Doug Murray's dark hair had begun to turn grey from the day he arrived. By the time that we left North Africa it was completely grey although he was only in his late twenties, but from then on he was known to us as 'Daddy'.

Barely two weeks after arriving at Boufarik our pleasant respite was rudely interrupted by a very hurried movement order. We were to pack up and prepare to move out in full battle gear.

Chapter 22

By Sea to Bone and on to El Aroussa,
24 January 1943

The Situation in January 1943

The brigade at this time was still without the 2nd Battalion, which remained in the Beja area. Moving out from Boufarik on 23 January 1943 were the 1st and 3rd Battalions, the 1st Parachute Squadron RE and the main body of 16 Parachute Field Ambulance.

*

From Boufarik we were taken down to the docks in Algiers where two Dutch ferries, now named HMS *Princess Beatrix* and *Queen Emma,** were waiting with the destroyers HMS *Wilson* and *Wheatland* as escorts. It was a tight fit as we boarded the *Wilson* and we were shoehorned into every recess of the ship. As we headed East, the word was passed down that we were returning to Bone and then on into the line.

Hammocks had been slung for those that had boarded first, but we were not sailors and there were many laughs and curses as lads fell out of them. The many unsuccessful, of whom I was one, shouldered our way back onto the deck where we sat with our backs pressed up to the superstructure.

As we sat on the deck the sea appeared to be very close with the waves racing by just below the level of the deck. This was emphasised further at the rear of the ship as the bows road high into the swell. The rails appeared flimsy as we watched the moving ocean and we dug our backs further into the steel. Until we got used to it there were quite a few mutters such as, 'Hell … look at this' every time a high wave rose up towards us.

It was cool on the open deck and we welcomed our first taste of naval catering when 'Kye', a thick cocoa, was ladled hot and steaming into our tin mugs –it was so thick that you could almost chew it. Our second surprise was when the crew relieved us of our rations to prepare a meal 'navy style', or so we were led

---

* Originally Dutch cross-Channel ferries, these vessels were requisitioned by the Ministry of War Transport in 1940 and converted to troopships at the Harland and Wolff yard in Belfast.

to believe. They opened our compo tins regardless of contents and heated them in a bucket before serving it out.* The dish comprised tinned meat stews with puddings and soups, the lot, but we were so tired and hungry that those of us who were not feeling sea sick ate it, and surprisingly it wasn't bad!

The reason given for our hurried departure was that the Germans were enjoying increasing successes with a series of probing attacks against the right flank of the 1st Army in the Bou Arada sector. We were told that our brigade was urgently required to reinforce it. Mobile and lightly armed and with no further parachute operations planned, it seemed to us that we were becoming very useful to the main army for plugging their gaps.

Just before leaving we had each decided to grow a moustache which we pledged to keep until we had returned to Algeria. Some of the lads managed to cultivate wonderful growths and Lucky's in particular curled up to his ears. Unfortunately, mine was a failure and disappeared shortly after Tamera, and I think it was 'washed' off in the Algerian baths where we later spent time scrubbing the ingrained red soil from our skin.

*

Germans on the Offensive

The latest German attacks were a direct result of the German Panzer and Italian Centauro successes against the French and US Army's II Corps around Faid. Suffering heavy casualties and having been pushed back 50 miles, the untried US troops were sent reinforcements from the Bou Arada sector. The Germans then took advantage of this weakening of the front and began making incursions around Bou Arada. Of particular concern were the German positions on Djebel Mansour and Alliliga. The 1st Parachute Brigade was being moved up to mount a counter attack which was scheduled to begin on 3 February 1943.

*

Creeping into Bone after a voyage of about 24 hours, we looked out on the bomb-damaged harbour which was littered with broken cranes and warehouses. It was very still. The water was reflecting the dieing flames of the fires that were still burning in the buildings from the last air raid. All was overhung with rising smoke.

We were disembarked quickly; the ships were always anxious to be away from the confines of the quay. As we were disembarking and amidst all the hurried activity, some wag was broadcasting Vera Lynn's 'We'll Meet Again' over the ship's tannoy. It was good and morale-boosting and we were quietly

---

* 'Potmess' is the Royal Navy slang for this particular dish.

laughing and in high spirits, and it was to the strains of this song that the destroyer pushed off and headed back out to sea.

All became quiet again as we left the docks. We had an overnight wait before a group of open lorries could be assembled to transport us into the mountains. It was late afternoon when the convoy eventually moved off on what was to be a wet and uncomfortable journey of 100 miles up to Ghardimaou.

Stretching above and below us, the long convoy of trucks moved into the mountains along narrow roads, of which many had precipitous drops. Our journey was mostly in the dark and the night was as black as pitch. As we climbed it began to rain and the intensity increased into a steady torrent and we were soon soaked to the skin. Occasionally, the trucks slipped in the mud and we had to get out and push, slipping ourselves and getting plastered in the process. It must have been a nightmare for the Royal Army Service Corps (RASC) drivers as they concentrated on keeping us on the road, visibility was poor enough with the blacked-out slit headlamps, but in those conditions it was atrocious.

We spent hours huddled down under our capes, singing as the trucks jolted, swayed and groaned through innumerable low gear changes as they climbed the tight bends. We sang for hours, all our old favourites and newly composed songs about our officers, most of which cannot appear in print. I remember our troop Lieutenant 'Ropey' Cox shouting back from the relative comfort of the cab, 'Don't you lot go making one up about me because it's too easy.'

We arrived at Ghardimaou as day was breaking. We were all damp and spattered with mud, but before we could continue our journey we had to hang around for a further day waiting for more trucks to arrive. Eventually, we reached our new camp near the village of El Aroussa where we were held in reserve behind the front line.

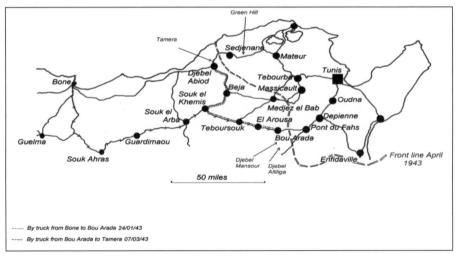

Truck journeys from Bone to Bou Arada and Tamera.

The Front Line

The brigade moved into the front line facing the Germans on the right flank of the British 1st Army where the sector met part of the US 2nd Corps. The 1st Battalion was the furthest along the hillside of Djebel Bou Arada with the Guards in reserve and a contingent of the French Foreign Legion alongside them. The 2nd Battalion had also arrived complete with its replacements from Sidi N'Sir. The company of the French Foreign Legion, strange as it may seem, mostly comprised men from Bavaria and Saxony, that is Germans who were completely loyal to France. Any of these legionnaires that had the misfortune to be taken prisoner by the Germans would expect to be shot.

Chapter 23

Bou Arada, Tunisia

B ou Arada was a small market town on a valley floor surrounded by high hills covered by scrub and trees. Immediately south of Bou Arada rose the large hill of Djebel Bou Arada, where across a raised valley at its southerly end it faced the twin hills of Djebel Mansour and Alliliga. On these hills the Germans had managed to establish a salient that protruded into the British forward positions.*

Back in our reserve positions on Djebel Bou Arada we continued to man the hilltops observing the enemy from fortified positions. From these strong points the brigade was sending out patrols to monitor enemy movements. Attached to these patrols there were usually several or more sappers from our squadron to defuse or lay mines if required.

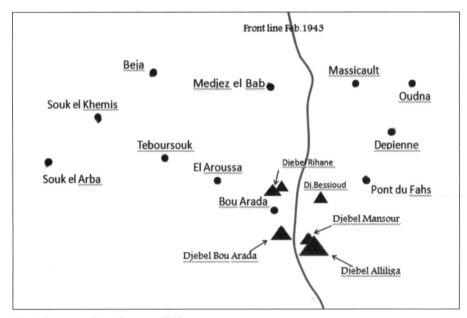

The Mansour salient, January 1943.

---

* A salient is a projection or bulge from an army's position towards the enemy lines. The hills Mansour and Alliliga projected into the British front line.

Hillside Battles

The 1st Parachute Brigade moved onto and along the hill feature of Djebel Bou Arada from where it could look across the valley to the German-held salient of Djebel Mansour and Alliliga. The 1st Battalion, which had been chosen to make the attack, moved forward at 0500hr on the morning of 3 March 1943. The first objective of Djebel Mansour was taken and the adjacent higher hill of Alliliga, the second objective, was crested at 0630hr.

The Germans recovered and counter attacked Alliliga forcing the 1st Battalion to withdraw back across to Djebel Mansour. The 1st was now hard-pressed and a battalion of the Guards was brought in to counter attack Alliliga to try and relieve the pressure, but this was unsuccessful. The Germans were able to supply reinforcements and managed to position their guns on the higher Alliliga from where they were able to bring down heavy fire upon the 1st Battalion on the lower Mansour.

Holding the high ground on Alliliga, on 5 February the Germans then attacked and took the French Foreign Legion positions on the flank of the 1st Battalion. Less than a dozen men returned after a desperate all or nothing charge at the German attackers.

The 1st Battalion's position on Djebel Mansour became tenuous; they were short of ammunition and water after losing their re-supply mules. Mansour could not be held unless Alliliga was retaken, and unfortunately this was not considered possible and as a consequence the 1st Battalion was withdrawn. The battalion lost 13 officers and 169 men killed, wounded or missing in this action.

The Parachute Brigade now regrouped facing the Germans along the sector, with their forward positions being little more than a mile distant. Both sides were now facing one another from their elevated hill positions in a wary stalemate.

*

The battalion paratroops had a healthy dislike of mines, as did we, but we had no choice, although we had many a laugh based on the black humour of handling them. We would arrive in a rest area of infantry and ask loudly enough for all to hear, 'Sergeant, can we borrow a couple of blokes?' You should have seen them scatter, the implication being that we wanted some help with the handling of mines. We also used our tapes and mine signage to keep the battalion paras out of our positions. From experience, we knew that they would pinch a comfortable spot in an embankment if we left it unattended, but a few mine tapes usually kept them at a distance.

I found the Americans to be a friendly and generous lot. We would often meet their trucks on the road and would drive up alongside until we were travelling two abreast. A thumbs up would often as not result in them throwing across a selection of tins – we were always on the lookout for extra rations. It was the first time that I had ever seen peanut butter, and we found that the large tins of it were virtually fluid when opened. This also happened with the tins of corned beef which were running with fat in the warm climate, but they still made a fine stew. The US base camps always had plenty of food, and we took every opportunity to 'stock up', but overall we considered our compo rations to be superior to their field rations.

*

Fighting Around Djebel Mansour

In mid-February 1943 the Germans attacked the US 2nd Corps along the southern flank of the front line and successfully took Gaftsa, Sbietla and Kesserine. To hold the attack reinforcements were sent from the British sector around Bou Arada.

The Germans, aware that the sector had been the weakened, attacked it on the morning of 26 February in the Agroub area, held by the 3rd Battalion. A force of Austrian and Italian Alpini reinforced by German troops came up through the scrub onto the 3rd Battalion's hillside positions. After fierce fighting, the enemy force withdrew into the cover of a wadi,* which ran back towards the foot of Djebel Mansour.

The wadi turned out to be a fortuitous trap. During the previous days the 3rd Battalion mortars had been ranged on the wadi together with its heavy machine guns (many of them captured German weapons). Luckily, the machine guns had been aimed on fixed sites along its rim. When they opened fire, such was the intensity that the enemy were frantically climbing out of the wadi to avoid the mortars and then jumping back in again to avoid the machine guns. The action, which ended in mid-afternoon, resulted in 250 enemy dead and 150 prisoners captured. The 3rd Battalion lost 2 officers and 12 men with 40 wounded.**

During the action B Troop of the 1st Parachute Squadron fought with the 3rd Battalion, while A and C Troops were despatched to assist the 1st Battalion, which was similarly engaged. After this defensive success, the Parachute sappers were put to work laying mines, barbed and trip wire on the gulley approaches in front of the brigade's positions. The objective was to hold the line until sufficient forces could be brought up to enable a decisive 1st Army attack. Shortly afterwards, during the first week of March, they were relieved by the Americans and were expecting and looking forward to being withdrawn for a rest period.

Following the action the enemy returned to their hill positions in and around Mansour and Alliliga where they continued to face the British line. Both sides were once again in stalemate.

*

---

*   A wadi is an Arabic word meaning valley or dry riverbed.
** Casualty figures taken from Ministry of Information, *By Air to Battle* (1945), p. 46.

During our periods of rest we usually caught up with our mail from home and wrote letters in reply. Ever since I had been in the army my mother had been sending me the *Barnsley Chronicle* and it found its way out to me in North Africa. I used to pass it on to 'Blackie' Severn who was a Royston lad with the 1st Battalion.* This time when I went across to have a chat and take him the *Chronicle* his mates informed me that he had been killed several weeks ago.

The war was never very far away, even when we had brief periods out of the line. I recall going fishing one lovely sunny day with Lucky. We were using wireless aerials as improvised rods in a small river that had a depth of about 5ft. After a while we put our rods to one side and went in for a swim. I noticed a green backpack beneath the water and dipped down to pull it out but it was too heavy. Lucky gave me a hand and we found that it was attached to the body of a sapper from a field company. Pulling him ashore, we identified him from his tags and brought the padre down, and after a brief prayer we buried him in a field grave on the river bank.** He had no obvious wounds other than blue blast markings on the side of his face, and in his pocket was a photograph of a young woman and a child. We never found out how or where he died. I always remembered his name, Thomas Pickering, and many years after the war I saw his grave in a Tunisian military cemetery where he had been reinterred.

At around this time I almost met up with my first cousin, David Hicks (my Uncle Bob's son from Widnes), who was serving with 1 Commando. The Commandos, like us, had assumed an infantry role. Hearing that they were in our area, I went across to where they were camped but unfortunately he was out on a job as the CO's driver, and our paths never crossed again.

During our time in the Tunisian hills we were not always aware of exactly where we were; the officers read the maps and had a greater insight into the strategic overview. The names of the features and towns were both heard and seen, names such as Djebel Mansour, Djebel Alliliga and Bou Arada, but to us the general picture was much simpler. We just soldiered on and carried out our engineering tasks knowing little about the details of the master plan in our theatre of war.

The German positions were always fairly close during this period, often just across the valley where they were dug into hillsides and camouflaged among the scrub and trees, very much the same as ourselves. We were occasionally attacked by air and very often the Germans warned us of an impending attack

---

* Albert 'Blackie' Severn was a corporal in the 1st Battalion of the Parachute Regiment and was killed on 3 February 1943, the day the 1st Battalion made their initial attack on Djebel Mansour. Aged 27, Blackie is buried in Medjez-el-Bab cemetery in Tunisia.

** Sapper Thomas Henry Pickering, 270 Field Coy RE was reinterred in Tabarka Ras Rajel cemetery. His headstone records his date of death as 20 March 1943, aged 26.

by firing white flares into the sky to warn their pilots of their own positions. We would copy them by firing a corresponding white salvo from our Very light pistols which confused their pilots.* With the confusion sown, they often managed to bomb and strafe their own positions. It gave us a good cheer when they scored an own goal.

We were again ragged and filthy, and one day a young lad came up to me who had just arrived as a replacement. 'Remember me?' he asked, and I was surprised to see it was Gordon Spicer who I had seen at Longmoor. I was already in the squadron and the last time we met I was visiting some of my old mates when on leave from Bulford. Gordon, an 18-year-old ex-Great Western fireman, approached me for information as he was considering applying to join the Parachute Engineers. I recall telling him that I enjoyed it but added the caution that it wasn't for everyone. I was glad that I was impartial with my advice as he was to lose his leg at Arnhem. Taken POW, he was later released by the Germans in an exchange of wounded. After the war, Gordon was found a job as a signalman on the GWR, being unfit to return to the footplate. I was always glad that I hadn't encouraged him to join as I would have been unhappy to have felt in any way responsible for his misfortune.

Rations were delivered to us by jeep or by mule when we were in the more inaccessible positions. Those delivering the supplies would try to get as near to us as possible before throwing off the boxes or tins. They did not hang about and would quickly disappear, never seeming to bother with how many men they were feeding. If there were three of us, we ate well, but if there were thirteen, we went hungry. Food was occasionally a problem, and although there was plenty in theatre it was just the difficulty of getting it to us. I remember crossing streams in the valleys where large tins of corned beef had been thrown in to be used as stepping stones, and I never passed one without thinking of the waste, such was the hit and miss situation of our ration supplies.

Our rations were light and compact and were intended to keep us going until we could forage for food or obtain compo supplies. Packed in our numerous pockets were hard tack biscuits and corned beef supplemented with tablets of Bovril chocolate, which was hard solid stuff and when eaten would sustain us for 4 or 5 hours. The chocolate was often stored beneath the webbing of our water-bottle holders, but having lost my water bottle on several occasions I preferred to keep mine in my smock, calculating that if I lost my bottle again, I would at least have my chocolate!

We also carried twenty or thirty Benzedrine tablets which we used when we were approaching the limits of our endurance. These stimulants were only

---

* The Very light was a pyrotechnic signal cartridge that exploded into an aerial flare when fired from a pistol. The cartridges were produced in a variety of colours and were invented by an American, Edward W. Very, in 1877. They were first used by the US Navy in 1882.

issued on operations when sleep was not possible. The tablets were supposed to be taken only on the command of an officer who would usually recognise fatigue, but in reality we made individual choices as officers were not always with us.

It was bitterly cold in the hills at night and our thin smocks and shirts were unable to keep us fully warm and dry. During the winter months, the rain was often prolonged and persistent and came down in sheets. We sheltered in pup tents that we placed over our slit trenches, but the weather meant that both the tents and our clothing seemed to be permanently damp. I always welcomed stand to an hour before dawn just to be able to move around and leave our cramped position.* Stand to was a time of increased activity in camp when muscles were stretched as men emerged from their sleeping positions, sentries were vigilant and patrols were sent out to relieve the forward listening posts. The lads would huddle down under their capes muttering, 'Africa, flippin' Africa' as the conditions were far from our perception of what Africa should have been like. It often rained for days and the pine and the cork woods were constantly dripping and the ground was threaded with rivulets.

Our parachute smocks had taken a battering and the anti-ballooning flap was left to dangle down at the rear of our thighs. The Arabs referred to us as 'men with tails' and it was this name that they would use when describing us to the Germans. The smock 'tails' were also useful in other ways. On occasions when we were closed up and moving in the dark we would hold onto the smock tail of the man in front to keep us together, like elephants in a Disney cartoon. Another improvisation that we used to keep in close contact on those dark and misty night-time patrols was to hang our white tin mugs on the back of our packs for the man behind to see. It was not unusual for men to get lost in the dark, especially in rain and if they became well spaced out and weary.

Back in camp near El Aroussa we spent our time training and sorting out our kit, and occasionally we came across French colonial troops in addition to the Foreign Legion. The French had the Regiment Spahis Tunisiens who were cavalry troops scouting our sector on horseback. Now firmly on our side, these troops were known to us as the blue patrol due to their light-blue uniforms and cavalry boots. Some of our officers took full advantage of the Spahis' presence and were seen borrowing a horse for a recreational ride when the opportunity presented itself.

While the officers were horse riding, we would repair to the small town of Souk-el-Khemis which was situated on the road between Beja and Souk-el-Arba and administered by the French. Here we would stroll around the stalls

---

* Stand to, the soldiers' 'stand-to-arms', was the signal for soldiers to man their positions in readiness to repel an attack, which historically often happened at dawn.

and shops, visiting the local estaminets and generally relaxing, and one of these trips remains vivid in the memory. On this occasion Sapper Redding had tagged along. In the short time that he had been with us he had already been in quite a few scrapes and smashed up several bars, for which he had been sent away to the 'glasshouse' more than once. He had become the blight of C Troop and it was potentially dangerous for anyone having the misfortune to be in the shadow of his company. This time Redding 'disturbed the peace' by starting to throw the furniture around an estaminet that we were in. The local French police chief was then called, and we thought, 'Oh no' and sat back in our chairs to watch the fun. To our horror, Redding picked the policeman up and threw him through the plate-glass window. Berserk ... we all jumped on Redding before the policeman was able to recover his wits, and dragged him to the truck and drove back to camp. We dared not go back for days as the policeman was sure to have called in the red caps.

Major Murray was at a loss what to do with Redding, nobody wanted him and we were all relieved when he was removed once again. He was sent away and returned several more times before, with a sigh of relief from within C Troop, he never returned. In quiet moments someone would say, 'Do you remember Redding?' and we would all have a good laugh.

*

Moving on from Bou Arada

The 1st Parachute Brigade left the Bou Arada sector on 5 March when they handed over to US troops. Almost immediately after being relieved by the Americans, the northern sector of the front line was hit by a German surprise attack. Successful, it drove the British 139th Infantry Brigade back beyond the village of Sedjenane. The 139th retreated back down the valley to the Tamera Gorge, through which passed the main road and railway linking the west of Tunisia to Mateur, Bizerta and Tunis.

This was considered a serious setback. The 1st Parachute Brigade, which was looking forward to a rest after the Bou Arada fighting, was now to be sent north to Tamera. The Tamera area, like much of Tunisia in which they fought, was mountainous and thickly wooded. The same principles were to apply in Tamera: whoever occupied the hilltops also controlled the passage through the valleys below.

Chapter 24

Tamera Valley, 7–14 March 1943

Our rest period was cancelled and we packed up to move out with full kit. The whole squadron was formed up and we were festooned with packs, weapons and capes as once again we were stood at ease waiting for trucks. Major Murray arrived and took one look at us and must have considered that we were overloaded. He snapped, 'Lighten your packs ... all German stuff and non-essentials out'. Reluctantly, our packs were 'lightened' as the lads jettisoned souvenirs and other loot that had been acquired over the past few months. Seeing us 'lightened', we were then issued with additional ammunition and other assorted ordnance to carry!

The trucks arrived and we loaded up to begin our move north to the Tamera area of the front. After a long overnight journey, we rested at Teboursouk for a day, before moving on again under cover of darkness. We passed through Souk-el-Arba and Beja. A hundred miles north of Beja our convoy finally stopped, we had reached our destination in the northern sector of Tunisia in a depression that became known to us as Happy Valley. This wide valley was spanned by a large stone viaduct which took a railway across, beneath on the valley floor snaked the Oude el Medane River and the road that led up to the Tamera Gorge, and on through the hills to the German-held town of Sedjenane.

The lesser geographical features along the edge of Happy Valley were soon anglicised and became known on our maps as Cork Wood, Death Ridge, the Pimple, Beggar's Bump with the adjacent flat-topped hill of Bowler Hat. Above these in a higher and more commanding position beyond Cork Wood were the German positions on the mountain of Djebel Bel Harch.

Once we had dug into the hillside in Cork Wood fighting patrols were sent out to establish exactly where the enemy was. Skirmishes were constantly taking place along our sector as we came into contact. The Germans frequently attacked our hillside with Stuka dive bombers, which emitted a hideous scream as they stood on end and hurtled down towards us. The Stukas were always accompanied by an escort of Messerschmidt or Focke-Wulf fighters which would also have a pop once the Stukas were on their way home.

As always as an air attack approached, up went the German flares to mark their positions, and they had also by this time taken to firing tracer into the air from their Spandau machine guns. But it was really to no avail as up went our own Very light flares and captured Spandaus in much the same manner, both sides were using captured weapons and with all the flares and smoke drifting around it was no wonder that they were often hit by their own aircraft.

*

The Situation in Tunisia

The German attack on the 139th Division had paused higher up the valley at Sedjenane. The newly arrived Parachute Brigade took up hillside positions above Tamera along Death Ridge and within Cork Wood. Alongside them were the battered remnants of the Leicesters and Sherwood Forresters which had retreated due to the strength of the German thrust. Behind and below in Happy Valley the British were supported by the troops and guns of the Corps artillery.

Although now contained in northern Tunisia, the German armies were still a potent fighting force tenaciously clinging to the hills through which the Allied army had to pass.

To relieve the pressure on their gradually reducing perimeter, the Germans attacked wherever they could detect a weakness in the Allied line. They would strike in the south, and when troops were rushed in to contain the attack from another part of the front, they would then go on the offensive in the north or the centre.

Despite the success of this recent attack in the northern sector, the overall German position in Tunisia was now desperate, and they were completely surrounded and outnumbered in troops, aircraft, artillery and tanks. The front line stretched across Tunisia from the north to the east coast, arcing from Enfidaville through the mountains and hills, where it passed in front of the towns of Bou Arada and Medjez until it reached the Tamera Gorge in the north. It was only a matter of time before the Allies would be in a strong enough position to push forward on all fronts.

*

We were dug in just below the ridge and now that the Germans had pinpointed our positions we were mortared and shelled. From behind us the air was rent by the scream of our own outbound artillery shells which were being fired by our gunners in Happy Valley, trying to hit the Germans who were shelling us. These outbound salvoes appeared to just clear the ridge and were so low that we dipped our heads every time one came over. In addition to this, we had to contend with the rain that was once again pouring down, filling our trenches and keeping us perpetually damp and mildewed.

We had had several lively fire fights with the Germans, who were so close that we could hear them shouting to one another across on the opposite hill. One evening we were on a scrub–covered slope in Cork Wood, and although

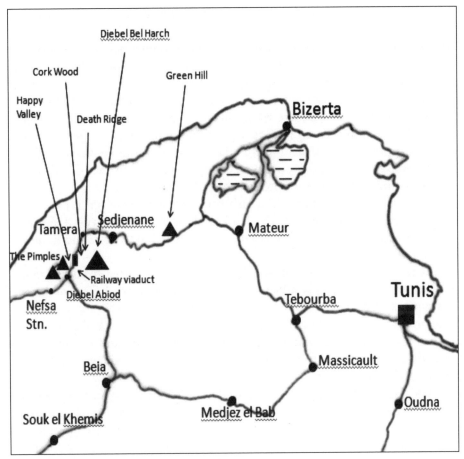

The area around Tamera, northern Tunisia.

overlooked by the higher Djebel Bel Harch upon which the Germans were similarly entrenched, it was a quiet evening. Lucky and I had carefully dug shallow trenches in a drier position in which we were determined to have a comfortable night. To finish off we had lined our 'excavations' with a swathe of leafy branches and covered them over with German ground sheets. When we stood back and admired our endeavours we were quite pleased with our labour. Just as we were settling in we were roused with a 'Hicks and Luckhurst' call, bemoaning our luck that we had been detailed to accompany a section from the 2nd Battalion on a night patrol.

Although C Troop was primarily supporting the 3rd Battalion, we were often detached to work with whoever needed us, but on this night we were to be blessed. On our return after tramping around in the night we found that the Germans had hit our positions with mortars, our carefully constructed pits were shredded and the whole area was peppered with holes.

Lucky was fortunate to have been detailed alongside me in this instance, for this job was usually a 'Hook and Hicks' turn. Hook and Hicks rolled easily off the tongue in our troop and it was easier to remember than 'Hicks and Luckhurst'. Len (Hook) and I were called out for numerous jobs due to the symmetry of our names. If a message needed carrying or a patrol required a couple of sappers from our troop, it seemed to Len and I that Hook and Hicks would get it. A message wasn't just a case of walking to the tent next door either, it would entail finding a position on an exposed hillside or in a dense, dripping wood, usually in the dark with both the Germans and our lads nervously listening for movement over gun sights. At times like these it's surprising how well you can tiptoe in hobnailed boots.

But not all of us were lucky, and early one morning one of our replacement officers was shot and killed by the 3rd Battalion out in the scrub. He was in front of their defences, which was a dangerous position to be in and we never found out why he was out there.

During my time in the Tunisian hills I began to suffer from abscesses, whether the cause of this affliction was due to the tinned food or having constantly to live in wet clothes I didn't know. Most of these abscesses were small and manageable but the one that I developed in Cork Wood was on my neck. It needed treating as it had swollen up rapidly and was giving me some discomfort. It was so large that when I was standing sideways it threw a shadow from the sun.

'Ropey' Cox arranged to have me sorted out. Picking me up in a jeep, he took me out of the line to a small convent run by French nuns which had a medical room. The sister who received us agreed to treat me but apologised for the fact that she did not have much in the line of anaesthetic, and being a paratrooper I shrugged it off as small beer, we were made of sterner stuff. I was sat in a chair and she quickly lanced and dressed it. Following this, I nonchalantly got up and sauntered out of the door where I promptly fainted. On recovery, I slumped in the jeep while Ropey bounced back along the tracks to our positions.

Out of the blue we told that we were leaving Cork Wood and were moving back down the valley. Gathering our kit to one side, we set about booby-trapping our trenches before leaving the hillside to walk down the valley to our new positions beyond Nefza. The final act on the way down had been given to C Troop which was tasked with setting charges in a narrow defile on a bend in the road, with the objective of preventing any German armour or vehicles following us down. On reaching the defile, we dropped our kit in the road and set about the task as our lads were filing past us on both the sides.

The technique that we used for setting the charge was known to us as a 'camoufler' for which we used the explosive powdered ammonal.* In order

---

* Camoufler was a French technique and simply means camouflage.

to crater the road successfully a large amount of ammonal had to be placed approximately 3ft below the surface. Our work would then be detonated or camouflaged depending on whether or not we were to blow it immediately or wait for a specific target. The setting of the camoufler was achieved by driving a hollow metal tube down into the road surface with a sliding hammer called a monkey, the tube was then removed together with the enclosed earth leaving a hollow pipe in the ground. A detonator was placed in the pipe followed by a small amount of ammonal which we gently tamped down. This charge was then set off which blew a hole about the size of a football at the base of the pipe. The charging procedure was then repeated. The insertion of a detonator was followed by a large amount of ammonal which was 'very' gently tamped down. The detonator was then attached to a wire that we connected to a battery box positioned about 50ft away. Finally, the pipe was refilled with earth and camouflaged with road soil.

*

Withdrawal

Approximately twenty days after arriving on 17 March the 1st Parachute Brigade had to withdraw from their positions on Death Ridge and Cork Wood due to a German attack that had been driven between the flanking French and Leicesters. A strategic withdrawal had to be made to prevent the paratroops being cut off, and their positions above the Tamera Gorge had to be abandoned. A new line of defence was established lower down the valley in the hills beyond Nefza Station to which they retreated.

*

Having been a member of the party that had prepared the charge, I was detailed to stay behind with Lucky Luckhurst, Len Hook and our troop Sergeant Fred Hoath. Our instructions were to detonate it when the last of our troops had passed through.

The Germans had by now realised that we were withdrawing and had begun firing shells over Cork Wood and down onto the area through which the road passed. Shells were also coming down the road and exploding in the valley below as they harassed the withdrawal.

By the time we had finished the last of our men had passed by a while before. Our last task was to connect the detonating wire to the detonating box which had been played out around the bend. It was a close-run thing because we had barely finished before the roar of engines and distinctive clatter announced that tracked vehicles were coming down the road towards us. The plunger was depressed which was followed by a huge explosion as the charge detonated. Being the last men up there, we were off down the valley without waiting to see what had happened. Unbeknown to us, it was a classic if fortuitous ambush.

As we ran down the track, shells were still coming in and we were lucky that many failed to detonate as their impact was cushioned by the wet ground. The rain had been heavy and everywhere was very muddy, and legging it across the valley floor we found the roughly ploughed fields particularly boggy and that the soil clung to our boots in great clods.

We caught up with the rest of the squadron behind the arches of the railway viaduct where they were sheltering from the shells that were still coming into the valley. Breathless, we were greeted with the usual tongue-in-cheek comments of 'Where the hell have you been?' and 'How long does it take to set a charge?' With the banter complete, our packs were shouldered and we moved on to new positions beyond Nefza.

*

Withdrawal Again

On 20 March the Germans renewed their attacks just north of Nefza station and were successful in driving the Leicesters off the hills Pimple and Bowler Hat. A counter attack was launched by the 3rd Battalion but had to be abandoned due to the Germans creeping in behind them and blowing the bridge over the Oude el Madene River, which they had previously crossed. A precautionary withdrawal was made as the bridge was their only means of re-supply.

*

In preparation for a further counter attack our squadron was tasked with hastily improvising a replacement bridge. This was achieved by placing oil drums in the river with their ends cut out to allow the water to flow through, with the upper depressions between the drums crudely filled with concrete which had been obtained from the French. The surface was then topped off with timber. It was strong enough to take jeeps and light trucks and the 1st Battalion was successful in using it to assault the hills Pimple and Bowler Hat in a night attack.

The brigade moved back up the valley after the successful counter attack of the 27th and we again passed the site where we had set off our camoufler charge in the road. The road had been repaired but a damaged German half-track was down in the gorge with several field graves alongside it. Apparently, we had cratered the road just as the leading half-track was approaching the bend. Unable to stop, it had fallen into the camoufler crater, rolled off the road and down into the gorge where it had turned over.

The brigade took over 800 prisoners, most of whom were Italian Bersagliari who had surrendered to the 1st Battalion. In a demoralised state, they had simply had enough. 'Digger' Howarth and I were given the job of escorting fifty of these Italians and two German officers back to a military police holding area. The Italians appeared to be well prepared for surrender as most were carrying small suitcases!

*

Counter Attack

On the night of 24 March the 1st Battalion was brought up from Tabourka where they had been resting. Crossing the improvised bridge, they put in the planned attack against the Pimple and successfully drove the Germans off. The way was now clear for a major offensive to be launched up the Tamera Gorge towards Sedjenane to regain the lost ground. Three days later on the 27th a big attack was launched from both sides of the river. The 1st Parachute Brigade with a unit of Goums drove forward on the left-hand side and 139 Brigade attacked from the right.*

General Lathbury, the 1st Parachute Brigade commander, had been ordered to advance back up the valley to open the road. To prepare the way before his attack, he was allocated the whole of the 46th Infantry Division's artillery.

Apparently, the Corps Commander, General Allfrey, was anxious about the crater that had been blown in the Tamera road by C Troop 1st Para Squadron (under brigade orders), however it was found that the Germans had partially repaired it to allow single-file traffic.**

The attack was successful and rolled the Germans back up the Tamera Gorge to the foot of Green Hill, passing the previously held positions of Cork Wood and Death Ridge on the way up. Green Hill was the position from which the Germans had started their attacks three weeks earlier and had precipitated the Tamera Valley battles.

*

We set off in single file like a crocodile of small school children eventually coming to a broad stream which we had to cross. Not wanting to get wet, we selected two of the biggest Italians and invited them to carry us across which they cheerfully did. The two German officers then started remonstrating that they also wished to be carried over the stream, but we were having none of

---

*   Goumier is a term used to describe a Moroccan soldier. The units (or Tabors) of Goums at Tamera were mostly irregular troops drawn from the mountains of Morocco and commanded by French officers. Among the Germans and Italians they had a fearsome reputation for not taking prisoners. When later used in Italy they became infamously associated with alleged war crimes against the civilian population.

** Discussion of phase two of the Battle of Tamera, John Frost, *A Drop Too Many* (1992).

that and made them plunge in and get wet, and they were playing steam as they waded across. On seeing them safely into the 'red-cap pen', we again borrowed the two Italians to carry us back across the stream, after which they went back across on their own to join their mates in the pen.

*

On the Move

139 Brigade continued to push back up the valley to the village of Sedjenane and the slopes around the base of Djebel Bel Harch. On 3 April, the 1st Parachute Brigade was then moved by lorry to the approaches of Green Hill where they spent a week on patrols in the area. On 14 April, the 1st Parachute Brigade was relieved by men of the US 9th Division and was withdrawn, travelling once again by rail back to Boufarik in Algeria.

*

Following our successful return up the Tamera Valley, our squadron and 3rd Battalion were moved up near Sedjenane where we were camped in and around old iron-ore workings. The area was particularly notable for the red dust that permeated everything we wore right through to our skin. We were still rinsing it out of our hair for weeks after we had left the area. If any period should have given rise to the name of the red devils, this should have been it!

We lost a lot of men in Tunisia, but at the time we did not realise just how many casualties our brigade was taking as we were well spread out during much of the fighting. Our squadron alone lost around 30 killed out of its approximate strength of 150. The three battalions were so short of officers at one point that some of our engineering officers were being transferred into infantry roles.* Platoons were at times down to two or three active men while the battalions were down to a couple of hundred. When we originally went into the line in Tunisia we quickly became aware that our brigade did not have enough men to carry out the job that it was being asked to do. This was apparent to the ordinary soldier through the situations that we found ourselves in week, week out. But we did it.

---

* 1st Parachute Squadron officer Lieutenant Dennis Simpson took command of the 2nd Battalion's B Company at the second Battle of Tamera.

Chapter 25

Returning to Boufarik from Tamera, 17 March 1943

All the rail journeys seemed to take between three and five days between Tunisia and Algeria and we were now experienced box-van travellers, having endured and enjoyed many days on the trains. Along our route the scenery was spectacular with the high hills around Ghardimaou and the passage through numerous deep gorges.

Outside Constantine we passed through a large railway junction at Khroub where the war still seemed to have had little effect on the Algerian railway system. The trains heading towards the front still had priority over those that were returning. At Khroub I recall observing a large French-built Garratt that was similar to the engines that I had fired back at Royston, which now seemed a long time ago. I also chatted to the driver of our train as best I could and recognising the loco man in me, he invited me to ride on the footplate – not likely, there was no way I was going to ride on the footplate in that heat when I could swing in my hammock with the breeze flowing by!

The route passed through the foothills of the Atlas Mountains and ran downgrade to Algiers. On approaching the outskirts of Boufarik, the railway came around a long loop within which there was a large POW camp holding what appeared to be thousands of German troops. As our train slowly negotiated the bend, both sides were looking at the other, we from the slowly moving train and the Germans up through the wire. A handful of Germans started clapping and then cheering, one or two at first then the volume rose as more crowded up to the wire – they were saluting us as we rolled past. It was a strange feeling as we found ourselves laughing with the Germans, we had been trying (and succeeding) to kill one another for months and now they were applauding us. They were German paratroops, our opposite numbers, the Fallschirmager.

We arrived at Boufarik for rest, recuperation and to take in replacements. The brigade began to build up its strength after its losses in the line. Many new faces arrived from home and had to be trained, acclimatised and fitted in. These new lads were keen and eager to impress and somewhat in awe of our well-worn appearance. We put them at ease (or wound them up) by telling them that it wouldn't be long before they would be looking like us given the pace of life that we had experienced.

It was at about this time that our C Troop commander Captain Tony Hewitt returned to Britain on leave.* We believed that he had never fully recovered from the head injury he had sustained on landing at Bone some six months previously. Tony never made it home as the aircraft in which he was travelling did not reach Britain. We didn't get the news until several weeks later. Lieutenant Ropey Cox was promoted to Captain and became our new troop commander.

*

The 1st Parachute Brigade in Action

Between November 1942 and July 1943, a period of nine months, the 1st Parachute Brigade sustained 1,700 casualties during the fighting in Tunisia.** These totals comprised killed, wounded and missing out of an original number of around 2,000. The 3 battalions that had arrived in North Africa in November 1942 had an individual battalion strength of between 540 and 550 men of all ranks, and of these original men there were little more than 200 left in each battalion. During this period the brigade received a total of 1,400 men as replacements in the form of transfers from the recently formed 2nd Parachute Brigade, newly trained volunteers from the Airborne Depot and the gradual return of its own wounded.

The brigade had taken part in more battles than any other formation in the 1st Army Group and had been accredited with inflicting more than 5,000 casualties among the enemy, and had also taken 3,000 prisoners.[†] In addition to the German Fallschirmager, they fought troops of the 10th Panzer Grenadier, Tunisian and Barenthin Regiments and the Italian Bersagliari.

*

Following our arrival back in Boufarik after the Tamera fighting, we were allowed local leave and weekend passes. To enhance our recuperation, a leave scheme had been arranged with the French civilians in Algiers, whereby they agreed to give soldiers lodgings in return for a small renumeration. As food was in short supply among the civilian population, it was also agreed that the soldiers would take their own rations.

The lodgings were allocated to us by the red caps (Military Police) who most of us avoided like the plague, but the scheme nevertheless appealed and so off we

---

*   Captain Antony Hewitt is remembered on the Brookwood Memorial under NKG (No Known Grave). Tom remembers Tony wearing a First Aid Nursing Yeomanry (FANY) cap badge on the right breast of his battledress. His wife was a lieutenant in the FANY driving ambulances.

** Casualty figures taken from http://www.paradata.org.uk/events/north-africa-operation-torch.

†   Figures taken from http://www.paradata.org.uk/events/north-africa-operation-torch.

went to sign up. By the time that my turn arrived some of the lads had already returned with stories of smashing lodgings in comfortable villas. Others had been less fortunate and found themselves fleeced. The common misfortune was that after handing over their rations on arrival and then going out for a stroll, they found their lodgings were locked and their rations were gone on their return!

My experience was somewhere in between. Chin Massey and I took the opportunity to 'holiday' with the French in Algiers and arrived at our allocated address in a poor part of town. Our digs were in a large run-down tenement and our hostess turned out to be an old crone in a head scarf with a dangling cigarette. Undaunted and determined to make the best of it, we were relieved of our rations and went out for a stroll. On our return, we had an awful meal that did not contain any of the food that we had brought in, and subsequent meals were of similar quality. However, things looked up when our 'hostess's' young niece came around, and as we had cinema coupons, we asked her out and she agreed. The communication was obviously very poor, in fact extremely poor, because the old crone got excited and it ended up with the four of us trooping out, with neither Chin or myself wanting to be seen escorting 'Madame Crone'.

Chin and I took some stick that evening on our way to the cinema. As we sidled along with the young girl and her aunt, the lads were shouting across the street, 'Which one's yours mate?' ... and the film was in flippin' French! We never did see our rations again during the whole of our stay. When the scheme started we wondered why the French were being so accommodating when previously most of them would not even speak to us. Now we knew, their amazing change of heart was due to the fact that we had become a meal ticket.

Chin Massey was famous within the squadron for having shot down a Stuka dive bomber with a Bren gun. The Stuka had come in low over the brow of the hill that we were on when Chin braced the gun against his hip and blazed away, and much to everyone's amazement smoke started billowing from its engine and it came down. It really raised a cheer among us as it was most unusual to hit an aircraft with a machine gun. It was good to get one back at them as they had been hitting us often enough.

*

German-held Tunis Surrenders, 7 May 1943

Finally, hemmed in on all sides, the German army had retreated as far as the Bay of Tunis. In order to escape it began taking Italian transport ships across to Sicily. Frantic efforts were being made to remove as much armour as possible before the British and US armies arrived.

The formal surrender and the end of the war in North Africa took place on 13 May. Thousands of Germans and Italians were left behind to surrender having failed to fight to the last man as Hitler had demanded. The Allied armies now began preparations to invade Europe via Sicily and Italy.

Chapter 26

Boufarik to Mascara for Training, May 1943

The brigade now moved from Boufarik to an isolated valley on a plateau 60 miles inland from Oran to begin training for the next operation. Our new camp was an airstrip located in a dust-filled valley which appeared to have been flattened out of agricultural land. Down both sides of the runway were the remaining dried stalks of what appeared to have been a wheat field. Our squadron arrived before the main body of the brigade to prepare the basics for the tented camp. We dug latrines and drains and erected tents. The US air and ground crews complete with Dakotas were already encamped with their usual 'up-market' facilities, towards which we cast envious eyes. As usual they were friendly, and being skilled at scrounging, we unashamedly took advantage of their hospitality whenever we could.

Arriving with the brigade several days later were the RAF Mobile Parachute Packing section. The section was made up of both packers and sewing machinists to repair our torn and damaged parachutes. The all-male packers and repairers worked in two large enclosed van-type lorries that were backed up end to end, within which they set up their workshop of packing and repair tables.

Our parachutes were originally made of white silk but by this time they had mostly been replaced by an olive-green nylon. Nylon had the advantage over silk in that it had a closer weave and held more air, and it didn't cling in folds and therefore opened more readily and dried more quickly. This was an advantage for the packers who were able to turn round our used parachutes much faster.

We found the weather to be extremely hot and dry at our new encampment and the area around the airfield was a dust bowl. The movement and take-off of aircraft created great clouds of red dust that hung in the air and coated our clothes, tents and hair. Great heaps of powdered earth several feet high were deposited at either side of the runway waiting for the next disturbance and everyone's discomfort. Further afield in the valley the landscape was very pretty with small French farms and towns surrounded by citrus groves and wild flowers. The main towns in the area were Mascara and Matemore.

There was not much to do when our training was over and so to amuse ourselves we began tortoise racing. There were numerous tortoises in the wadis ranging in size from tiny, perfectly formed ones the size of a penny to the old timers that had carapaces bleached white by the sun. Many of the lads carried the small ones around in cigarette tins when they had found a 'galloper' and they were guarded as closely as any Newmarket thoroughbred, for money was wagered on the outcome of the races. These events were so well organised that we even attached an upright bristle to the rear of the shell to carry a miniature racing number. In between races the runners were corralled in a tortoise paddock outside our tent. Several even did parachute jumps, so keen were their 'trainers' to hang on to them, but eventually they were released and allowed to wander off. So unconcerned were these creatures that they would often enter our tents through the front flap and out the other side. I even recall one purposely walking across the blanket of a card school.

As well as tortoise racing, time was spent familiarising ourselves with enemy weapons. We also carried out several training exercises jumping in and around the valley in various strengths which culminated in a brigade drop. Each of the drops was followed by a simulated attack on a bridge. Although we were not aware of it, these exercises were working us up for our role in the invasion of Sicily.

On one of these drops we came across an anomaly that we had not experienced before, and this created a great deal of ribaldry. Due to the rising thermals, some of the lads were suspended in the air about 100ft from the ground, neither moving up nor down, just hovering above us. Those of us that were down were shedding our webbing and preparing to move off, the activity of which made several of the 'hoverers' quite anxious. Looking down from their elevated predicament, they were shouting for help only to be greeted with catcalls from below to stop skiving and worse. They all came down eventually.

Following these exercises our parachutes were collected and taken to the mobile packing units for repair and repacking, but retrieval had to be quick due to the high value that the local Arabs placed on both the parachute silk and the nylon. They were always watching on our periphery and would have one away if the opportunity arose. Several thousand parachutes were collected and repacked by the small RAF packing section in the short time that we were training in the Mascara area.

Sometimes on route marches we traversed large areas of salt flats which kicked up salt which stuck to the sweat on our legs. On halting we were able to peel it off in sculptured sheets. Several of the lads developed abscesses which were attributed to salt exposure. And it was just my luck to develop another abscess, this time on my thigh. I had the good fortune, or should I say misfortune, to be treated by the Battalion Medical Officer who was visiting our area on his rounds. He was a big, bluff, no-nonsense Scotsman who after a cursory inspection instructed me to lie down and the watching lads to hold my arms and legs. An anaesthetic liquid was dropped onto a gauze mask and held over my nose and mouth and I was out. When I came round gingerly touching the protective dressing, the lads began their banter, 'Well, you should have seen it, Tom ... it ran yellow all over the place', and, 'You'll not want your dinner tonight ... it's steak and kidney pudding ('compo') ... you'll not be wanting yours then'. But steak and kidney pudding was my favourite and undaunted by the al-fresco surgery, I recovered sufficiently to claim my share.

Chapter 27

Mascara to M'Saken, Sousse, Late June 1943

Following our training around Mascara, we were moved down to M'Saken in Tunisia by road and rail. We arrived on 30 June 1943 after yet another five-day journey and joined a huge canvas encampment dispersed among the olive groves. An enormous sea of tents housed our 1st Brigade together with the 2nd and 4th Parachute Brigades and 1st Air Landing Brigade – it was a tented town of over 10,000 men. The camp was situated alongside the main road linking Sousse to Kairouan near the large Arab village of M'Saken. The weather was even hotter down in M'Saken than it had been up at Mascara and we were seared by the wind that blew in off the desert, but despite this we preferred our new camp as we were only 30 minutes from the sea.

We had always been distrustful of the local Arabs during our time in Tunisia, and from the beginning we suspected that they considered our presence to be an unexpected bounty from which they could prosper. We believed that during the up-country fighting they gave the Germans information on our movements and then scuttled down the valleys to give the positions of the Germans to us, therefore collecting a double bounty. We also believed that they would take advantage of our wounded if left unprotected in the field, and it was rumoured that some of our dead had been dug up for their clothing and boots. Given the severity of the times, any Arabs found wearing British uniforms ran the risk of severe unofficial retribution if caught. Such was our low opinion of them that any buildings or roads that we built were often burned or blown up when we pulled out of the area.

Our camp near M'Saken therefore presented a windfall for the locals and we began losing a lot of our stores through pilfering. This came to a head one night when a local was shot by a sentry for failing to respond to a challenge. He was found to be carrying a large tent out of camp on his shoulders. Shortly afterwards, a raid was carried out on M'Saken under cover of darkness to search Arab houses in an attempt recover stolen stores.

Apart from these serious issues, we were in daily competition in our day to day bartering at which the Arabs were unsurpassed at skinning us. We initially dreamt up ruses to get our own back by selling them two left or right boots as a pair, or by trading used tea leaves with a covering of fresh ones, but I think overall they got the better of us.

Background to the Invasion of Sicily

The decision to invade Sicily was part of the strategy to win the battle for the Mediterranean and to provide a springboard for the invasion of Italy. The operation to be launched from North Africa was to form part of a massive assault by both British and US troops, numbering 180,000 men in total. The Americans were to land in the west of Sicily and the British in the east. It was hoped that a pincer movement would cut off and defeat four divisions of German troops before they were able to escape cross the Messina Gap into Italy. The Allied operational plan was called Husky. The British part of Husky was to be Fustian, and the 1st Airborne Brigade's assault on the Primosole Bridge was named Marston.

We were now confined to camp in M'Saken, all independent leisure being curtailed as we concentrated on preparing our equipment for what we knew was a pending operation – it could only be Sicily. Replacements were coming in and old faces were returning from hospital. The division had a visit from the US General Eisenhower, who was a popular figure with the troops, and our spirits were high.

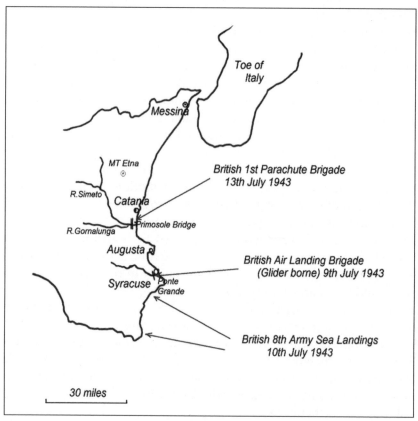

British landings on the east coast of Sicily, 10–13 July 1943.

The Hicks family on the steps of the Railway Inn, Ditton, 1920s. Left to right, back: Tom's mother Anastasia, father Fred and grandmother Margaret; front: a friend, Tom and brother Bob (standing in front). (*T. Hicks*)

Young loco cleaners, Royston Shed, 1936. Tom is on the extreme right. (*T. Hicks*)

The cleaners and passed firemen at Royston shed pose on the running plate, 1936. Tom is sitting on the left. (*T. Hicks*)

Tom, aged 20, on the tennis court prior to joining the army, 1939. (*T. Hicks*)

A pre-war photograph of a Beyer-Garratt on a mineral train. The front tank was solely for water. It has two 2–6–0 arrangements (2–6–6–2) at both the front and back. The enormous coal bunker can be clearly seen sitting squarely at the back. The loco weighed over 155 tons. (*Brian Stevenson*)

1898627 Sapper T. Hicks, aged 20, at Longmoor, 1939. (*T. Hicks*)

Tom on the barrack steps at Longmoor, 1939. (*T. Hicks*)

A 0–6–0 War Department locomotive on Longmoor shed, 1940. This engine has a steam condensing system indicating that it had been previously modified to work on the London Underground before it found its way to Longmoor. (*T. Hicks*)

A mobile platform in use at Hardwick Hall, August 1942. Note the rubber rimmed protective helmets worn by these parachute troops during training. (*IWM H22891*)

Leaving the whole in the floor of the balloon basket from 800ft, 1942. The static line attached to the parachute can be seen clearly.

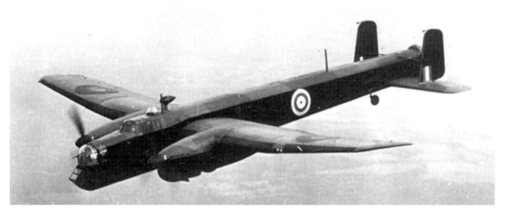

An Armstrong Whitworth Whitley bomber, 1941. Tom made his first parachute jumps from this type of aeroplane. (*Pen & Sword Archive*)

Paratroops inside a converted Whitley bomber, 1941. The interior of the Whitley was not comfortable – no windows, dark, cold, cramped and you couldn't stand up so your back was against one side with your feet against the other. Imagine ten men in full webbing attending the call of nature! (*Airborne Assault Museum*)

Paratroops dropping from a Whitley bomber, 1942. (*Pen & Sword Archive*)

Paratroops on parade during a training exercise, 1942. (*Airborne Assault Museum*)

Tom, aged 23, and Bob Hicks, aged 18, with fellow trainees, 28 September 1942. Tom is in the centre and Bob is at the back on the left. Bob was undergoing aircrew training in Blackpool at the RAF Radio School and Tom was visiting him while on leave.

A Douglas C47 Dakota, *c*. 1943. Introduced to the paratroops in late summer 1943, Tom recalled it was absolute luxury after the Whitley and it is still fondly remembered by him. (*Pen & Sword Archive*)

Paratroops making preparations, 1944. (*Pen & Sword Archive*)

Dakotas dropping paratroops on a training exercise, 1944. (*Pen & Sword Archive*)

Paratroopers attach an equipment container to the fuselage of an RAF Dakota, 22 April 1944. (*IWM H37727*)

Tom, aged 23, in Boufarik, Algeria, 1942. (*T. Hicks*)

Tom's pal Len Norman Hook in Boufarik, Algeria, 1942. 'Hicks and Hook' was easily remembered when 'volunteers' were required. (*Mary Hook*)

The sergeant seen here is carrying a weapons valise. He is holding the webbing loop in his right hand which is attached to the 20ft length of rope with which he had to lower the valise once the parachute canopy had deployed. The rope was secured at waist height on the right-hand side of the harness, visible just below and left of his right cuff. Once the canopy had deployed, the cord retaining the release pins was ripped away allowing the heavy valise to fall away. It was then lowered on the rope to hit the ground before the paratrooper. Landing with the valise attached could result in serious if not fatal injury. This is how Tom jumped at Arnhem with his Bren gun inside the felt-lined case.

Parachute containers being assembled at an airfield near Kairouan, Tunisia in preparation for the assault on the Primosole Bridge in Sicily, July 1943.

The bridge at Arnhem, *c.* 1938. (*Dutch National Aviation Museum Aviodrome*)

The three photographs seen here are stills from the film *The Battle for the Bridges* and show the 1st Airborne Division parachuting into Holland and landing at Arnhem in September 1944. (*Pen & Sword Archive*)

Three sappers from the 1st Parachute Squadron RE after being taken prisoner at Arnhem on 21 September 1944. 'Ginger' Pratt (left) and George Needham (right) assist 'Wag' Papworth.

Lance Sergeant Harry Padfield, B Troop 1st Parachute Squadron RE (left) and Corporal G. Roberts, 16th Parachute Field Ambulance (right) help carry a wounded comrade, 19 September 1944.

Members of 1st Parachute Squadron RE, east of Arnhem bridge, 20 September 1944. Left to right: Sapper J. Dinnie, Sapper C. Grier and Lance Corporal Dick Robb (wounded). Although a member of A Troop, Dick always knocked about with Tom in C Troop. (*IWM HU002131*)

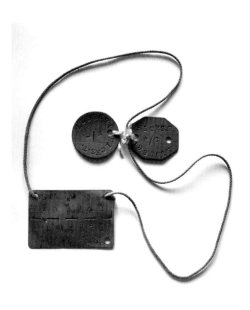

Tom's army and POW dog tags. (*N. Hicks*)

Tom's battledress top displaying his parachute wings and divisional patches. (*N. Hicks*)

After returning in rags from the POW camp in Germany, this top was issued to Tom on 23 April 1945. It was then worn regularly at Longmoor from June 1945 until demobilisation in June 1946. The top was made by M. Craps & Sons in 1942. (*T. Hicks*)

The 1st Parachute Squadron reunion, 1954. From left to right: Jonah Jones, Lucky Luckhurst, Dick Robb, Tom (holding the flag) and Len Norman Hook. (*T. Hicks*)

An 8F hauling a short 'tripper' towards Carlton Yards from Royston shed, 21 March 1967. This beautiful, clear photograph was taken just seven months before the end of steam and shows Monckton pit on the left and its stack on the right. (*Steve Armitage*)

Tom taking part in his last parachute jump with the Red Devils on Ginkel Heath, near Arnhem, September 2007. (*T. Hicks*)

Tom, aged 88, at Arnhem, September 2007. (*T. Hicks*)

Tom, aged 93, playing tennis at Notton
Tennis Club, summer 2012. (*N. Hicks*)

Tom walking on the now-landscaped Monckton stack with Royston and the forested railway site below. (*N. Hicks*)

Chapter 28

Sicily, July 1943

O ur next operation was to cross over to Sicily to drop as a division in front of 13 Corps (8th Army), which was to come in by sea lower down the coast. The sea landing was set for 10 July, three days before we were to drop. The 1st Airborne Division was given three objectives in an operation that was quintessentially what the Airborne Forces were created for, to drop ahead of the advancing army and to hold an objective until relieved. If the operation was successful, the momentum of the main army's advance could be maintained. We were again upbeat and excited.

*

Divisional Objectives on Sicily

The division's objectives were to capture the Ponte Grande Bridge south of Syracuse, the port of Augusta and the Primosole Bridge. The Ponte Grande was to be taken by the glider-borne 1st Air Landing Brigade, Augusta by the 2nd Parachute Brigade and the Primosole Bridge by the 1st Parachute Brigade under the command of Brigadier Lathbury, who had previously commanded the 3rd Battalion.

The 1st Air Landing Brigade took off in gliders on the night of 9 July and succeeded in taking the Ponte Grande Bridge. Disaster was averted after almost eighty of the brigade's gliders landed in the sea, and those that struggled ashore from the sea were exhausted and without weapons. In addition to this, many of those that made landfall were widely scattered and the gliders that actually made the landing zones (LZs) hit banks and walls killing and maiming many of the pilots and troops.

Nevertheless, such was the superiority of the invasion that the 2nd Parachute Brigade's operation against Augusta was cancelled. The reason for this was that elements of 13 Corps that had been landed by sea had advanced so rapidly up the coast that the town was taken, making the 2nd Para Brigade's assault unnecessary.

The third objective was given to the 1st Parachute Brigade, the strategically important Primosole Bridge. The bridge was set in a defile spanning the Simeto River on the approaches to the Catania Plain and was a gateway into the heartland of Sicily. It was to be taken and held for 24 hours to allow the infantry and armour to move up from Augusta. The superior forces of 13 Corps would then cross over the bridge to engage the Germans on the Catania Plain.

The assault on the bridge was to be made by the 1st, 2nd and 3rd Battalions supported by 1st Para Squadron RE, medics of 16th Parachute Field Ambulance and men of 21st Independent Parachute Company, a total force of around 1,800 men. The elements of the 1st Parachute Brigade mentioned above were still under strength at this time following the fighting in Tunisia. The essence of the operation was as in all parachute operations to be one of speed and surprise.

Chapter 29

Primosole Bridge, Sicily, 13 July 1943

We were briefed that the objectives of our squadron were to accompany two platoons of the 1st Battalion in the *coup de main* attack on the bridge. Once on the bridge we were to remove the demolition charges. The squadron would then clear any enemy mines and lay defensive mines on the bridge approaches.* If the bridge was blown before it could be taken, we were to find an alternative bridging point on the Simeto River. The rest of the brigade was to assault a nearby anti-aircraft battery and set up a perimeter around the bridge which they would defend until relieved.

Our containers and stores had been packed several days before in preparation for the operation. We moved down to the airfield outside Kairouan on 12 July only to have our departure postponed for 24 hours. Returning to M'Saken, we passed through the 2nd Parachute Brigade camp and they gave us some stick as they assumed that our operation had now been cancelled as theirs had been (Augusta), but we were only delayed for 24 hours and were back down on the airfield the following day.

When we arrived at the airfield I could see that the operation was going ahead by the purposeful activity around the Dakotas. Once olive green, they were now repainted in a desert sandy brown. Dusty and faded, they looked well seasoned to the job. All had names painted below the cockpit windows and these were mostly girly, as the US crews had personalised their aircraft in keeping with USAAF custom. One of the aircraft carrying the sappers of B Troop had been affectionately named 'Miss Carriage', as opposed to the more exotic and glamorous names around her.** Now fully kitted up and with boarding imminent, the Roman Catholics among us came together in the shade of the aircraft for a short service with our padre Father Egan.[†]

---

*   Most of the squadron's A Troop and HQ Company were not on the operation.

** Ironically, 'Miss Carriage' was the only aircraft carrying members of the 1st Parachute Squadron RE's B Troop that would drop the sappers in the correct place. See Peter Stainforth, *Wings of the Wind* (1952).

[†]   Among the first wave of Dakotas to take off for Primosole were the 6 aircraft carrying 95 men of the 1st Parachute Squadron comprising B Troop (44 men) and C Troop (49 men).

Transportation

The 1st Parachute Brigade was to be carried by 105 Dakotas of the American Troop Carrier Command and 11 RAF Albermarles with 16 gliders in tow.* The brigade took off from six airfields located between Kairouan and Sousse. Problems always beset the operations and three of the paratroop-carrying Dakotas did not take off or had to turn back shortly after becoming airborne due to malfunctions. Many more were to turn back later without reaching the objective.

*

Squadron Diary Extracts, July 1942

The following extracts are from the diary of the 1st Parachute Squadron RE in July 1942. The entry for 13 July briefly states the objective and the squadron's situation on the night of the operation. The parachute sticks for five of the six aircraft carrying the sappers are given together with the dropping order. Tom is listed in aircraft No. 2. The sixth aircraft is referred to in Captain Houghton's report as only being able to drop twelve men from its stick of eighteen.

13th July 1943

Moved to airfield to emplane for FUSTIAN. Planes took off between 19.45 & 20.10. A/a fire encountered & planes damaged. 2 planes returned including Capt Livesey Lieut Buchanan Assault sticks returned. Radio reports that 1 Bde took its objective – no news of Major Murray but plane returned. Capt Brockington's plane not yet returned, may have been forced down. Squadron tasks to ensure that charges taken from Ponte Primosole in Catania on R. Simeto, clear mines & if bridge blown recce new crossing.

First Aircraft

This stick of seventeen comprised sappers from C Troop together with the Squadron Commander Major Murray and his batman Gordon Spicer.

---

* Figures taken from Ministry of Information, *By Air to Battle* (1945), p. 60.

A/C No. As on Para G5 30

Dropping Order	Army Number	Rank	Name and Initials	Unit
1	106883	Major	D.C. Murray	1st Parachute Squadron
2	2126374	Sapper	Marshall W.	
3	5726981	Sapper	Spicer G.F.	
4	2094258	L/Sgt	Smith J.W.	
5	1876084	Sapper	Hulme G.R.	
6	1909450	Sapper	Jones C.T.	
7	1991285	Sapper	Synclair R.	
8	1911774	Sapper	Hammond W.C.	
9	2075982	Driver	Howarth F.	
10	251037	Lieut.	C.E.P. Sankey	
11	2113379	Sapper	Massey H.	
12	1919212	Sapper	Poulson S.	
13	2009868	L/Cpl	Lane P.G.O.	
14	1875757	Sapper	Warren H.	
15	5335778	Sapper	Hobbs J.	
16	2114011	L/Cpl.	Pratt R.	
17	6398554	L/Sgt.	Hoath F.G	

Second Aircraft
Stick of sixteen comprising sappers from C Troop.

A/C No. As on Para G5 63

Dropping Order	Army Number	Rank	Name and Initials	Unit
1	1875223	L/Cpl.	Littlejohn R.	1st Parachute Squadron
2	1871084	Sgt.	Naylor K.I.	
3	224554	Capt.	Brockingham T.C.	
4	1882755	Sapper	McDonald R.	
5	1991310	Cpl.	Clayton R.	
6	1911778	Sapper	Luckhurst F.	
7	1898627	Sapper	Hicks T.	
8	1943421	Sapper	Hook N.L.	
9	2228870	Lieut.	Cox C.G	
10	2189799	Sapper	Brookes T.	
11	2114032	L/Cpl.	McBernie J.	

Dropping Order	Army Number	Rank	Name and Initials	Unit
12	1880946	Sapper	Taylor G.	
13	1906435	Sapper	Davies W.	
14	2148914	L/Cpl.	Cameron C.	
15	1906288	Sapper	Johnstone A.B.	
16	2073654	L/Cpl.	Cosadinos G.	

Third Aircraft

Stick of fifteen comprising sappers from B Troop.

A/C No. As on Para G5 88

Dropping Order	Army Number	Rank	Name and Initials	Unit
1	1871091	L/Sgt.	Thornton H.J.	1st Parachute Squadron
2	326272	Sapper	Clark J.H.	
3	Not listed	Sapper	Grier C.	
4	2054820	Sapper	Morgan L.G.	
5	1911484	Sapper	Hall R.	
6	1941192	Sapper	Madden W.	
7	226295	Lieut.	P.T Stainforth	
8	2144443	Cpl.	Simkins J.	
9	2077436	Sapper	Gray D.	
10	1911650	L/Cpl.	Neville D.	
		Sapper	Brookes T.	
11	1915644	Sapper	Wickham J.	
12	1918461	Sapper	Chaney E.E.	
13	1916611	L/Cpl.	Newton G.H.	
14	1919918	Sapper	Snelling H.	
15	1906288	Cpl.	Padfield H.	

Fourth Aircraft

Stick of sixteen comprising sappers from B Troop.

A/C No. As on Para G5 89

Dropping Order	Army Number	Rank	Name and Initials	Unit
1	232100	Lieut.	A.H. Scott-Fleming	1st Parachute Squadron
2	1985259	Sapper	Christie G.	
3	1910707	L/Cpl.	Wilkinson L.	
4	5121848	Sapper	Hanlon R.	
5	1894154	Sapper	Downing G.	
6	2141624	Sapper	Butterworth N.	
7	2126716	Sapper	Hirst W.	
8	2435621	Lieut.	Buchanan G.C.	
9	2050678	S.S.M	Bannerman J.	
10	1911649	Sapper	Kill W.C.	
11	2193549	Sapper	Jones G.	
12	2058826	L/Cpl.	Slayton J.V.	
13	13039572	L/Cpl.	McCutcheon D.	
15*	2000989	L/Cpl.	Mcgivern G.	
16	1881520	L/Sgt.	Gillie T.	

* Position 14 not listed.

Fifth Aircraft

Stick of thirteen comprising sappers from B Troop.

A/C No. As on Para G5

Dropping Order	Army Number	Rank	Name and Initials	Unit
1	222702	Capt.	Livesey T.J.M.C	1st Parachute Squadron
2	2135069	Sapper	Carr S.F.	
3	2068682	L/Cpl.	Malley J.	
4	2135815	Sapper	Hookway J.A.	
5	2150311	Sapper	Todd J.T.H.	
6	2091594	L/Cpl.	Ings E.	
7	2066603	Sgt.	Clelend R.L.	

Dropping Order	Army Number	Rank	Name and Initials	Unit
8	2141593	Sapper	Long T.	
9	1871921	Sapper	Oldbury J.T.	
10	2125282	Sapper	Bennett G. Kill W.C.	
11	1874858	Sapper	Hendy J.	
12	6469132	L/Sgt.*	Lewis W.	
13	2000549	Cpl.	Halliwell S.	

* A British army corporal acting in the rank of lance sergeant. This was an acting appointment which could be removed by a colonel, whereas a substantive sergeant could only be demoted by court martial. The rank was abolished in 1946. The rank of lance corporal remains and became a substantive rank in 1961.

The following are further extracts from the squadron diary giving brief reports on the two aircraft that returned:

Captain Livesey's Report on Stick Number 90

Troops
Total No. in Stick 13
Number who jumped -----
Number who did not jump 13
Reason Plane was fired upon. Pilot was shot in thigh or stomach, Navigator in head. Co-pilot refused to continue as he said a/c was damaged & he would be unable to make the return journey, & was not sure of his location.
Statement of injuries
  (a) in a/c Pilot & Navigator (Slight)
  (b) on dropping

Captain A.E. Houghton's Report (Stick Number Not Stated)

Troops
Total No. in Stick 18
Number who jumped 12
Number who did not jump 6
Reason No. 12 in stick had his static line caught up about 8ft from door. The rest of the stick were held up & pilot refused to cross D.Z. again. There was considerable A.A. fire over D.Z. Plane was hit in tail and port petrol tank. N.B. The R.E. personnel were Nos 16, 17, 18 and consequently did not jump.
Statement of injuries
  (a) in a/c
  (b) on dropping

In summary, two of the six aircraft carrying members of the squadron returned to Tunisia due to damage with troops still on board. A third crash-landed in Malta and a fourth dropped (Tom's) its troops miles from the DZ before crashing into the sea. The fifth, Captain Peter Stainforth's aircraft 'Miss Carriage', dropped the paratroops in the correct place and the sixth only managed to drop twelve men, probably not on the DZ. We took off at dusk on 13 July shortly before 2000hr. We took off at dusk on 13 July shortly before 2000hr. The aircraft flew in Vics of three with a solitary navigator in the lead aircraft.* By this time we had an all-American crew with USAAF navigators having replaced those of the RAF. Navigators were still in short supply and hence on this operation we only had one for every three aircraft that were carrying the brigade.

The pilots' briefing was to approach Malta where a cone of searchlights would be lit as a beacon to indicate to them to bear left for the coast of Sicily. The aircrew had specific instructions to avoid an area where the Royal Navy were positioned along the Sicilian coast to prevent the possibility of attracting a friendly fire attack from our own ships.

It was a lovely, cool evening, and flying low with the large Dakota door open, we were eating corned beef sandwiches and were quite relaxed. Our three aircraft found the searchlight cone on Malta and altered course in the direction of Sicily as planned; the sixteen of us inside were having an uneventful flight. But the peace and steady drone of the aircraft engines were to be short-lived, as shortly after Malta all hell broke loose when we were surprised by a series of large explosions. Our aircraft bounced around and pieces of shrapnel came up through the floor. The pilot began weaving around as he tried to take evasive action and then there was a blinding flash and all the lights went out. In the dark we were thrown on the floor. Fully kitted, we were in a right tangle of limbs and webbing, disorientated and not quite knowing where we were.

*

Friendly Fire

Unbeknown to the sappers and crew the aircraft had strayed into the area off the Sicilian coast above ships of the Royal Navy that were protecting and supplying the landing beaches of the seaborne invasion. Having earlier endured German air attacks, the ships' gunners had mistakenly opened fire on the airborne assault aircraft.

---

* The term Vic was used to describe a group of aircraft flying together in a V-shaped formation, that is a lead aircraft with two others slightly behind an either side. The word echelon was also used which is an aviation term to describe aircraft in a diagonal line of flight.

The Royal Navy shot down several of the low-flying Dakotas carrying the paratroops, and a few more were badly damaged and had to turn back to Tunisia. The havoc caused by the anti-aircraft fire scattered the airborne armada of over 100 aircraft as pilots took evasive action. The result was that many of the Dakotas were now without navigators, leaving the pilots trying to locate the parachute DZs in the dark.

*

When the pilot eventually steadied the aircraft we found that we were on our own, the other two aircraft accompanying us had disappeared taking with them our only navigator. As we straightened ourselves out, the US crew chief came in and confirmed that we were on our own 'but we would manage'. Eventually, the dark landmass of Sicily appeared beneath us, our pilot had managed to re-orientate himself and was now attempting to find his way to our DZ. Once again we were flying steady and as we pressed on, the USAAF jump master was passing along a commentary of our progress. In the distance we could clearly see the dull glow from the cone of Mount Etna from which the pilot had been able to get his bearings.

We were then in for another surprise as a German airfield (Catania) lit up out of the darkness below. I later read that the Germans had switched on their ground lights in the assumption that as we were flying low we were one of their own aircraft coming in to land. Realising their mistake, the airfield lights were quickly doused to be replaced by searchlights and rapid shelling from their anti-aircraft guns. We were illuminated and could see one another clearly inside our aircraft's fuselage. Searchlights look like pin pricks on the ground but in the sky they cover an area of a football pitch, and we felt truly vulnerable.

The pilot's navigational skills may have been questionable but his evasive technique was top of the class – we flew sideways, dipped and climbed, while the night was full of orange-coloured tracers sweeping the sky. A searchlight came onto us and then went out for some reason and we thought we had got away with it as we were still climbing. However, there was a sudden loud bang and flames started flowing past the open door through which we were shortly to jump, a flak fragment had hit the port engine. Fortunately, no one sustained an injury but we had a lot more holes in the fuselage and after a few minutes the flames died down and were replaced by a leaking oily mess that was lit up by showers of sparks that were streaming past the door. The pilot must have found his bearings because shortly afterwards the white light came on in the dark, prepare to jump. It was a relief to stand up with a purpose. Standing close, we hooked our static lines onto the anchor cable and gave a quick tug on the man's line in front to check that it was securely connected, then the feel of a tug on your own from behind, right hand on the shoulder of the man in front and we closed up tight as a spring.

With Lucky in front and Len Hook behind, we were connected as one. There is a comfort in going together. The aircraft was rising and falling and we were swaying around having some difficulty standing up. I was willing the stick to get moving. The light then changed to green and the relief was palpable, 'Great,' I thought, 'we're out'. Adrenaline-charged, we started to move forward in a rapid hunched shuffle. We were going as fast as we could when the light changed to red. The red light meant stop jumping as it was unsafe, usually meaning we were over a hillside and the altitude had changed, but we were in an aircraft with a burning engine that was shooting sparks and oil past the door.* One man was jumping every 2 seconds following the despatch of containers. There was no way we were going to stop and out we went past the red light. It really was dark out there, a pitch-black night with no recognisable landmarks.

Among all this drama we were later to hear of a humorous incident concerning my mate Lance Corporal George 'Cossy' Cosadinas. Cossy was positioned last in our stick and was shuffling along in the dark with his head down. On reaching the door he mistook the US jump master for one of our boys that was refusing to jump. Cossy told the story that he incredulously thought, 'We can't have one of our boys refusing to jump … I'm not having this' and grabbed the American and mistakenly pulled him towards the door. Without a parachute the jumpmaster was reluctant to move. Realising his error, Cossy jumped seconds behind us but it was enough to detach him and we didn't see him for a couple of weeks after leaving the aircraft.

The front half of our stick, which included myself, landed in the dark on a hard and rugged hillside, the rear elements were not to be seen and Cossy unbeknown to us was miles away. We were scattered, and we could hardly see one another it was so dark. We knew we were in the wrong place and the few of us that were present began to try and locate the rest of our stick. We didn't have clickers or any other location aids so the method of regrouping was to follow the line of fall. You knew which direction the aircraft was travelling in and your number in the stick, so if you walked in the opposite direction to that of the aircraft you trusted to meet up. Walking quietly in the dark with eyes and ears straining, we quietly whistled and called to form up. We found out later that German paratroops had landed on the same hillside as us some 2 hours earlier, and we came across their discarded containers and equipment as we were searched for our own.**

---

* After dropping us our aircraft was to crash into the sea on its return journey to Tunisia due to damage to the port wing and tail sustained on the run in.

** Elements of the German 4th Parachute Brigade had been parachuted in to defend the bridge and the road to Catania in front of the advancing British forces.

After Landing

In the confusion caused by navigational errors and being fired on by friend and foe the aircraft and battalions were widely scattered. There were eleven aircraft lost and twenty-seven returned back to base in Tunisia without dropping their paratroops.

The B Troop sappers from 'Miss Carriage' were first to land on the DZ, followed by Brigadier Lathbury with Brigade Signals from a second aircraft and then the Brigade Defence platoon from a third. Only three aircraft managed to drop the paratroopers on the DZ. Brigadier Lathbury ordered that they form up into ambush parties of ten with the intention of attacking the bridge at daybreak.

Before the attack went in the sound of marching feet was heard. Hunkered down in defensive positions, the order to hold fire was given. To their relief it was Lieutenant Colonel Pearson with remnants of the 1st Battalion.

The bridge was attacked and taken at dawn by the much-reduced 1st Battalion *coup de main* force commanded by Lieutenant Colonel Alastair Pearson. It was left to elements of B Troop led by Captain Stainforth to follow the attack in and remove the explosives from the bridge.*

*

Moving quietly, we managed to form up into a small group and located our containers in the darkness, greatly assisted by the small blue lights that were now fitted into their base plates. In addition to the lights, we had chalked a marker on our particular container to save time. Once our equipment and arms had been found we felt much more comfortable and were able to move off. We hadn't got very far when we came across the body of one of our lads from C Troop who had been flying in another of our aircraft.** We presumed he had been dropped too low on the raised area of the hill. We paused only long enough to mark his position with his rifle and helmet and then took his rations and identification disc and moved on down the hillside.

Out of the sixteen that had dropped from the aircraft about eight of us had linked up, and the rest of our stick was nowhere to be seen. Before the operation we had studied the area and memorised the main landmarks, but it was so dark that we were unable to orientate ourselves and were lost.

---

*   See Peter Stainforth's *Wings of the Wind* (1952) and the personal account of Lance Sergeant Paddy Padfield, also of B Troop. Under orders from Lieutenant Stainforth, Paddy Padfield (then Corporal) was part of the stick that removed the charges on the left-hand side of the bridge. Sapper Billy Madden was part of the stick on the right.

** This was the body of Lance Corporal Ramsay Pratt, aged 26. He is buried in Catania War Cemetery, Sicily.

In the distance, we could see flares (Very lights) and tracer going up, so we thought that's where we ought to be. We placed our kit on an airborne trolley and started to walk down the hillside hoping to pick up the Simeto River, which would lead us to the bridge where we assumed we would find our squadron.

As we descended the slope it became a series of flat terraces, 40ft wide followed by a drop of 5ft or more. Along the terraces were vines supported on horizontal tension wires. Well, we had some tangles getting through these obstacles, swearing like troopers as we gradually made our way down the hillside.

Little by little, we started picking up lads that had been scattered by the drop, not of our squadron, but a machine-gun section from the 3rd Battalion without any machine guns. They had not been able to locate their containers. Eventually, we had a group of about fifty men all trying to get down to the river in a long, well-spaced crocodile.

It was still dark and my thigh was hurting from having landed heavily on the hillside, I placed my hand down inside my trousers and it was wet. 'Oh, hell!' I thought, 'What have I picked up here?' I withdrew my hand and tasted it – water, what a relief as I had initially thought it to be blood. Fortunately, it turned out that I had fallen on my water bottle and had cracked it and the water had seeped down my leg.* 'Phew,' I thought, 'I can cope with that.' My chocolate was also safe as I had it stowed in the pocket of my smock.

In the dark we continued to lose and collect men. We met an officer from the 3rd Battalion and after a brief conversation with Ropey he decided to take his men off in another direction. Ropey informed him that his lads had no weapons or ammunition, to which he replied, 'Never mind, we'll get some from somewhere.' When they had left we realised that there were now only four of us out of the eight that had landed, and we assumed that some of our lads had mistakenly left with this detachment from the 3rd, which was now well strung out. There was no point in chasing after them.

We continued downwards towards the fighting still hoping to find our squadron in the vicinity of the bridge; from a distance we couldn't determine if the bridge was still being held. As we approached, the Germans put in a big attack and we had to scramble out of the way to avoid being overrun. The Germans had dislodged our troops from the side of the bridge that we had just struggled down the hill to reach, and we now found ourselves on the side held by the Germans – we were cut off.

---

* An occurrence that was not uncommon, but always a surprise, due to the way that the bottle was attached to the webbing.

Battle for the Bridge

Earlier on the 14th the German 4th Parachute Brigade with a force of 2,000 men attacked the weakly held bridge from the west, the north and down the river valley from the east. The Germans were also able to bring up 88mm assault guns. By 1700hr the small force on the bridge was in serious trouble as they were low on ammunition and the enemy's superior firepower had begun to take effect. In addition to this, the surrounding cornfields and scrub were on fire removing any cover. A decision was taken to withdraw the bridge force and this took place at 1930hr.

The 1st Battalion withdrew from the north end and then had to abandon the southern end, from where they retreated to a small perimeter on high ground to the south. Later that night and during the early hours of the 15th, help began to arrive in the form of a company of the Durham Light Infantry and several tanks spearheading the 4th Armoured Brigade.

The Germans had forced the paratroops to withdraw from the bridge but were unable to damage it due to the gunfire being put down on them. The Durhams put in an attack at first light but were unsuccessful due to the mines and vehicles blocking their way, and for the rest of the day both sides were content to mortar and snipe at one another without putting in any further attacks.

*

From then onwards we did not see any more of our troops, and there were now only three of us with Captain Cox. Moving away from the bridge, we went along the river bank for about a mile to see if we could get across and back to our troops on the other side. However, we were unable to cross as the river was too wide and the opposite bank was now thick with Germans who were crossing in boats.

We were trapped, and the only option to extricate ourselves was to climb away from the river and up into the hills and then to try to work our way around the German troop concentration. We climbed a hill and threaded our way down the other side into a valley where we came across a wide, dry irrigation ditch about the size of a canal. After following this for a while we saw a large, stone farmhouse on a rise in the middle distance, and as it was a large building we decided to give it a wide berth, reasoning that it was probably occupied by Germans or Italians.

Continuing along the ditch, we came to a vast orange grove. The trees were about 8ft high and covered in unripe fruit and stretched for as far as the eye could see. Beneath the trees the grass was dry and standing about 2ft high so we crawled in to get our bearings. It was then that we heard the dogs. Looking through the grass, we could see a party of Germans with three Doberman-type dogs on long leads walking along the top of the ditch from the direction that we had just come. The dogs were straining on their leads and baying and we presumed that they must be following us. Ropey uttered a 'bloody hell' in a forced whisper and momentarily pausing said, 'Hicks, if they see us, you get the dogs, we'll handle the lads … just get the bloody dogs, we don't want them in among us'. I'd been given the job because I had my Bren gun sited on them and the Bren is a much heavier and effective weapon than a Sten.

We lay still watching as they came closer, and the dogs continued to bark but they stayed on top of the bank. Fortunately, they carried on straight past. The dogs appeared to have been attracted by something other than us, and straining they eventually made their way up to the farmhouse.

It was July and stinking hot, and we were getting short of water, mine having previously disappeared down my leg from the crack in my bottle. In addition, we hadn't slept for a couple of days and had eaten only hard rations. In the distance we could hear the firing and assumed that something was still going on, but we didn't want to move on in daylight as the dogs and Germans were still at the farmhouse and would surely spot us. We were still not certain if they were hunting for us specifically or paratroops in general.

Then a head came up out of the grass about 30ft away, a bald head, and we reasoned it could not be one of us because none of us had seen a para with a bald head before. We did not want to shoot and reveal our position so Ropey Cox said, 'Hicks, crawl over and see who he is.' 'Bloody hell,' I thought, 'flavour of the month I am.' I crawled tentatively towards him through the long grass. When I was about 15ft away I could see that he was a para, 'Are you all right?' I whispered in a low voice. 'No, I'm lost,' he whispered back, 'I've been here all day, you can't bloody move for dogs and the troops going by.' 'Come across and join us', I beckoned. So we crawled back and he explained to Ropey how he had become separated when jumping and was now trying to make his way back to where the firing was coming from.*

There were now five of us, hungry, thirsty and tired. We were carrying Benzedrine tablets in our smock pockets for times such as these so we took several each. The energy surge was quick and we felt we were able to climb mountains within half an hour of taking them. Revitalised, we waited until dusk and crept out of the orange grove in the direction of the ridge. Sometime after we were on a hillside and saw two peasants with shot guns looking up at us, and armed as we were, they still had the cheek to have a go at us with buck shot but we decided not to shoot and continued on our way. Later, we came across a hut in a cultivated area with a plentiful supply of pomegranate trees, watermelons and tomatoes so we had a good feed in the garden. We were in those hills all night trying to find our way out.

---

* Parachute troops were told in training that when on an operation they were to avoid unnecessary contact with the enemy wherever possible, and that their task was always to seize the objective and to hold it until relieved. Any diversion to the main task was considered to be a waste of resources and prejudicial to the operation.

The Bridge is Retaken

Also withdrawing were the sappers of B Troop who had successfully parachuted in on the designated DZ from the Dakota aircraft 'Miss Carriage'. After removing the explosives, they withdrew from the bridge on the 14th. Unable to withdraw with the 1st Battalion, they also began walking a circuitous route over the hills, eventually making contact with British forces several days later on the 17th.

In the interim the bridge had been retaken. Before dawn on the 16th, a second attack was mounted by a combination of the Durham Light Infantry and the remnants of the 1st Airborne Division and was successful, the bridge was retaken. The route onto the Catania Plain was opened up for the advance of the 8th Army.

*

When dawn broke we came across an old stone cottage with a few outbuildings which appeared to be deserted. We approached the building and went in kicking the door open like you see in the films. Nobody was inside. It had an unusual interior with a fully made up big brass bed with decorative knobs on it in one corner, and in another a well with a donkey looking on from inside a fenced area. Making ourselves at home, we had a drink from the well, shaved and changed from our long jumping denims into the shorts that we carried in our small packs.

Having slaked my thirst, I attempted to fashion a replacement water bottle from my lifebelt. We had been issued with a 'totally useless' deflated rubber ring before take-off, which was carried around our necks and under our arms to assist in buoyancy should our aircraft come down in the sea. It was useless really, but we were carrying so much kit that we would have sunk anyway. Improvising, I opened up the tube and filled it with water thinking that I had found a clever replacement for my water bottle. Ingenious were it not for the fact that the lifebelt had an inner coating of talcum powder producing a milky white unpalatable fluid – I would have to remain thirsty.

We made our way down into the next valley and saw a couple of armoured cars travelling towards us along a road and as they got closer we identified them as our own. Approaching slowly, they recognised us and stopped. They were Durham Light Infantry from the Armoured Brigade that had come up from the coastal landing, and after introductions they informed us, 'We have been picking up your lads from all over the place ... scattered like confetti you are ... all over the hills'. We began to realise at this point that something had gone badly awry. We climbed aboard the hot metal body of the car and had a dusty trip down to the port in Syracuse, where upon arrival we climbed down and lay under some trees. Dusty, dirty and tired, we slept. When we awoke we found that someone had kindly thrown blankets over us. We were told that we had been asleep for about 18 hours amidst all the noise, activity and bustle of the port.

After the Operation

The 1st Parachute Brigade lost twenty-seven killed and seventy-eight wounded at Primosole with many more missing who were presumed to have been lost at sea or in the remote hills.* For the 1st Parachute Brigade the invasion of Sicily was a disappointing operation. Out of the 1,800 men that took off from Tunisia less than one-third reached the bridge, more than one-third were taken back without jumping and many were dropped up to 30 miles away from their designated DZs.

Following the airborne operation, the 1st Parachute Brigade was withdrawn from Sicily. US and British forces advanced and pressed the Germans back to the area around Messina. Although they were successful in defeating the Germans, they were unable to prevent them from withdrawing most of their troops and equipment across to mainland Italy.

*

For days afterwards our lads came into Syracuse – we had been well and truly scattered. Due to the shelling and navigational deficiencies, the Americans had dropped us all over the place. From our point of view, the operation had not gone well, although the bridge had been taken, been lost and retaken. Our perception as a brigade was that too few of us had been dropped by the bridge and we were disappointed that we had not been more actively engaged. The enemy's demolition charges had been successfully removed but we hadn't been there in sufficient numbers to hold the bridge from the outset. The Germans had been able to bring in armour against our light weapons and our glider-borne troops had taken too long to arrive. At this time as we tried to piece together the events of the past few days, we were unaware of the disastrous events that had befallen our glider force.

Our depleted brigade (three parachute battalions, sappers and field ambulance) was gathered around the harbour in Syracuse. Eventually, we were loaded onto several tank landing craft where we were to spend the night before returning to Tunisia. Having bedded down in the cavernous hold, the harbour came under air attack during the night and the ships around us began making smoke to obscure the ships in the harbour, but unfortunately for us, it was sucked in through the air vents which were open to the warm July night. We were nearly gassed by the oily, black smoke before they managed to get the vents closed. Retching and with stinging eyes, we could barely see a yard in front of our faces. The raid passed and we gratefully climbed up onto the deck for fresh air, and on the deck we decided to stay!

---

* Figures taken from Hilary St George Saunders, *The Red Beret* (1950), p. 137.

The next morning the sky was clear and the sea was a Mediterranean blue. The water in the harbour between the shipping was dead calm and the landing-craft ramp was lowered from which we were able to swim. Later that day, we got under way and out to sea. Not long after this we started passing through the wreckage of gliders and the bodies of the troops that had ditched into the sea three days before.* Sections of Horsa gliders were recognisable together with what seemed like hundreds of bloated white bodies floating in shorts. Standing quietly, we watched as the craft we were on ploughed straight through them on a flat, calm sea. We were not allowed to stop.

---

* On 9 July 1944 troop-carrying gliders transporting the 1st Air Landing Brigade were towed off from airstrips close to Kairouan with 1,727 men aboard. Only 56 of the 144 gliders reached Sicily, 73 coming down into the sea off the coast after being released too early into a head wind. Encumbered by full battle gear consisting of webbing, ammunition, heavy boots and as far as 5 miles from the coast, 326 men were drowned. These were the bodies of the men that Tom's tank landing craft sailed through.

Chapter 30

Returning to M'Saken, Tunisia

On our return to Tunisia we were taken back to the tented encampment that we had left at M'Saken. Travelling from the docks in open trucks we once again passed through the tented lines of the 2nd Parachute Brigade and put on a bit of a show, yelling and cheering as we hung over the sides of the truck waving Nazi flags and armbands. We knew only too well that this would wind them up as they were disappointed that their Augusta operation had been cancelled.

Further to this and much to our chagrin, in our absence the 2nd had designed a flag sporting a 'red devil' which they had duly run up their flagpole. The same night members of our 1st Battalion crept into their area and pinched it because the 'red devil' (Die Roten Teufel) soubriquet was earned by the 1st Brigade and no way were they going to share the German-bestowed compliment with the 2nd Brigade.

On our return hundreds of us were still missing and every day lads were returning in twos and threes and small groups, most relating a similar tale of being scattered over hills and mountains followed by very long treks. As we were reunited, spirits were raised by the renewed comradeship and banter as our experiences were shared.

In Tunisia our wounded were being treated in British, US and New Zealand field hospitals, and those of us who were lucky enough to get into the latter two did not want to come out as the conditions were so comfortable. This was borne out when I visited my C Troop mate Len (Hook) in a Kiwi hospital and corroborated later by Lucky (Luckhurst) who was in an American; both had picked up wounds in Sicily. Len was languishing on a balcony with his feet up on the rail when I walked onto his ward. Clothed in a dark-blue dressing gown, sunglasses and waving a cigar, he didn't quite create the image of the wounded soldier I was expecting. When I sympathetically enquired, 'Are you all right, Len?', he whispered, 'Shhhhh, it's great', and he then regaled me with the paradise he had found himself in. 'Clean sheets, nurses in white stockings, [a] plaster dance with music, orange juice and some form of booze.' At the dance apparently the ambulant 'wounded' shuffled around to music with the nurses 'holding them up'! The lads were in no hurry to be discharged, so Major Murray had to go around the wards in the various hospitals badgering the medical staff to chase them all out.

From M'Saken we were taken down to the coast to Hammamet where we spent a week by the beach in open-sided tents. Here we were told to do nothing, just rest, swim and when the bugle sounded for meals to eat. No duties or training, just rest. It was extremely peaceful down there, the sun shone and the breeze filtered under the canvas during the long afternoons. Every day we swam out in the blue waters to the superstructure of a partly submerged ship, and in the evenings we strolled and were able to idle around the local cafes.

During our rest periods in Tunisia the Salvation Army opened snack bars wherever they were able to provide us with small comforts such as tea, snacks and cigarettes. Mostly free, their efforts were greatly appreciated by the troops. So we rested until our week had elapsed before moving back into camp at M'Saken where we began training again.

In between training we had periods that were quite loosely supervised, mostly as a result of the reorganisation following our return from Sicily when troops were coming and going. This period provided the opportunity for one or two of us to wander off on unauthorised absences. Chin Massey (C Troop) befriended some aircrew in a bar and hitched a lift to Malta over a weekend to visit his father, while Johnny Seers (HQ Company) claimed to have gone one better by hitching a flight with some US aircrew to London, bringing back newspapers to prove it. Both absences went undetected. Lucky and I were not so adventurous but chanced our arm by travelling to Tunis without a pass. Stopped by the red caps, our subsequent punishment was to be confined to camp with the additional field punishment of digging a 5ft-deep trench out in the sun – how we regretted our little trip out to Tunis.

Back on camp we said goodbye to Corporal Curly Clayton who had been with us from the beginning; Curly had applied for a commission. Papers had arrived calling him forward to attend an officers' selection panel and so he was leaving for Britain. Curly never came back to us.

We stayed at M'Saken until September when we were informed that we had another 'job', this time it was to be Tarranto in Italy. We were briefed that the operation was to be a sea landing and we were once again to be used in an infantry role. The brigade was still under strength after Sicily and the required number of replacements had not come through. I was again suffering from an abscess, this time in the area of my stomach and it was becoming extremely painful. Trying to make light of it, I had taken to bandaging an upturned cup above it to prevent it from being chaffed by my uniform and webbing, but to no avail. I was beginning to feel really unwell as our move across to Italy approached.

Chapter 31

Malaria in Tarranto, Italy, September 1943

We started packing up in anticipation of moving when in addition to the abscess on my stomach, I started experiencing the first symptoms of what I later found out to be malaria. I was feeling quite ill. When the squadron began moving out for the port on 9 September I was determined to go and believed that my illness would pass. The lads encouraged me saying, 'Come on, Tommy, we'll help you along' and they helped me to pack and load up. I made it to the port of Bizerta after a journey of several hours where we boarded a ship.

I was getting worse as we set sail in the early hours of the morning for Tarranto. We arrived later that afternoon and after having spent many hours on deck, I knew I couldn't continue. I had now been ill for three days and was all in. After disembarking I was re-embarked and taken back to Tunisia where I was transported to a tented hospital near Sousse where I found myself in the company of quite a few others.* I was exhausted after the long return journey by ship and by truck. Malaria was rife at the time and I was hospitalised for four or five weeks.

*

The Situation in Tarranto

The 1st Parachute Brigade had no opposition on its arrival in Tarranto and was kept in reserve behind the 2nd and 4th Parachute Brigades, which had landed several days before them. Following the operation in Sicily, the squadron and the three battalions were kept mainly on perimeter duties with some patrolling in the mountains. The 1st Parachute Brigade was withdrawn back to Tunisia two months later in November.

*

When the brigade returned one of the main topics of conversation was the misfortune that befell the 6th Battalion (2nd Parachute Brigade) on HMS *Abdiel*. The minelayer had been carrying them into Tarranto harbour two days

---

* This was most probably the 71st General Hospital outside Sousse.

before we arrived back in September. The *Abdiel* had struck a mine and her magazine holding her own mines went up and she broke in half, and as a result a great many men were killed and over a hundred wounded. Bodies were still floating in the harbour uncollected after several days and had become grossly swollen. The troops were so sickened that some began firing rounds into them to make them sink until stopped by the padre. Men from our 1st Battalion had the sad task of assisting in the retrieval of the bodies.

By November 1943 we had been in North Africa for twelve months and it was welcome news when we were informed that we were to return home. The brigade was still under strength as we packed up in preparation to leave, with many of our lads still recovering in the various field hospitals.

After travelling to Algiers, we boarded a large troopship that was painted in a drab grey camouflage, which turned out to be the requisitioned P & O liner SS *Samaria*. We were bound for Liverpool in a fast convoy. There were thousands of troops milling around both on deck and in the port and it took two days to get us all packed in. In addition to our brigade, there were large numbers of the 8th Army who were returning home to prepare for the invasion of Europe.

The voyage took the best part of a week and is memorable only for the overcrowding and the anticipation of seeing Britain again. Below decks we were surprised to see that the sleeping arrangements were rows of tightly packed hammocks. These were slung so close together that they had to be synchronised to the roll of the ship to prevent them colliding. It was a strange sight to see all the hammocks swinging as one. Many men chose to sleep on the decks despite the cold nights in order to escape the cramped conditions below. During the day there were queues for everything. The NAAFI queue started early in the morning and lasted until late afternoon. Otherwise, the voyage was uneventful except for the escorts depth charging an area of distant sea on one occasion.

Chapter 32

Back Home Again – Donington, Lincolnshire, December 1943

The *Samaria* entered the Mersey after six days at sea, arriving in Liverpool during the early morning. The weather was fine and no one was expecting us. The river was full of shipping, both merchant vessels and convoy escorts. As we edged into the roadstead, the whole mass of troops crammed to the port-side rails to gaze at the Liverpool skyline, and the ship developed a terrible list to port but nobody seemed to bother in the general excitement of being home.

For reasons of security we had been ordered to cover our uniform badges and put away our distinctive red berets in an attempt to disguise our arrival. However, we needed little disguising as our uniforms were in rags, and having been lived in for months with only rudimentary attention they were soiled and creased. Our only distinguishing feature was our faded parachute smocks.

After disembarking, we were marched in a long, ragged column through the streets to Liverpool Central station for transportation to our new camps in Lincolnshire. The normal bustle of the city was disrupted as surprised shoppers and office staff came to the kerbside to clap. One of these spectators was the wife of one of our sergeants, a Liverpool lad. She was by chance out shopping that morning and on spotting him, joyfully grabbed him and marched alongside with her arms locked around his waist.

On reaching Grantham our squadron left the battalions to be billeted at Donington, a small Lincolnshire village situated between Spalding and Boston. Donington was to be our new 'home' and we were dispersed in various buildings in and around the village. Shortly after arrival, we were issued with replacement uniforms before going on leave for Christmas.

The replacement of our uniforms was welcome, but the replacement of our airborne smocks was a personal loss. Although badly faded and repaired, those of us who could hang onto them did so, nobody wanted to hand them in for a new replacement. The smocks had become a symbol of our esteem as fighting troops and having shared our experiences had also become 'good luck' comforts. Many a stain and a tear held a story. In addition to this attachment, most of us had customised the rear inside hem into a large pocket that was used to carry personal items such as socks or a towel. Little did we know that our new smocks would soon become well seasoned.

On returning to Donington in January 1944 the squadron had settled into an old school house and a collection of Nissen huts. The school house became the sergeants' mess and the Red Cow public house became the officers' mess. Our headquarters were in a house named Komani which had South African connections, and I clearly recall the inner door as it depicted a coloured African landscape in leaded glass.

Our Nissen huts were situated adjacent to the HQ but the cookhouse was across the village and when we were hungry it seemed miles away. We used to take a shortcut over the fields collecting mushrooms on our way which were duly fried up on our arrival.

The squadron's three troops each had a pub of their choice, C Troop frequented the Peacock, B Troop the Bottle and Glass and A Troop the Providence and we all used the Red Cow Tap, an annexe behind the officers' mess. Within our pub the Peacock the landlady created a homely atmosphere by allowing us to use her lounge for reading and letter writing. In addition, there was a piano that we used for many a lively sing–song, especially on the nights of our inter-pub darts matches.

The close proximity of the seven pubs in the village saw the introduction of new rules: we were not allowed inside until after 1700hr. Some of the lads that were married brought their wives down for long weekends, which worked quite well for them but our squadron commander's wife also used to come down for longer periods. Unfortunately for us, she used to sit in the upstairs window of the Red Cow that faced our pub the Peacock. If she saw anyone sneaking in before 1700 hr, she would 'blow the whistle' by phoning the old man. So when she was in residence a pint before 5 had to be downed quickly and a timely exit made through the back rooms because we knew that a couple of sergeants would shortly arrive followed by additional fatigues or worse. So fleet were our lads that it must have been quite a frustration for old Doug when his good lady asked if the 'drinkers' had been apprehended.

As replacements came in from the airborne training depot and the wounded returned from Tunisia, the squadron was coming back up to strength. Building up to around 150 men, the 3 troops of the 1st Parachute Squadron were once again a becoming replete. Among the replacements was a Cornishman, Lieutenant Tim Hall, and as we were both Catholics I was asked if I would like to be his batman. 'Not likely' was my unspoken response as I much preferred soldiering with my mates, but politely declining it was left as, 'OK, just keep an eye on him then'. There were only four Catholics in our squadron and instead of attending the main church parade ours was a little less formal, and we went off for a drive to our church in Spalding in a jeep with our new Lieutenant Tim. Maybe I was too close to him as he was later to select me to accompany him on the Driel ferry reconnaissance at Arnhem.

The 1st Parachute Brigade was to stay in Lincolnshire for nine months and the squadron remained at our base in Donington. The 3rd Battalion was based near Spalding and the 1st Battalion went to Grimthorpe Castle, while the 2nd Battalion was in and around Stoke Rochford Hall. Although the brigade had been separated, we were still fairly close together geographically and the sappers of our squadron continued to support the battalions.

Soon after arriving, Major Murray called me to one side and showed me a letter he had received from army administration. The letter stated that the railways were desperate for trained locomotive men and I was given the option of leaving the squadron to return to my job at home on the railways. This offer had been made once before at Longmoor. I didn't need time to think about it as my answer was immediate, I wanted to stay with my mates. The squadron and C Troop had become part of my family and I couldn't and didn't want to leave. 'We had better lose this then,' he said and refolded the letter and placed it in his pocket, and that was the last that I heard of it.

Shortly afterwards there was a request for ten men to attend a course at Longmoor to learn the best ways of disabling steam locomotives. I quite fancied this as I had visited Swindon railway works on a similar exercise when I had first joined the squadron, so both Lucky and I applied. Lucky went but I was told, 'You're not going on this one as you know all about steam engines', so that was one that got away.

We used to travel into Spalding for our nights out and had the old soldier's problem of how to get back to camp after the pubs had shut, a distance of 10 miles. Public transport was non-existent and if we missed the last liberty truck it was a long walk home unless we could pinch a bicycle. Many a bicycle was stolen along the way between Spalding and Donington to be thrown over a hedge on arrival.

One cycle in particular never got home. Chin Massey had a girlfriend who had loaned him her cycle, and we tried to get four on it outside the pub and it collapsed. In slow motion, the spokes buckled and sank around the hub of the front wheel. Surveying the damage, Chin said in a small, low voice, 'Maggie won't half grumble'! From then on it became a buzz word when a silence descended and tensions were mounting, someone would pipe up quietly, 'Oh, Maggie won't half grumble'! Then Chin would pull out his stonemason's chisel and ask if anyone wanted an epitaph.

Training continued at Donington with regular PT and route marches of a standard 20 miles, which were usually inflicted upon us on Monday mornings. Monday mornings were specifically chosen to blow away the hangovers from any weekend excess. They were a good barometer of our fitness as many lads would have only just returned to camp several hours earlier from a weekend pass.

In addition to fitness and soldiering, our engineering skills were also put to good use. We constructed bridges over the fen dykes and were often called upon to put up Nissen huts for the three battalions. When building a Nissen, we would arrive in a truck with the prefabricated parts and have it up within hours.

There used to be double entertainment at the cinema in Spalding as the 3rd Battalion RSM, J.C. Lord, used to parade defaulters in the cinema car park in full kit. We often enjoyed gloating at the defaulters on parade more than we did the film, but we had to be careful not to catch J.C.'s eye or we would be invited to join in. J.C. Lord was a big man, and was a Grenadier Guardsman before volunteering for the paratroops and appeared to be about 6ft 4in with a large moustache. We always gave him a wide birth because just to catch his eye made us feel guilty, even when we were innocent!

The squadron had one or two local dramas, the first being when the police had a purge on the stolen bicycles that were turning up in Donington from the local area. The second was when it was suspected that one of our lads had demolished the toilets in the Dial Community Hall with a hand grenade. This village amenity was used as a venue for dances and was frequented by the squadron and girls from the village and Land Army. The Dial toilets smelled awful and their demolition should have been considered a public service. Nevertheless, a different view was taken, and although it was never proven that it was us that wrecked them, a weekly deduction was taken from our wages for their restoration.

We were by now well settled in the village and two of my pals had developed a profitable little undertaking supplying rabbit pies to the officers' mess in the Red Cow. These two lads were friends and great characters hailing from the east of the country. 'Bulham' Brooks was the son of a gamekeeper from Leigh-on-Sea and 'Ginger' Holland was from the other Royston in Hertfordshire. Bulham was a crack shot, the best in the squadron and not averse to a bit of poaching. We often saw the two of them slinking off down the lane towards the woods with Bulham's concealing a .303 rifle under his gas cape. Ginger acted as beater by scaring up the rabbits and Bulham with his marksman's eye would shoot them.

The rabbits were then taken to Donington's butcher, Mr Wyvers, who skinned and dressed them for his wife to bake into pies. The pies were then taken to the officers' mess in the Red Cow and sold through the back door to the sergeant cook. The sergeant cook, however, was constantly wheedling the price down, much to Bulham and Ginger's indignation as Mrs Wyvers' pies were of an extremely good quality, so they contrived to put him in a spot. They bought a cat collar and a bell in Spalding and inserted it into a freshly baked pie. A rumour was put around that the butcher also crimped the edges of these pies with his teeth, untrue, but such was the pattern on the pastry edge it could appear to a credible story. Strangely, Bulham and Ginger were not asked for any more pies by the sergeant cook and, on enquiry, an officers' mess steward told them he'd been posted.

Mrs Wyvers was a good cook and a kindly lady who sometimes had as many as five lads round during an evening, and several of the lads walked out with her daughters. Many of the lads from the battalions and squadron courted and were to marry local girls.

Ginger had a bullet crease in his red beret and a nick in his cap badge, where he claimed Bulham had creased him in error while out after rabbits He carried the beret around as a spare and was always telling the story of how his mate nearly killed him. This tale became the oft-told story of the 'Ginger rabbit' and when related would be greeted with hoots of derision. Ginger would then indignantly produce his damaged beret as evidence.

Bulham's poaching first came to light in the early days of the squadron at Bulford when he kept a ferret in a cage under his bed. Quick-witted and a charmer, he even earned praise from our late CO Major Dorman who strode into our billet unannounced. Catching Bulham, he rasped, 'What's that under your bed, Brooks?' 'A ferret, Sir,' replied Bulham. 'A ferret …,'repeated the Major, and as quick as you like Bulham was in with a, 'Yes, sir, we're keeping down the vermin.'* 'Good man', said the Major and strode out the other side of the hut. Anyone else and they would have been on guard duty for six weeks!

Our lanyards were getting a little worse for wear at this time so the lads used to get replacements made up for them by the girls that manned the anti-aircraft guns in London. We would supply the parachute rigging cord from which they would plait them up. One 18ft length was sufficient for one lanyard. We would then dye them to the colour of our unit.

The 2nd Battalion used to soak their lanyards in a solution of water and dissolved mepacrine tablets which they had found created a yellow dye, and they always looked smart and fresh.** So I decided to freshen up mine and duly bought some royal blue dye from Spalding market, soaking it in a bucket and stirring it with my bayonet. Unfortunately, it had the unusual effect of changing the blade of the bayonet to a golden colour. I was the only one in the Squadron with a golden bayonet and it raised many a comment on parade, but of course I did not have the faintest idea how how it happened.

In May a stick of ten from C Troop was sent to visit a US unit camped at Burbage village, just south of Hinckley. The detachment was for ten days during which time we were to pass on the techniques that we had developed during our time in North Africa. The US lads were a new unit and were

---

*   Bulham was sadly killed at Arnhem shortly after getting married. The nickname 'Bulham' originated from a story he told us about a sergeant in his RE field company who had a tendency to refer jovially to his sappers as 'me old Bulham'. When we heard the tale he was of course stuck with it.

** Mepacrine Hydrochloride tablets are used for treating giardia infections and protozoal infections of the gut, and also used for water purification in the field.

enthralled with our experiences and the tricks that we had learnt. At the end of our stay we joined a march through the village as part of a 'Salute the Soldier' parade. This was a government initiative intended as a morale booster for the civilian population who were encouraged to line the parade routes in appreciation of the army.

The ten of us stuck out like sore thumbs as we marched through the village behind a US company. Extremely suave in their smart uniforms together with felt hats and rubber-soled boots, they floated along without so much as a squeak. Then we came along with our hobnailed boots sparking the gravel and making one hell of a clatter, which together with our helmets and airborne smocks caused quite a stir. The Americans had never seen our distinctive camouflage smocks before and the locals had never heard of us, so we were sure that they thought that we were Germans. We were an unusual sight and caused quite a bit of interest.

Returning to Donington, we were still waiting for our next operation. We worked hard during the day and continued to amuse ourselves during the evenings. Bulham and Ginger were now a pair of likely lads and were always out on 'business', and they were rarely short of money so we decided to wind them up. Having recently returned from our liaison with the Americans, we decided upon a plausible ploy. Our squadron clerk was a corporal and as one of the lads was not averse to a little sport; he would often provide us with unauthorised passes complete with the CO's signature and a unit stamp. Enlisting his help, we typed up an 'official' notice stating that Sappers Brooks and Holland were to be seconded to America as part of a team to demonstrate British parachute-engineer techniques. The document was stamped and signed and posted on the billet noticeboard in the late afternoon. They fell for it, and all that evening they were strutting around preening and glowing at their good fortune, convinced that they had been selected due their showing during the recent Hinckley liaison visit. But by next morning the notice had gone and Bulham and Ginger new they'd been had!

The brigade was held back in Lincolnshire, and we suspected something was going to happen but did not know what. We used to listen to German radio propaganda broadcasts during the evenings which we treated with great fun and derision. The announcer once told us that they knew where the 1st Airborne was, and they then played a song with the lyrics of 'we are waiting for you over here' which then became a sing-song as we all joined in. On a more serious note, the German radio tried to sow seeds of discontent by stating that the Americans were taking our wives and girlfriends while we were away. Although we laughed, there were some anxieties.

During our training in Lincolnshire we were introduced to the concept of parachuting with our weapons and lighter equipment attached to our bodies. Previously, our weapons had been dropped inside the containers, which on occasion caused some anxious moments when they could not be quickly located. An example of this was the machine-gun company that we met in Sicily that were wandering around in the dark without their machine guns. It had therefore been decided that we would practise jumping with our weapons while still using the containers for the heavier equipment. To facilitate this we were to start jumping with our weapons in a bag that we held in our arms.*

The bag, or the weapons valise as it officially became known, was basically a kit bag on a 20ft length of rope. The valise was attached to the body by two webbing straps that were fastened around the neck and lower right leg, both of which were released by pulling a cord at the front. In practice, we were to jump with these bags loaded with light weapons, ammunition and other equipment. Once out and with the parachute deployed, we could release the valise and lower the rope to ensure that it hit the ground before we did.

We discussed the practicalities and possible modifications to the valise with our officers Ropey Cox and Tim Hall. Many of the lads adjusted the webbing and modified the valise to suit whatever they would be carrying. I chose not to have the webbing strap around my neck feeling much more comfortable with a shortened version attached to my chest straps. The word valise was quickly lost from our vocabulary as we had taken to calling it the Bren sleeve.

As the summer of 1944 progressed, we were now carrying out more training drops (three in total) in both brigade and larger numbers as part of the newly formed 1st Airborne Division.** During these drops we practised the new method of jumping with the weapons valise and lowering it down before we hit the ground, and apart from a few mishaps this worked well. Weights were increased and some lads were loaded up to as much as 100kg (220lb).

To keep us in trim we were taken with the 3rd Battalion on a live-firing exercise to the moors beyond Holmfirth, and travelling by truck we passed close to the villages around Barnsley. Lucky, an East End Londoner, was amazed to see colliers returning home from the pits with black faces. 'Who are these blokes?' he enquired as he looked out from the back of our truck in wonderment, 'Why are they all black?' he asked. When I told him he said, 'You're joking … why don't they have a wash?' When I explained that most of them washed in a tin bath at home in front of the parlour fire, and that many

---

*   Elements of the Parachute Brigade first started jumping with their weapons in kitbags during the Mascara exercises in Algeria. The method was again used during the Primosole operation when elements of the 2nd Battalion (John Frost) found it to be a big advantage. Hilary St George Saunders, in his book *The Red Beret* (1950), also stated that this method was used by parts of the 3rd Battalion when jumping in Sicily. These instances were small-scale trials organised by individual commanders and had not been formally adopted by the brigade.

** The 1st Airborne Division comprised the 1st and 4th Parachute Brigades, the glider-borne troops of 1st Air Landing Brigade and with the addition of the Independent Companies totalled a fighting force of over 10,000 men.

were so tired that their wives washed down most of them, he was astounded. Lucky was equally surprised by the half-ton loads of coal that had been tipped outside the houses in the streets, because in London coal was delivered in sacks and he couldn't see the point of tipping it in the street. Before joining up many of the lads had never travelled before and every movement around the country was a new experience that provided an insight into a different way of life.

At Holmfirth we were billeted in an old mill that was memorable for its rotten floorboards and leaking roof. On the moors it rained. We lived in the mill for a week and used live ammunition in an exercise with a unit of commandos that stood in for our enemy. On the last day of play a sheep was accidentally shot in no-man's-land and it was watched covetously by both sides. At the 'final whistle', several of the commandos started to move towards it but A Troop's Joe Simpson was up in a flash and started sprinting for the carcass. Before they had realised what was afoot, Joe was in first and had hoisted it across his shoulders before jogging back to our lines. Joe was as hard as nails and was one of those lads who preferred not to wear socks in his boots. That evening the sheep began its journey back to the mess at Donington in one of the A Troop trucks. As we returned, we came down through Barnsley and our troop commander Doug Murray allowed me to drop off and spend a night at home. I returned back to camp the following day using my railwayman's pass.*

Following the invasion of Europe in June, we were briefed for a series of operations that were mostly in France. There were about seven of these in total, but all were cancelled.** This happened for a variety of reasons, sometimes the army fighting in France had advanced so fast that it negated the need for us to go in, and on other occasions the Germans had occupied our landing fields before we were due to take off. Time and again we had packed our equipment and were ready to go only to be cancelled at short notice, following which we had to unpack and in some instances retrieve our containers from the airfield. We were getting really fed up, especially since the 6th Airborne which had not been in action until the invasion of Europe had dropped into France on D-Day. We were impatient to be off again.

With the cancellations we had packed and unpacked so many times that the billet had become a shambles. Our NCOs and officers largely turned a blind eye to the turmoil as we were now once again at a high pitch of readiness. High spirits were still to the fore and during this period we were plagued by A Troop, which had taken to raiding our billet as they returned from the

---

*   This was the concessionary rail pass held by serving ex-railwaymen in war time.
** Records state that over a dozen operations were proposed for the 1st Parachute Brigade and then cancelled during the latter part of 1944. Some of these were called off in the early stages of planning and others when the troops were virtually in the aircraft.

pub. Intermittent at first, these sorties began to take the form of a nightly raid whereby a handful would charge in and overturn as many beds and their occupants before dashing out again. After one such raid we determined to respond. The following evening we wired up our metal door handle to the ceiling light. Sure enough, later that night we heard the scuffle of boots followed by an almighty yell, and a great cheer from us, which seemed to take the edge off their forays.

There were also one or two scuffles within the troop and I recall Mac McBurnie and Jeb Taylor fighting over a game of cards like a scene from the Wild West. Punching and scrapping over beds, down the corridors and from room to room, it seemed to go on for an hour until Smudger Smith came in and said, 'All right, lads, you've had your fun.' Bloodied and battered, they shook hands and went off for a wash! Soon all our energies were focused on pulling together.

We had one more inexplicable experience several weeks before we flew out when our fighting knives were taken off us. We were never given a specific reason why they were withdrawn other than a vague suggestion that it was at the request of a Red Cross or Geneva Convention. Whatever the reason, it was not very well received for many of us had become quite attached to them. The knives had been carried through North Africa, Sicily and on many exercises, but as always we did as we were told and prepared to hand them in at the quartermaster's store.

When I reported to the quartermaster to hand in my knife, the store's sergeant already had a pile of knives on his counter. As I stated my name and placed my knife down, he turned to answer a question from someone behind in the store. I quickly picked up my knife and flicked it through the adjacent open window. Turning back to me he said, 'Hicks wasn't it?' and signed in his book. I then scampered out and retrieved my knife from the grass outside. I took my knife home with me on my final pass. We were instructed to use our folding jackknives in the event that our rigging lines needed to be cut.

*

The next and last wartime operation that the 1st Airborne Division was waiting for was Operation Market Garden, which was to be put together within a week using the plans of the abandoned Operation Comet.

*

Chapter 33

Arnhem, Holland, 17 September 1944

In early September we were informed that our next operation was going to be in Holland. We were going to a town named Arnhem with the objective of capturing and holding the road bridge over the Rhine. Our first briefings outlined a plan whereby we would drop in brigade strength onto the polder at the southern end of the bridge, which was on the opposite side of the river to the town. Immediately preceding our drop it was proposed that two gliders would touch down on the ramp approaching the bridge.* The gliders would then career along with their momentum carrying them into the entrance where their wings would be knocked off. The glider-borne troops would then leave the aircraft and deploy to secure both ends. We would then drop in to reinforce its defence.

We were optimistic that this time we would be off, briefings were given and an atmosphere of anticipation was building, then a couple of days later the operation (Comet) was once again cancelled.

*

Operations Comet and Market Garden

Operation Comet intended to use only the 1st Airborne Division and the 1st Polish Independent Parachute Brigade to capture and hold all three bridges over the Waal, Maas and Rhine. It was cancelled on 10 September 1944 due to a changing situation on the ground and the serious concerns of the various commanders that the force would not be sufficiently strong enough.

Within a week the plan was back on as Operation Market Garden which would use three divisions, one British and two US, to take and hold the three bridges, which were 60 miles behind enemy lines. The planning was mostly in place from the cancelled Operation Comet. The British 1st Airborne Division would now drop at Arnhem on 17 September 1944.

Market was the airborne element of the operation and consisted of the British and two US divisions, Garden was the relieving ground forces of the British XXX Corps. The drop by the British 1st Airborne Division to capture and hold the bridges over the Rhine at Arnhem was a bid to end the war by the Christmas of

---

* A similar assault to the successful attack made by the glider-borne Oxford and Bucks on the bridge over the Caen Canal on D-Day (Pegasus Bridge).

1944. The plan was to take the three bridges and hold them for 48 hours, which was considered the amount of time that the advancing XXX Corps required to advance and relieve the airborne forces. The road bridge, the last major obstacle before entering Germany from Holland, was the primary objective; the other two were the railway bridge and a floating pontoon bridge. However, before XXX Corps could set off along the road to Arnhem there were several canal and two river bridges that had to be taken and held by the US 82nd and 101st Airborne Divisions. The British 1st Airborne Division consisted of over 10,000 men made up of paratroops, glider-borne infantry and specialist support troops.*

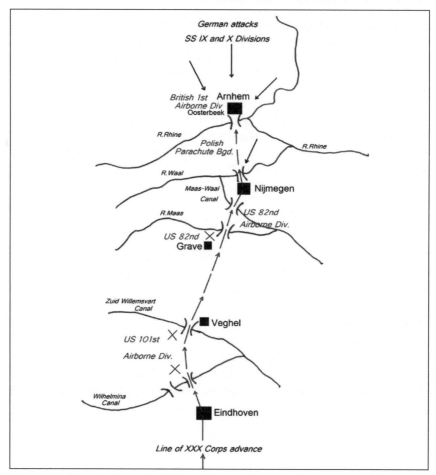

Bridge objectives for Operation Market Garden, 17 September 1944. The red crosses indicate the Dropping and Landing Zones of the US and British forces. The arrowed line shows the route that XXX Corps were to follow on their ill-fated advance to relieve the British 1st Airborne Division at Arnhem.

---

* The number of the airborne troops that were landed north of the Rhine varies in accounts, some stating that there were over 10,000 men, others that there were little fewer than 10,500. The lower figure has been used here.

Within a week we were briefed one more, and again it was Arnhem. This time the plan was for us to go in as a division in preference to the smaller strength of a brigade. The operation was definitely on and with less than a week to go our briefings began to give us a breakdown of the tasks that the squadron was required to carry out.

*

The Role of the 1st Parachute Squadron RE

The primary task of the 1st Parachute Squadron RE was to move in with the assault companies under the command of the 1st Parachute Brigade, to remove the explosives from the main road bridge, the rail bridge and to secure the pontoon bridge if possible and to assist in the defence of the bridges as necessary.

On the second day two of the three troops were to rendezvous at the power station where they would revert back to the command of the CRE;* the third troop was to remain under the command of the 1st Parachute Brigade. In addition to this, there were numerous allotted tasks associated with the DZs and LZs. However, within hours of the landing the unfolding events were to change most of the plans.

*

We were to drop onto the flat heathland some 8 miles distant from the bridge, and in order to reach it we would have to pass through built-up areas held by the enemy. We were lightly armed and it was stressed that both speed and surprise were essential. Once on the bridge we were to hold it and its strategic approaches for 48 hours until XXX Corps spearheaded by the tanks of the Guards Armoured Division arrived to relieve us. Originally, we were to drop onto the polder adjacent to the bridge and now the change of plan to drop us 8 miles away was discussed with some reservation among the lads.** Although many were heartened to be part of a division, many felt that this could still be a tricky operation.

---

*   Commander RE (at Arnhem), Lieutenant Colonel E.C.W. Myers.

**   The reason given for being dropped 8 miles away from the objective was due to the RAF opposing the original plan. This objection was based on aerial reconnaissance photographs that had identified German ack-ack batteries close to the bridge and on the nearby Deelen airfield. These guns were considered to be too much of a risk to the slow-flying tugs and gliders. There were also reservations about landing parachutists on the soft polder adjacent to the bridge, although the Polish Brigade was to be dropped several days later near Driel on similar terrain.

However, if there were any among us that were disconcerted, these feelings were over ridden by the desire to be off and the belief that we could do the job. As our preparations gathered pace, we were informed that the opposition would probably be light and that the enemy morale was low.* Our initial reservations were largely forgotten in the hectic activity to be ready. There were containers to check and load, weapons to prepare, parachutes to be issued and webbing adjusted. Communications, maps, more briefings and a multitude of smaller issues were ticked off as we geared up to leave for Holland.

In the final days before we left Donington our CRE Brigadier Henniker (known as Honkers) came to the squadron to bid us farewell as he was not going with us. Gathering the squadron around, he gave a short speech. He wished us good luck and then pointedly said to us, 'C Troop, put your berets on the back of your heads, loosen your collars and pull them around a bit, scruff up, that's it … that's just how I will remember you'. C Troop was the junior of the three engineer troops in the 1st Parachute Squadron and as such was the butt of many jokes, but we gave out as good as we got!

*

Logistics

The historian Martin Middlebrook (author of *Arnhem 1944, The Airborne Battle* (1995)) recorded that 143 members of the squadron flew out of RAF Barkston Heath to drop at Arnhem. There were however a further twenty-eight squadron members that travelled overland by lorry as part of the sea party and these comprised mostly young sappers together with several old hands.** The younger element had come in as replacements and had arrived too late from the airborne depot to gain the experience required for an operational drop. In addition to the replacements, the squadron sea party included drivers, admin staff, jeeps and lorries, with several of the latter carrying the miscellaneous equipment and personal kit. All the personal kit was to be lost as the sea party were never to reach Arnhem.

The squadron sea party was in fact part of the sea-tail that was the overland transport operation of approximately 1,000 vehicles carrying the equipment of the 1st Airborne Division that could not be taken by air.

*

---

*   The intelligence briefings were wrong and German morale was later reported to be high and the SS 9th and 10th Panzer units were in and around Arnhem taking in replacement troops and overhauling their tanks.

**   The number twenty-eight was provided by Sapper Jack Hobbs, a veteran of B Troop who travelled with the sea party.

Chapter 34

The Plan of Attack

Day One, 17 September 1944

The Airborne Division of over 10,000 men was to be delivered by parachute and glider onto the heathland outside Arnhem and north of the River Rhine. It was planned that the transport of troops and equipment, or the lift, was to be completed over a period of three days. The Independent Parachute Company, 1st Parachute Brigade and glider-borne 1st Air Landing Brigade, together with part of divisional headquarters, were to arrive on the first day, 17 September.

The first to drop were the Independent Parachute Company who were to mark the DZ. This was to be followed shortly afterwards by the glider-borne 1st Air Landing Brigade, the Reconnaissance Squadron of which was to make a dash for the bridge in jeeps, while the main body secured the DZ and LZs (glider landing zones).

The parachute element of the 1st Parachute Brigade started jumping at around 1400hr and within 20 minutes was on the ground. Once on the ground and with the DZ secured, the brigade's 2nd Battalion was to take a lower route through Arnhem towards the road bridge. En route a company was to be detached to take the railway bridge. On arrival at the road bridge the 2nd were to relieve the Reconnaissance Squadron and take up defensive positions at both the north and south ends. The 3rd Battalion was to take the middle route along the Utrecht road by way of Oosterbeek. On arrival in Arnhem they were to take up defensive positions to the north-east of the bridge. The 1st Battalion had been allotted the task of taking the high ground to the north of Arnhem to defend against German counter attacks. They were not to move off the high ground until both the 2nd and 3rd Battalions were near to their objective, the bridge.

Day Two, 18 September 1944

The 4th Parachute Brigade, together with elements of the glider-borne South Staffordshires and the division's remaining guns and vehicles, were to arrive to form a larger defensive perimeter around Arnhem.

Day Three, 19 September 1944

The 1st Polish Parachute Brigade of 1,500 men were to drop south of the bridge to act as a reserve and to reinforce the divisional defensive positions. They were to cross the river into Arnhem as the situation required.

In summary, the bridge was to be taken and held for 48 hours, and once taken the outer areas surrounding the bridge (the bridgehead) were to be held to prevent German counter attacks retaking it. The Airborne Division would then be relieved by XXX Corps (main British army) approaching along the road from Nijmegen.

Chapter 35

RAF Barkston Heath, Lincolnshire, 17 September 1944

We left Donington by truck for the short journey to RAF Barkston Heath on the morning of Sunday 17 September 1944. It was a lovely, clear day on what was to be my third operation. Arriving early, we gathered in small groups and after all the activity were able to laze on the grass – we even had time for a cup of tea before kitting up in preparation for our aircraft number being called. We were at ease and ready to be off.

We were heavily weighed down and festooned with all manner of kit. Attached to our webbing were both Mills and phosphorous grenades together with pouches of ammunition. We had rations for 48 hours, a water bottle, a dixie, an entrenching tool and a rain cape. We then had our weapons, which in my case was a sleeved Bren gun with its 20ft length of cord.

On our chests we carried an anti-gas respirator, although I had cheated a little on this one. My respirator was back in the billet but its case was still fixed to my chest having been stuffed with hard-tack biscuits and corned beef, I had decided that I was far more likely to be hungry than gassed. Finally, we had a weighty parachute and harness.

*

Troop Strengths

Alongside 1st Parachute Squadron RE flying from RAF Barkston Heath were the 1st Battalion of the Parachute Regiment (548 men) and 16 Parachute Field Ambulance (135 men). The 2nd Battalion of the Parachute Regiment (525 men) and 3rd Battalion of the Parachute Regiment (588 men) flew from RAF Saltby. Brigade HQ and its Defence Platoon (82 men) flew out of Barkston Heath (paratroops) and Blakehill Farm (Horsa glider-borne troops).* Out of the 2,000 parachute troops flying out with the 1st Parachute Brigade only half of the men were left from the originals that had previously fought in Tunisia only 14 months ago.

*

---

* Figures taken from Martin Middlebrook, *Arnhem 1944, The Airborne Battle* (1995), p. 456.

Numerous other small items were stowed in our pockets which included a jackknife, toothbrush, razor and soap, local money and a yellow recognition triangle. There was also a phrase sheet in several European languages to assist us to get help in the event that we were cut adrift.

As had become our custom, the padre took us to one side and held a short Roman Catholic service in the shadow of the aircraft. With the padre's blessing, we lined up to board. This was no easy matter as we were carrying so much kit that we had to be helped up the steps of the aircraft by the US ground crew.

NOT TO BE PRODUCED IN PUBLIC

ENGLISH	DUTCH
I am (we are)	Ik ben (wij zijn)
British; American	Engelsch, Amerikaan
Where am I?	Waar ben ik?
I am hungry; thirsty	Ik heb honger; dorst
Can you hide me?	Kunt U mij verbergen?
I need civilian clothes	Ik heb burgerkleeding noodig
How much do I owe you?	Hoeveel ben ik gij schuldig?
Are the enemy nearby?	Is de vijand dichtbij?
Where is the frontier?	Waar is de grens?
BELGIAN:	BELGISCH
Where are the nearest British (American) troops:	Waar zijn de dichtst-bijzijnde Britsche (Amerikaansche) troepen?
Where can I cross this river?	Waar kan ik deze rivier over-steken?
Is this a safe way?	Is dit een veilige weg . . .?
Will you please get me a third class ticket to . . .?	Wilt U mij alstublieft een derde klas kaartje bezorgen naar . . .?
Is this the train (bus) for . . .?	Is dit de trein (bus) naar . . .?
Do I change (i.e. trains)?	Moet ik overstappen?
At what time does the train (bus) leave for . . .?	Hoe laat vertrekt de trein (bus) naar . . .?
Right; left; straight on	Rechtsch, linksch, rechtuid
Turn back; stop	Keert om; halt
Thank you; please	Dank U; Alstublieft
Yes; No	Ja; Nee
Good morning	Goedenmorgen
Good afternoon	Goeden Middag
Evening; Night	Avond; Nacht
CONSULATE	Consulaat
Out of bounds	Verboden toegang
Forbidden	Verboden

This communication leaflet contained questions and phrases in Dutch, German, Spanish and French.

Eventually, with much shuffling and bumping, we settled in, ably assisted by the crew chief who offered help as our kit snagged everything we passed. We were now ready, we were kitted and loaded. Below the aircraft our containers were secured in the racks where they had been hung the previous day.

Once airborne and looking out through the window there was a sight that has remained imprinted on my mind ever since. All around us were aircraft, Dakotas in a clear, blue sky, and there appeared to be hundreds of them rising and falling as they slowly flew in formation. Below and moving more slowly were combinations of tugs and gliders over which we seemed to be quickly passing. Above flew numerous RAF and US fighters, just dots in the sky that were zipping around like flies protecting our passage into Holland.*

Sitting down both sides of the aircraft we were a mass of khaki and olive green, sprawled be-webbed bodies and packs with not an inch between us. We were handed out cheese sandwiches and a bottle of beer, some lads ate and some were unable to eat. As the flight progressed, some read newspapers while others bantered. A few smoked quietly, reflective and alone with their thoughts, each man seemingly dealing with the future in his own way.

Passing over the Dutch coast, I could see miles of low-lying ground that had been deliberately flooded by the Germans, a measure taken to prevent any coastal invasion by infantry and armour. Here and there red-roofed houses could clearly be seen standing above the water, and there were several German ack-ack batteries lifeless and smoking from earlier attacks and a flak ship was burning on a river. We had a quiet flight over the North Sea and into Holland with no attacks or sightings of any German aircraft.

In addition to our normal kit, we were jumping for the first time with the heavy equipment bags.** Although we had tried it in training, we were now kitted up heavier than ever before and were latticed with webbing and straps. Wedged in shoulder to shoulder the Bren valise (sleeve) rested heavily at my feet waiting to be attached to my right leg and chest. Also coiled and wedged in at my waist was its 20ft length of lowering cord.

More than the usual concentration would be required during the drop. Once the parachute canopy had deployed we were only seconds in the air

---

* In the first wave of aircraft leaving Britain that Sunday morning there were 157 carrying paratroops. Of these, 73 left Barkston Heath, and this included the 9 aircraft carrying the 1st Parachute Squadron RE. Flying from other airfields were a further 358 aircraft towing the gliders that carried the troops and equipment of the 1st Air Landing Brigade. A further 2 waves were planned to follow during the course of the next 2 days. This information is taken from Major General C.B. Urquhart, DSO, *Arnhem* (1958), Appendix IV.

** The equipment bags, officially termed weapons valises, contained a variety of weaponry and ammunition and in some cases included 45lb mortar base plates. Bren guns were carried in a felt-lined sleeve, which was a modification of the valise.

before hitting the ground so the valise had to be released from its fastenings by a quick-release wire, and then lowered down fairly quickly to the full extent of its 20ft to ensure that it landed before you did. Care had to be taken when lowering the cord hand over hand, if it was lowered too fast you were liable to sustain cord burns to your hands, but lower it too slowly and you risked a heavy landing as the weight pulled you in hard.

When we jumped some of our valise harnesses failed to unclip causing many of the lads to land very hard as they were unable to jettison the extra weight, and most were to sustain injuries. Other lads, having unclipped the valise, lost the cord completely allowing it to plummet in free fall posing a risk to others below. But most of us were able to land with our weapons close at hand, which as planned proved to be a time-saving and reassuring advantage.

When we were about 20 minutes away from our DZ we stood and followed the well-practised procedure of hooking up and checking the lad in front. The hook up was a little more involved as the valise had to be attached and the parachute line checked. As we approached the DZ at around 1400hr, we began to hear flak bursts, but it was nothing much and didn't alarm us. We checked again and bunched up closer together, I placed my right hand on the shoulder of the man in front and felt the reassuring clasp of Lucky's hand on my shoulder behind – our whole stick was compressed up as one. I didn't think that my heart was the only one that was beating a little faster.

Chapter 36

Landing on Renkum Heath, DZ-X

The red light came on first (red on), followed 5 minutes later by the green and our whole stick began moving towards the door. As we shuffled forward, the Bren valise felt momentarily ungainly tied into my body by the webbing on my chest and right leg. I had no time to dwell on it. The void of the door appeared quickly as the man in front went out leaving the sharp light of day. There was a powerful rush of air and an increase in noise as I dropped my right hand to the valise, threw my static line away to the left, tucked in my elbows and kicked my right leg over the threshold. In one quick movement I was out.

Our whole stick was out in a little more than 15 seconds. The blur of the exit was quickly arrested as my parachute deployed and seconds were spent checking that my rigging lines were OK, followed quickly by the release and lowering of my valise which began swinging wildly around like a pendulum on the end of its cord. I had hardly any time to look at my rigging lines before I was rolling into the ground, and that was before any thought was given to meeting an enemy. Somewhere close by would be my mate Lucky with more magazines and our spare gun barrel.

It took as little as 20 seconds to reach the ground and an immediate awareness came over you as you took in what was happening around and above you. Men, containers and other loose debris were still rapidly descending.[*] Looking up, the canopies were still falling around me presenting a colourful sight of reds, yellows, olives and browns. There were numerous containers swinging among the men, together with radio packs and such diverse items as crated miniature motor bikes, all floating down among the hundreds of drab olive greens of our own. On the ground men were wrestling with all sizes of canopies in various stages of collapse.

I had a good landing on Renkum Heath and all seemed pretty quiet in Holland except for the crackle of canopies, our own shouts and the rustle of kit around us. The squadron formed up on our blue smoke rendezvous point (RV), and despite our heavy loads we had sustained only four injuries. We were then divided, two troops went with the 2nd Battalion, one troop with

---

[*] Men were liable to be injured during a mass parachute drop, not only through bad landings but also because the supplies and equipment broke loose from the men still in the air.

the 3rd, leaving a party of twelve of us from C Troop with Captain George as the DZ clearing party. The clearing party wasn't part of our operational brief as we were all supposed to be heading for the bridge, however, on landing it was realised that there was too much debris on the DZ and we were detailed to deal with it. The selection was made with a rapid 'you, you and you' and then we quickly moved off.

The 2nd Battalion set off for the bridge along the lower route with its usual support of our lads from B Troop and on this occasion some of the lads from C Troop (including my mate Tony Jones). The remainder moved off towards Oosterbeek with the 3rd Battalion.

The main task allotted to the sappers en route to the road bridge was for one party to detach from the 2nd Battalion to remove the explosive charges from the railway bridge. Another group was to be detached similarly to tackle the pontoon bridge. The main body was to continue with the 2nd Battalion to remove the charges from the road bridge and once it was taken to assist in its defence.

Our first job was to clear the DZ of the debris of the drop to enable the gliders to land safely the following morning on the second lift. Our orders were to stay on the DZ overnight and to catch up with the 3rd Battalion heading into Arnhem once the gliders were down. Arnhem power station had been planned to be the squadron's ultimate RV.

The DZ was covered in discarded parachutes, both empty and damaged containers, ammunition, weapons, abandoned live mortar bombs and broken radios. Much of it was smashed as many of the containers and weapon valises had broken loose during the drop, and other equipment had not been collected in the urgency to move off. There were also troops on the ground that had been injured on landing and were therefore unable to get away.

As we sorted ourselves out at the RV, a Dutch girl brought us milk from a nearby farm that was named Klein Amerika. The farmer also came out with a big black horse harnessed to a flat wagon, 'I help,' he said, and he did. Quartering the area, we threw the debris on his cart together with several injured lads using the front garden of his farmhouse as a collection point.

After we had finished clearing the DZ we went out to check the adjacent farmsteads for German troops. On entering one of the farmhouses, we were appraised by two little old ladies who were sitting inside, one of whom spoke to us in passable English and said as she wrinkled her nose, 'English ... we can tell you are English because of your smell'. We replied, 'No ... no ... the English don't smell, it's the Germans and Italians who smell' but she insisted that we smelled. There were no Germans and it seemed to be pretty quiet in this part of rural Holland so far.

As ordered, we remained on the DZ at Renkum Heath that Sunday night alongside the Border Regiment which was providing the main defence of the landing grounds, and they like us were waiting for the second wave to come in early the following morning.* It was a cold night and we used the discarded parachutes to huddle up and keep warm.

*

Situation on the Ground

Almost immediately things started to go wrong with the predetermined plan on the afternoon of the first day. Only half of the Reconnaissance Squadron's jeeps had arrived due to several gliders failing to make the LZ, and those that did arrive proved difficult to unload making them late in starting their dash for the bridge. Once they did get on their way they ran into stiff German opposition which blocked their path.

Even 5 hours after the initial landing the first British troops had still not reached the bridge and a German Reconnaissance Battalion of the 9th Waffen SS Panzer Division was able to cross it and move towards Nijmegen.

The 2nd Battalion reached the bridge by the lower route at 2000hr after leaving the DZ 4 hours earlier at 1500hr.** On arrival, they took up defensive positions in the buildings overlooking its northern end, and they were to be reinforced by small groups from other units making an approximate total of 700 men. They were gradually surrounded by superior German numbers, self-propelled guns and tanks, and unable to communicate with their Brigade HQ they fortified the buildings and prepared to defend them.

*

Still on the DZ. On Monday morning we started taking rifle and machine-gun fire from the nearby woods and then some mortars started coming in. We in turn began taking up positions to return fire, acutely aware that our slow-moving second wave gliders were shortly to arrive.

The farmer's stable block was hit and caught fire and his unfortunate black horse was killed. We were not aware of the horse's demise until later when we saw the farmer come out of the smouldering building with a huge knife in one hand and a haunch of meat in the other, which he had apparently taken from the dead animal.

Later that morning a flight of Messerschmidts came roaring in low over the DZ strafing the empty gliders that had landed the previous afternoon. We were fortunate that the second lift had been delayed or they would have been caught on the ground.

---

*   Unknown to the waiting troops the second lift was delayed and wouldn't arrive until early afternoon.

** This information is taken from Ministry of Information, *By Air to Battle* (1945), p. 102.

Monday 18 September 1944

The 3rd Battalion advanced as far as the Hartenstein Hotel in Oosterbeek on the Sunday evening, where they then spent most of the night before moving out again during the early hours of Monday morning. On reaching the outskirts of Arnhem near the St Elizabeth Hospital, the 3rd met determined enemy resistance. The several hundred men of the German Battalion Krafft blocked the streets giving time for the 9th SS Panzer Division's Kampfgruppe Spindler to bring in their tanks and self-propelled guns. With more troops arriving by the hour, the 3rd Battalion was heavily engaged and was unable to make any further progress towards the bridge.

The Germans were already aware of the objective as the battle plan for the whole of Market Garden had been retrieved from a crashed US glider of the 82nd Airborne Division. In addition, the element of surprise had passed and the enemy had now had 12 to 14 hours to get organised and they were moving fast and easily along open roads into Arnhem.

*

During the early afternoon the second wave started to come in to a fusillade of machine-gun and rifle fire from the Germans in the woods. I was set up with the Bren in the farmer's kitchen garden firing into the trees from the cover of his bean trench. The German mortars then started to rain in on us again and we took a few casualties. Geordie Hall had some toes blown off by a mortar burst and was then the subject of some gritty bantering, 'You won't be dancing in Arnhem town hall tonight then, Geordie' one of our wags was shouting across at him with more mirth than sympathy as a dressing was applied to his foot. None of us were to dance in Arnhem town hall.

Looking up at the second lift, I had never seen so many closely packed aircraft before. The sky was full of them. The gliders that had now been released had been towed in by Dakotas, Halifax and Stirling bombers which were now high above and wheeling away. The released gliders came in low over our heads. Ponderously slow with whistling sounds like a deep and prolonged gust of wind, they were so low that we could read the white chalked graffiti messages scrawled upon their fuselages: 'We are the vestal virgins', 'I'm here mum' and numerous rude instructions to Adolf. Heaven knows what the dour Germans would make of this artwork when they were later to inspect our debris.

Some of the gliders clipped the treetops as they came in and a few turned over, while several more ran off the DZ into the woodland but the majority managed to land safely. The Germans were driven back from the woodland and melted away as members of the Border Regiment came across to clear them out. The large gliders were Hamilcars carrying a 17-pounder with a jeep as a tow. The smaller Horsas were carrying the glider-borne infantry of the South Staffs.*

---

* Over 200 gliders came down onto LZ/X on the second lift, with a further 70 on LZ/S. In total, approximately 10,000 men were to arrive north of the Rhine over the first three days.

On the arrival of the second lift our orders were to leave the DZ on Renkum Heath and catch up with the 3rd Battalion, which was strung out on the road into Arnhem ahead. As we set off, smoke was drifting low across the DZ from a nearby barn that was blazing furiously. Well spaced out on either side of the road, we met no further German opposition as we moved towards Oosterbeek. However, we were greeted with celebrating and joyous Dutch civilians who were throwing orange flowers and offering us glasses of milk and apples. They were under the misapprehension that they had been liberated, but we couldn't stop and we politely sidestepped them and moved on.

Further along, we passed a German staff car at the side of the road riddled with bullets with what appeared to be a dead high-ranking officer hanging out the rear door; his aide and driver were also dead. We later learned that the senior officer was Major General Kissim, the Arnhem town commander who had had the misfortune to run into the forward elements of the 3rd Battalion ahead of us. Several Dutch women were sweeping up broken glass from the road as we passed.

On reaching the junction with the main Arnhem–Utrecht road, we turned left where a tram car lay on its side. The lads were strolling along in the sunshine, well spaced out on both sides of the road, and we had still not met any opposition since leaving the DZ.

This information is taken from Martin Middlebrook, *Arnhem 1944, The Airborne Battle* (1995), p. 235.

Chapter 37

The Oosterbeek Perimeter

Our forward progress was halted further along the Utrecht road in Oosterbeek where we met elements of the 3rd Battalion withdrawing back towards us from Arnhem. The sound of the battle ahead was very distinct. German troops with armour were reported to be pouring in, and we were out gunned and unable to get past them due to the closely packed buildings that had high wire fences in the gardens. Subsequently, we were ordered to fall back on the Hartenstein Hotel, where we reinforced the South Staffs and Border Regiment that were now in the adjacent woods. The Hartenstein had previously been the German HQ until we had landed on Sunday, and it had now become the HQ of our divisional commander, General Urquhart. The fighting in and around Oosterbeek was increasing in intensity but we were still feeling quite confident as we believed that XXX Corps would soon be arriving from Nijmegen.

In the sky above us numerous Dakotas and Stirling bombers were circling trying to drop in supplies. We were all laying out our yellow cloth recognition triangles and some of the lads were spreading out bed sheets and parachute canopies in an attempt to guide them in. The re-supply aircraft were having a pretty rough time, the sky was black with flak bursts as the Germans fired on them with increasing accuracy. They were coming in low and far too slowly and we could see them taking hits, but they still kept coming and several were trailing smoke and flames.*

Looking up we felt helpless and detached, but we were in awe of their courage as we watched in slow motion their terrible predicament. They seemed to be moving so slowly among a sky full of flak bursts, yet our feelings were tempered by a sense of futility as the containers with our supplies were mostly floating down into the German positions.**

We didn't have any air support in the form of strafing fighters that I could see, and we were desperate to have the pressure of the German guns taken off

---

* The RAF was to lose 66 aircraft on the re-supply flights with 222 aircrew and despatchers from the RASC killed. This information is taken from Martin Middlebrook, *Arnhem 1944, The Airborne Battle* (1995), p. 398.

** It has been estimated that several hundred tons of parachuted supplies came down into positions that were held by the Germans.

us as they were shelling us at will. Whether this was due to the failure of our radios being unable to call them in I don't know, but I didn't see any of the hundreds of fighters that had escorted our armada across from Britain.

*

Tuesday 19 September 1944

By the afternoon of the 19th General Urquart realised that his airborne forces in and around Oosterbeek were not going to be able to reach the bridge. The German forces that had been reinforced with armour were just too strong to fight through. The decision was taken to form a defensive perimeter within the suburb of Oosterbeek backing down onto the Rhine, and once formed it was to be held until XXX Corps arrived. It was reasoned that if a section of the river bank could be held then a crossing might still be possible.

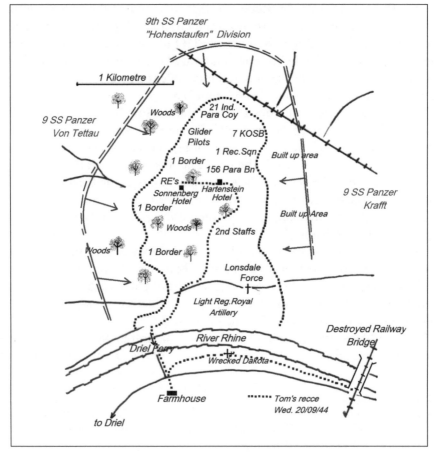

The Oosterbeek perimeter. Members of C Troop 1st Parachute Squadron were dug in immediately east of the Hartenstein Hotel.

The new perimeter took the form of a large horseshoe and all the outlying groups began to fight their way into it, but as the pressure of German reinforcements grew, many of the outlying groups were either wiped out or taken prisoner. With the desperate decision to make a stand in Oosterbeek came the realisation that the bridge and its hard-pressed defenders would have to be abandoned.

The troops within the Oosterbeek perimeter became the remnants of the airborne division. Fighting side by side were paratroops, the glider-borne troops of the Border, Kings Own Scottish Borderers and South Staffs Regiments including their glider pilots, men from the Pioneer Corps, RASC (drivers and mechanics), gunners from the Light Regiment Royal Artillery, Provost and HQ Companies together with a handful of RAF aircrew that had the misfortune to have parachuted in from their damaged aircraft.

*

Other problems were also becoming apparent. Due to the failure of the radios our officers were unable to communicate and did not know the exact dispositions of the other battalions, or the opposition that they were facing, and because of this neither bad nor good news affected us. All we knew was that our war was in front of us. Trusting in ourselves and the knowledge that XXX Corps were coming up to relieve us, we dug into the woods and prepared to hold our ground.

The perimeter was formed in the neatly housed suburbs and woodland around Oosterbeek from where it extended down onto the River Rhine, which at this point was deep, fast flowing and about 150yd wide. Smaller groups were cut off outside the perimeter around the railway, and these lads had to fight their own battles and many didn't survive.

We were mostly moving through wooded areas, making stands in the lanes, bungalows and houses before moving on again. In one position I was in a party of six searching a large house. I was halfway up the stairs when it was hit by a shell from an 88.* The corner of the house was taken off causing the stairs to collapse. I was pitched down onto the floor where I landed heavily onto my wrist (twenty years later it was diagnosed as an untreated fracture of the scaphoid). Lucky and I quickly came out among clouds of plaster dust. There were six of us that went into the house, including our CO Doug Murray and his batman. Both men were uninjured and survived, but such was the confusion that Lucky and I didn't see them again until after the war.

Just before dark our section began digging in around the ruined brick walls of a large house (Sonnenberg Castle) to the left of the Hartenstein Hotel;

---

* The 88 was a German self-propelled gun.

most of the section that I was with were either wounded or killed there. Our Sonnenberg trenches were now on the edge of the newly formed perimeter. The situation appeared to be extremely fluid and disorganised. Groups of men were still coming in towards us away from the German fire. They came running through the trees in ragged groups and either passed through our positions or jumped into our trenches to catch their breath before moving off again. They were at great risk of being shot by us who were covering every movement in front with the traverse of the Bren. Many of the groups were without officers or NCOs and it seemed that they were led by the biggest or the fittest. Once into the perimeter, these troops were reorganised and allocated to defensive positions.

It was obvious to us that things were beginning to fall apart. The Border Regiment that had taken the high route had been driven off the high ground and had retreated into the perimeter. In our area the Germans seemed to be content to just to sit back and shell us. Some close-quarter fighting took place in the area of the perimeter that encompassed the suburbs but in the woods it was the constant barrage of mortars – they were shredding us. It was difficult actually to see a German, and our mortars were ranged to attack the position from which we estimated their mortars were sited. We were firing our Brens in controlled bursts at any movement or flash that we observed. The wrist that I had injured in the house was by now swollen and was very uncomfortable, jarring painfully with each vibration of the gun.

During a lull in the fighting, I went to the Hartenstein to try and obtain some water, but they had none to spare and were down to draining the toilet cisterns and pipe-work. On the lawn outside the Hartenstein I passed the sobering site of the bodies of our lads, faces grey and partially covered with blankets, there were around 200 laid out in lines on the ground. German prisoners were laying out more, and they were also carrying out and settling down the wounded that had been attended to inside the hotel which had now also become a casualty receiving area. Our NCOs were chasing out men that had lingered too long with their wounded mates after carrying them in, and others with minor wounds were also being ousted to be positioned in trenches.

More German prisoners were locked in the tennis courts and they were visibly unhappy with their situation as we were all being heavily mortared. Shovels were thrown in and they were told to do what we were doing and 'get digging'. All they had to do was stay alive. In the lulls they were asking for food but we had none to give them as we had none ourselves, the 48-hour rations that we carried having all been eaten by now.

We kept having to move around to reposition the Bren to avoid the Germans pinpointing our position. On one of these movements we were running low when we passed Colin Cameron in a ditch by the road. Crouched low and on his own, we paused to ask if he was OK and he mumbled something about

'Fishing for a tank'. The Germans were now bringing in tanks and we were using Hawkins and PIATs to prevent them getting in among us.*

We believed that we were holding our own as the perimeter was intact. On Tuesday night Lieutenant Hall came across to Cossy and me and indicated for us to follow, 'a job for you Costadinas and Hicks', he informed us. As we left our trenches zig-zagging through the trees to keep up with him we could hear the Borders shouting and firing behind us in the woods. We followed him into the Hartenstein for a briefing on the task ahead. We were introduced to a Dutch guide who was to accompany us, a young lad of about 15 years of age who was wearing a yellow scarf and appeared to be from some form of boy scout group.

Our job was to see if we could find a way to cross over the river to the opposite bank, and if possible to visit the damaged railway bridge to assess its condition. We already knew that the railway bridge was down in the water as it had been blown up on the first day, but we didn't know how badly smashed up it was. We were told that an assessment was required to be passed down to the army group that were fighting their way up to us. Could it be bridged was the question, and what sort of bridging equipment would be required to repair it, what was the depth of the water, the speed of the current and the state of the bank seats?**

Leaving my heavier Bren, I was given a Sten gun and we left in a jeep. With Tim driving we made our way down behind the Hartenstein, skirting the battle that was taking place at the nearby crossroads. Entering the woods we descended down through the trees towards the Rhine with friend and foe taking odd shots at us. The boy told us that he had never been down to the river in the dark so we kept him crouched down in the foot well.

On reaching the river we located the Driel (Heveadorp) ferry, left the jeep in the trees and let the young boy go. Surprisingly, it was still being operated by an old Dutchman named Pieter, and we gave him cigarettes and he took us across the river. Fortunately, the crossing was a quiet one as the ferry had no engine, relying on its rudder, an underwater cable attachment and the current for propulsion.

---

* Colin was in charge of what was called a 'Hawkins necklace' which was a string of mines attached at intervals along a length of rope. The mines were hidden at one side of the road and the rope was placed across it, and as a tank approached the rope was pulled across the road drawing the mines under the tracks. PIAT, Projectile Infantry Anti Tank. This was a portable anti-tank weapon firing high-explosive shells, operated by one or two men. It had a range of 100m and could penetrate 4in of armour.

** The area of the bank that was firm enough to support a bailey bridge which could possibly be used to bridge a broken span.

Once across, we climbed up the bank and onto the road which separated the river from the polder, from where we made our way to a nearby farmhouse and enquired if any Germans were in the vicinity. The farm was occupied by two or three families with children. They gave us a cup of milk and a biscuit and informed us that Germans passed by now and again but not recently. Leaving the farmhouse, we continued along the bank in the shadow of the raised road in the direction of the railway bridge, passing a wrecked Dakota on our way. The aircraft had a cloying sweet odour emanating from it and we gave it a wide berth; I had come across the smell several times before in Tunisia when we had passed wrecked tanks holding their dead crewmen.

On reaching the railway bridge, Cossy and I took up covering positions some distance apart on either side of the tracks. Tim took the bank measurements and then climbed out onto the collapsed girders to measure the depth and the current. The depth was taken by tying a hand grenade to parachute cord with knots tied in the line at foot intervals and then dropping it into the water. The speed of the current was estimated by throwing a piece of wood into the river and timing its passage between two points. We were under instructions not to get involved with any German patrols, but to elude them and let them pass by if at all possible.

It was still a very dark night and above our positions on the opposite side of the river the sky was lit up with searchlights and tracer, it looked quite beautiful and not unlike one's first sight of Blackpool illuminations. The Germans were using red, green and white tracers and together with the flash of the mortars and artillery bursts, it all appeared unreal when viewed from the relative quiet of our current position.

As I crouched on the bank looking towards Oosterbeek, the moment was disturbed as I heard the swish of footsteps coming towards me from behind. Alarmed and alert, I dropped, turned and lay flat in the wet grass facing the oncoming sound with my heart beating ten to the dozen. Clutching my Sten, I reasoned that, 'If I can't see them then they can't see me'. I was relieved to see a cow approaching me out of the darkness.

The animal came right up to me and stopped, inquisitively bending its neck as it emitted clouds of misty breathe from its nostrils. Its muzzle was dribbling as it stooped lower and gave my face a tentative lick. 'Push off', I whispered, or some such strained expletive. It must have been attracted by the salt in the rivulets of sweat on my forehead. I didn't need this, I was already sweating with my heart still pounding fit to burst from its initial approach, but fortunately it lost interest and wandered off.

I felt a tug on my lower leg and Tim Hall whispered, 'Come on, Tom, we're off.' I rose from the wet grass and we picked up Cos and retraced our steps to the ferry. Pieter was still waiting for us and we re-crossed the river, retrieved the jeep from the woods drove back up into the perimeter again without further mishap. The strange thing was that during the first three days that we were in the perimeter the ferry was open and could have been used to get men across the river, and we could have reached the opposite side of the bridge. We were not aware of the ferry's existence before our reconnaissance sortie, it is an anomaly, and I have never understood why it was not or used or known about.*

Tim Hall returned to the Hartenstein to report on our findings and Cossy and I picked up my Bren and returned to our position. As we arrived, we got a blast and a grin from Smudger Smith in his broad Sheffield accent, 'Weer the 'ell 'av you bin … it's bin like Bulford Naafi on a Sat'dee neet eer', referring to the rattles and bangs that were still going on around us. We got back into our trenches among the trees in the Sonnenberg woods and resumed firing at the flashes of the German muzzles in the darkness. We were still being constantly mortared and were getting thinned out. By this time the Germans had realised that we were on the back foot and were beginning to come in much closer.

*

Under Pressure

The Market Garden plan was now 36 hours behind schedule. The advance of the Guards Armoured Division, the vanguard of XXX Corps, was stuck at Nijmegen over 12 miles away, and the bridge over the Waal that they needed to cross had still not been captured.

Major General Urquhart wrote in his memoir that Wednesday 20 September 'arrived as a drizzling dawn'.** Later that morning he concluded that, 'With the exception of the 2nd Battalion at the bridge the 1st Parachute Brigade had to all intents and purposes been wiped out, the South Staffords had ceased to exist as a unit and the 11th Battalion had disintegrated. I realised that whatever prospects there had been of reaching Frost (at the bridge) were now gone.'

*

It was here in the grounds of Sonnenberg that I had a close call. We were away from the ruins but still under trees covering a lane with the Bren gun. Lucky was on another job so Jock Sherwood was standing in as my no. 2, changing the magazines as I blazed them off. German shells were screaming in with air

---

*   Lieutenant Colonel John Frost, the 2nd Battalion commander, stated in the final chapter of his memoir, *A Drop Too Many* (1992): 'We had not been told that there was a ferry at Driel, though the capture and subsequent operation of this would have been an ideal task for some of the RE. The failure of the planners at all levels to identify and make use of this useful asset is hard to understand.'

** Major General Urquhart's memoir was published as *Arnhem* in 1958, see p. 103.

bursts hitting the tree canopy above and shredded twigs and red hot shrapnel were coming down on our helmets like rain. Mixed with incoming mortars, there was a general pandemonium.

We had been out there for quite a while and were running low on ammunition when two lads ran out with another Bren and more magazines to relieve us. Dropping down into our position, they breathlessly told us, 'We're here to give you a break, Tom.' We got up and sprinted back across the open ground to our previously dug slit trenches by the castle. Jock, who was a faster runner than me, jumped into my trench which was the nearest and I had to jump over him to get into his trench a few yards further on. I had just got down when there was a loud crump and my trench with Jock in it took a direct hit from a mortar shell, and he was killed. Jock was new to the squadron and had only been with us for three months having recently arrived as a replacement before Arnhem.* I was hit by a small piece of shrapnel in the back of the neck, just below my helmet, and this drew blood but I luckily escaped a serious injury.

Some of the lads had built roofs over their trenches by improvising a half section of a container filled with earth, however these were in short supply in our area and all that we could do was to curl up tight and weather the intensity of the bombardment.

We were desperately short of water and were having to fill our water bottles from a slime-covered bird bath adjacent to a small grotto in the woods. The Germans had deliberately cut off all the tap water in and around our area. As the day lengthened on Tuesday, the RAF re-supply flights continued, while the German flak bursts were becoming much more concentrated as they became more organised and brought in more guns. The bulk of the supply containers and panniers were still not reaching us. The question that was now being asked by all of us was, 'Where were XXX Corps, and how long would they be?' The maximum period of 48 hours for which we were expected to hold for had long since passed.

Among it all humour still surfaced. Quite close to our position was a group of RAF aircrew in their blues manning a slit trench having apparently baled out of an aircraft. Compared to us, they were comparatively clean, and much to our amusement the story went around that they were dressed up in their best blues under their flying gear in preparation for a night out in Boston, which they had hoped to dash off to on their return home.

---

* Sapper Jock (Henry) Sherwood, aged 26, was buried in a field grave in the trench where he was killed and wasn't discovered until 2006 by the Dutch Army Recovery and Identification Service. Tom was instrumental in locating his grave. After the war, he was listed on the Groesbeek Memorial for those with no known grave. He has now been reinterred in Oosterbeek Airborne Cemetery, 23.C.19.

Thursday 21 September 1944

On the evening of the 20th the 2nd Battalion troops with Lieutenant Colonel Frost and attachments were still holding the north end of the bridge despite heavy fighting. The bridge over the Waal at Nijmegen had at last been captured by the US 82nd Airborne Division. However, infuriatingly, the Guards Armoured Division had not started moving towards Arnhem, preferring instead to wait for its infantry support to catch up before setting out towards the beleaguered 1st Airborne, much to the disbelief of the Americans.

The Germans finally defeated the airborne troops at the north end of Arnhem bridge on the morning of 21 September, which was the fifth day of the landing. Of the 700 or so men that had arrived at the bridge in the first two days, there were now little more than a 100 still resisting on the final night of its defence. The buildings in which they were fighting were either on fire or had been reduced to rubble. Without food and sleepless for days, they were down to the last of their ammunition, with many of those that remained standing carrying wounds. They were simply overwhelmed. The survivors were ordered to break out of the German encirclement in small groups to try and reach the Oosterbeek perimeter, but most were taken prisoner or killed.

The last assault began at dawn when five German tanks came over the bridge supported by panzer grenadiers. They commenced firing shells into the remains of the houses at point-blank range, and by 0900hr it was all over. In Oosterbeek the perimeter still held.

Later that afternoon after the defence of the bridge had ended, the 1st Polish Independent Parachute Brigade arrived. They were two days late having been delayed in Britain by fog. During this period the battle had changed and they were now urgently required to cross the river from their DZ to reinforce the Oosterbeek perimeter. They had hoped to cross the Rhine using the Driel ferry, however by now it had been cut loose from its mooring and had drifted down the river.

While the Polish Parachute Brigade's 1,500 men were in flight to Arnhem, a coded message had been sent out to the pilots of their transports instructing them to return to Britain. Weather conditions were deteriorating and it was considered unsuitable to proceed to Holland, but due to a mix up in the radio codes only a third of the force received the correct signal and turned back, the rest continuing on to Arnhem and dropping 1,000 men. The Polish reinforcements were hit by German flak and small arms fire as they landed. They were stuck on the opposite side of the river to Oosterbeek lacking boats, and less than 200 were able to get across into the perimeter to assist the beleaguered airborne division during the next two days.

*

Sometime on Wednesday I spoke to Ropey Cox and he told me more of the lads had been killed, Fred Hoath, Barney and Wallace Morrison.* Our actions in Africa and Sicily had never been as prolonged and intense as this and we had never experienced so many casualties.

In our positions in Oosterbeek we began to hear the guns of XXX Corps firing into the surrounding German positions from across the river.** As well as German shells coming in at us, we now had our own shells screaming overhead from the opposite direction, some of which were dropping short into our positions. 'Jeb'† had been killed and many of us were carrying wounds. There were now no doubts at all that the Germans were far stronger than we had been led to believe. This day was particularly bad and it appeared that the Germans were content to just sit it out while they sniped and mortared us from cover. It was later recorded that the rate of enemy fire was five mortar bombs every 20 seconds and that these bombardments were sustained for hours at a time. However, while they were mortaring we knew they would not try to come in among us so we just kept our heads down. When they stopped we raised our heads above the parapet and engaged them again. When the fire slackened off into a lull we moved back our wounded and tried to obtain drinking water and something to eat.

Friday 22 September was our sixth day on the ground and we were still under heavy bombardment. We now knew that we were completely surrounded and with our backs to the river the perimeter was shrinking. It began to drizzle and we were able to drink the rain water. We were still hanging on and there was no thought of giving up.

The Germans were now confident enough to bring up a radio van from which they began broadcasting the popular songs of the day, 'Pistol Packing Mama', 'In the Mood' and Vera Lynn came over a tinny loud hailer, interspersed with calls for us to give up and think of our wives and sweethearts at home. The

---

*   Driver Wallace Morrison, aged 20, was killed on 18 September 1944 and was buried in a field grave near St Elizabeth Hospital. He is now reinterred in Oosterbeek Airborne Cemetery, 15.B.12. Sergeant Fred Hoath, aged 27, was killed on 20 September 1944 and was buried in a field grave in the garden of the family Ter Horst near the church in Oosterbeek. He has also been reinterred in Oosterbeek Airborne Cemetery, 2.B.13.

**   These were the guns of the 64th Medium Regiment in Nijmegen. Following the capture of the Waal bridge, they were able to cross the Waal River from where they made radio contact with the beleaguered Airborne Division in Oosterbeek. Positioning their guns, they commenced firing into the surrounding German positions from 12 miles away.

†   'Jeb' Gilbert Taylor, aged 24, was killed on 21 September 1944 close to Tom's position. He was a tall 6ft-plus Scot who was given the name Jeb, as in DJebel, the Arabic name for mountain. Jeb arrived as a replacement in Tunisia in 1942. He has no known grave. Also on the 21st, 'Bulham' Thomas Brooks, aged 24, was hit in the thigh by the fin of a mortar bomb in the same location as Jeb. He later died, but also has no known grave.

firing died down when the broadcast came on and it did more to sustain than demoralise, it was like an impromptu concert and was greeted with hoots of derision in our area. However, it didn't survive for very long as it attracted our fire and went dead after a loud bang as if a PIAT had struck.

*

Trapped in the Perimeter

The survivors of the 1st Airborne Division in the Oosterbeek perimeter were now outnumbered 4 to 1 by the surrounding German forces who maintained the heavy barrage of mortars accompanied by intermittent shelling. It was estimated that there were now approximately 3,600 men left.* Their predicament deteriorated further when German forces cut the road between Nijmegen and Arnhem, delaying the relief force by another 24 hours. To add to their problems, low cloud and rain prevented further supplies being dropped in by air.

On the afternoon of Saturday 23 September, the road from Nijmegen to Arnhem was opened once again, but the survivors of the Airborne Division were now in a very bad state. The next day the road from Nijmegen to Arnhem was cut again for a second time and was to remain blocked by the Germans until Tuesday 26 September. It was now realised that there would be no relief of the beleaguered airborne troops by XXX Corps, and a decision had been taken to get the survivors out of the Oosterbeek perimeter and across the river.

*

It is difficult to remember an exact sequence of events during these last few days. We were now very tired, dirty and hungry. I recall one of our lads, Jock (John) Campbell, moving from trench to trench as he brought us soup in a large tin, bent double he was spilling it everywhere. We later saw Jock's tin in a tree but we never saw him again.**

The incoming mortars had sensitive fuses and many were exploding in the trees above sending down showers of shrapnel and splintered branches. One of these air bursts exploded well nigh on top of me and I was hit by shrapnel in the back of the neck below the rim of my helmet, almost in the same place where I had been previously hit, boy was I numb. I lost the sensation in my legs and I could feel the blood running down my back. Curly (Plummer)

---

*   Figure taken from Martin Middlebrook, *Arnhem 1944, The Airborne Battle* (1995), p. 339.

**   Sapper John Campbell, aged 24, was killed and buried in a field grave south of the Hartenstein Hotel near the sports ground. He was reinterred in Oosterbeek Airborne Cemetery, 20.C.19.

helped me out of the trench and Lucky dashed across a clearing to get a jeep. My last recollections were of mortar bombs bursting everywhere, but I was helpless. I made a mental note to thank them for looking after me when this was all over then I passed out. I didn't see Lucky again until after the war, he was taken prisoner shortly afterwards and was transported to Merseberg POW camp near Leipzig.

I was stretchered with the other wounded to a nearby house, which I later learned was named 'Gelder's Hof'. Situated across the road from the Sonnenberg, it was one of the many houses serving as a first-aid station. On arrival, I was placed on a table and my wound was probed in an attempt to remove the shrapnel, after which it was left open and packed. I was then placed on the floor in a corner of the lounge among the other wounded. When I came round I found that my head was locked to one side and my neck and shoulders throbbed, and my legs were still not responding.

The next day, Monday the 24th, a medical officer came in and told us that the division was pulling out of the perimeter and moving across the river.* We were told that they would not be able to take the wounded. We half expected that this would be the case as our wounded had been left behind before in Tunisia with our medical orderlies. One of our lads came into the aid station to see if I could be moved, but my system was shocked and I was still unable to walk. His visit only confirmed that I would have to stay and wait for the 'Jerries' and be taken prisoner. There were many more of us, including the padre and the medics from 16th Parachute Field Ambulance, who were still busy working among the wounded.**

I lay on the floor in Gelder's Hof for two days during which time the house was hit by shell fire several times, and some of the wounded were wounded again. All the windows had been blown out. My recollections were very hazy. There were wounded men in every room, on the stairs, on the landing and in the bedrooms. Men were moaning and some were screaming. Also in the room with us were a Dutch civilian and his wife, both were wounded. I was positioned in a corner opposite a blown-out window with sheets of hardboard hanging down from the ceiling, and lying next to me was a severely wounded SS Sergeant who was also moaning and kept repeating, 'Wasser ... wasser', asking for water. I always carried two water bottles and we were fortunate

---

*   The RE War diary records that on 24 September there were only eight men and one officer from C Troop among the defenders still standing in the perimeter.

** Of the 135 men of the 16th Parachute Field Ambulance who went into Arnhem, 6 were killed and 129 were posted as missing. Most of the latter became POWs having voluntarily stayed behind to care for the wounded; none were recorded as being evacuated across the river. This information is taken from Martin Middlebrook, *Arnhem 1944, The Airborne Battle* (1995), p. 456.

that I had enough to share. I was able to give him a drink of rain water and he was very grateful, 'Danke, danke komrad, danke komrad', he thanked me over and over and kept hold of my hand. Two of my mates came in to see me before they were due to leave the perimeter in the attempt to break out across the river. We chatted and then they left with a wave and a final, 'See you, Tom … when we get home'.* The SS man kept holding my hand throughout the night.

*

Monday 25 September 1944

The Germans ordered the evacuation of all Dutch civilians from Arnhem. As a result, 95,000 people were forced out off their homes and the town and left to fend for themselves.

On 25 September the remains of the Airborne Division slipped down through the woods to attempt the hazardous crossing of the River Rhine. In all, approximately 2,400 men got across out of the 10,000 men who went in. They had to leave behind 7,600 men, out of which 3,000 were wounded and 1,400 dead. The rest were prisoners with a small number in hiding with the Dutch. The accepted German casualties were 3,300, which included 1,300 dead.**

Of the 143 men of the 1st Parachute Squadron RE that dropped at Arnhem, 20 died, 13 were evacuated across the river and 110 were missing.† Most of the missing were carrying wounds and were taken prisoner. C Troop had 9 men killed and 25 wounded out of the 39 men that went in.

The Battle of Arnhem was the largest battle that the 1st Airborne Division fought during the Second World War and it was the most costly. Lightly armed and with rations for only 48 hours, the Airborne Division's objective was to capture and hold the bridge for 48 hours. They managed to hold it for almost five days and the Oosterbeek perimeter for nine days. The division faced the formidable German Tiger tanks and Type 88 self-propelled guns of the 9th and 10th SS Panzer Divisions.

Many viewed the operation as a disaster, but this did not reflect on the troops who went into Arnhem to do a job at very short notice. The US

---

* One of these friends was 19-year-old 'Wakey', Allan Wake, who had been teamed with me on the Bren as my No. 2 following the death of Jock Sherwood. Tragically, he was also shot while making his way back to join the withdrawal across the river. I was later told that Wakey was taken to Apeldoorn Hospital. I don't know if he died there or was moved to a German or Dutch Hospital, but he died after the battle on 22 December 1944. Allan is buried in Oosterbeek Airborne Cemetery, 18.C.14.

** These figures are taken from Cornelius Ryan, *A Bridge Too Far* (1974), p. 459.

† These figures are taken from Martin Middlebrook, *Arnhem 1944, The Airborne Battle* (1995), p. 456.

Commander in Chief General Dwight D. Eisenhower said, 'There has been no single performance by any unit that has more greatly inspired me or excited my admiration than the nine-day action by the 1st British Airborne Division between September 17th and 25th.'

Lieutenant Colonel John Frost (later Major General), commander of the 2nd Battalion, paid tribute to the 1st Parachute Squadron RE, stating in his memoir *A Drop too Many*, 'As usual the men of the Royal Engineer Parachute Squadron fought through to the end. Throughout the war we of the Parachute Regiment thought it was almost a waste to use them as sappers when they were so good at killing the enemy.'

The Battle of Arnhem is regarded as one of the most admirable defensive actions in the history of modern warfare.

Part Three

Prisoner of War

Chapter 38

Early Days as a POW

The final part of the account of Tom's wartime experience remains true to the POW diary but includes recollections to improve the flow of the story. The dates and sequence of Tom's entries remain as they were written.

*

Tuesday 26 September 1944

During the morning after my second night on the floor at Gelder's Hof we heard the distinctive rumble of an approaching tank. A 60-ton Tiger came across the garden and up to the house sticking its gun barrel through the blown-out window. The intrusion of the barrel was followed by a tank crewman dressed in the black uniform and forage cap of the SS Panzer troops. He looked to be fresh and very young. Leaning in from the body of the tank, he spoke at us in broken English, the gist of which was, 'Ha! I am the gunner on this tank, the best tank in the world … we will win this war.' He was arrogant, but we were too weak or too tired to reply and those of us that were conscious just looked at him blankly, in our exhausted state he was just an irrelevance.

The tank barrel withdrew and an SS officer came into the room accompanied by three other soldiers. I observed that they were wearing the 'Viking' insignia in raised gothic script on the cuffs of their tunics.* The officer noticed the SS sergeant lying on the floor next to me and came across and shook his hand. I could tell he was asking if we had treated him well, 'Ja, Ja', he replied pointing at me and repeating, 'Komrad, Komrad', explaining that I had given him water. The officer said, 'Gute' and then surprisingly shook my hand and wished me good luck before leaving.

Wednesday 27 September 1944

After our third night in Gelder's Hof more German troops came in and started to move out the wounded, some of whom were on stretchers and some

---

* Probably elements of the SS Viken Battalion comprising Norwegian Waffen SS.

were walking. Before our transportation began, we were searched but I had nothing of interest for them, most of my kit having disappeared during our days in the Oosterbeek woods.

We were loaded onto flat-bed trucks and taken to an improvised hospital in Apeldoorn, which was a former Dutch army barracks now being used as a field hospital. Some of the lads had terrible wounds. The trucks were driven at speed through the cobbled streets and we were bounced around on the hard, flat floor. The troops transporting us were not the troops that we had fought and appeared to be some form of auxiliary unit who were not inclined to the sensitivities of our wounded.

On reaching the hospital at Apeldoorn, we were placed in a large barrack room from which the beds had been removed and the floor was scattered with straw. There must have been between 400 and 500 of us. Men were holding each other up, I say men but most of us were in our early twenties. Everyone looked older, unshaven, red-eyed, dirty and almost all were bloodstained in some way, but I could still sense the edge that the paratroops among us retained. We were visited by two medical officers, a British colonel and a German together with other German army personnel. As they passed among us they were deciding who would stay in the hospital and who would be moved to Germany. The colonel was trying to convince the Germans that we were worse than we were, but they were not taken in or distracted. The German medical officer took a cursory look and pointedly made a decision stating 'krankenhaus' (hospital) or 'Deutschland' (Germany) and that was that. I was recovering and although still shaky had regained the feeling in my legs and was able to stand.*

From the moment that we were assembled the Germans told our officers and NCOs that anyone that tried to escape would be shot. We spent five nights on the straw before those of us who could be moved were taken into Germany. Our futures were to be varied, some lads were moved to the camps in great discomfort where their wounds were treated in makeshift POW medical huts, while the seriously wounded were taken into Dutch and German hospitals.

---

* Apeldoorn barracks had been taken over by the Germans and 1,700 of our wounded were taken there and attended to by 250 of our own Field Ambulance assisted by Dutch medical staff. The Field Ambulance lads had voluntarily stayed behind to care for the wounded and none were evacuated over the river. The walking wounded were gradually transferred into Germany in ambulance trains. The more seriously wounded remained in German hospitals, and Tom's pal Tony Jones from York spent the rest of the war in a German hospital with a serious head wound and was well treated. The figures quoted here are taken from Martin Middlebrook, *Arnhem 1944, The Airborne Battle* (1995), p. 437.

Thursday 28 September 1944

I met some more of our lads today, and we were cheered by the sight of hundreds of US Fortress bombers passing over head.

Monday 3 October

We were paraded outside the barracks. The numbness had left my legs and although I was shaky, I was now able to stand. I was beginning to feel much better with the exception of the wound to my neck, which was very stiff and had locked my head to one side. My wrist was still swollen but settling down. We were extremely dirty and hungry having been fighting and living rough for sixteen days, and our uniforms were torn and bloodied, but the Germans did not feed us.

Having lined up and been counted, we were then marched through the streets of Apeldoorn to the railway station with German troops on either side of our column. Our spirits were not broken and we were singing as we marched. Along the route Dutch civilians threw us apples and risked being hit by the guards.

As I looked around as we marched through the streets, I was conscious of the mess that the Germans and we had made of Arnhem. Trees were down along the road sides, burnt-out jeeps and tanks were scattered around and dead bodies from the fighting were still to be removed. The neat houses and gardens were completely wrecked with broken fences and rutted lawns and many houses were charred and smoke was still drifting around. It was a battlefield.

We arrived at the station where a long train of cattle vans were waiting at one of the platforms. This was designated as an ambulance train and the roofs of the vans were draped with red crosses. We were herded in forty men to a van with a great deal of counting and shouting by the German guards. The straw on the floor of our van was filthy, still soiled from the last occupants. We were each given a loaf of black bread for the journey and a bucket of water for drinking to be shared between all forty of us.

The upper part of the van had barred apertures that had been wrapped with barbed wire and once we were inside the doors were closed and bolted. We were entrained in daylight on Monday and were locked in the stationary vans overnight. Cramped with little room for comfort, our wounds and bodies began to smell as we wiled away the hours in the dark.

Tuesday 4 October 1944

The train moved off in daylight on Tuesday morning and we travelled all that day and night. On Wednesday at daybreak the train stopped in a station, possibly for a toilet break. Some of the vans were opened but we were still locked in when we heard the guards firing. Later, I saw the body of an officer draped over the buffer beam of a wagon on an adjacent track; he had obviously been placed there as an example to the rest of us.* We presumed that when the doors were opened he had tried to slip away beneath his van.

Later that day an aircraft flew low over our train and a flak gun started firing. Locked inside we listened in apprehension as we hoped that the pilot would see the red-cross symbols on the van roofs. Nothing more happened and we all sighed with relief as the moment passed.

Thursday 6 October 1944

We were offloaded and taken into the middle of a field, there were no latrines for us. Looking back at the train we could see that there were two Tiger tanks draped in camouflage netting on a pair of flat wagons behind the locomotive, which in our eyes compromised the train's red-cross status. We presumed that they were being taken clandestinely away from the front for repairs.

We were on the train for three days being transported into Germany. The going was slow with frequent halts as we were held in loops to allow other trains to pass. There were no toilet bins in the van, but fortunately most of us were unable to go anyway and the water we passed went between the boards in the van floor. Very hungry, we chewed on the black bread which was hard and pretty sour. Little did we know it was to be our standard fare for the future.

During the night our train passed through Hanover in the middle of a big air raid. The train had increased its speed to get through the city and the cattle vans were swaying and bouncing as we crossed numerous points. We had one particular moment when debris from the explosions rattled down on the roof of our van. As we swayed in the darkness, low voices were muttering somewhat incredulously about it being the RAF up above and that we were running the risk of being bombed by our own aircraft.

When the train finally stopped and the doors were opened we found that we were at a place called Fallingbostel in Lower Saxony. It was here that about 400 of us arrived on Friday 7 October, dishevelled, dirty and ravenous, and all talk was of food.

---

* The officer concerned was possibly Captain John Keesey, a medical officer from 16 Parachute Field Ambulance who was reported to have been shot jumping from an ambulance train. This information is taken from Martin Middlebrook, *Arnhem 1944, The Airborne Battle* (1995), p. 436.

Treatment of Prisoners of War, 1939–45

The third Geneva Convention in 1929 specified that prisoners of war be treated humanely. Germany and Italy together with the Allies, Britain, the USA, the commonwealth countries of Australia, Canada and New Zealand, were signatories of the convention. The Soviet Union and Japan were not.

Under the Geneva Convention to qualify for prisoner of war status the captured soldier, sailor or airman must have been operating in accordance with the custom of war, that is he or she must be part of a chain of command, wear a uniform and openly bear arms.

If soldiers of lower rank were made to work, they must be paid, but their work must not contribute to the war effort of the country imprisoning them. Officers and NCOs of sergeant and above were not required or made to work.

When one thinks of prisoners of war the question of escape often comes to mind. However, in the camps that were holding the lower ranks the men were malnourished and hard labour was often inflicted, and for these men survival became their primary concern.

The Germans and Italians by and large treated Allied prisoners whose governments had been signatories of the convention without brutality. However, escapees risked being shot and those that fell into the hands of the German Gestapo (secret police) often experienced brutality and were killed. The harshness of the camps in Europe was reflected by the difficulties and privations being endured by the civilian populations, especially in the latter stages of the war.

The main grievances of Allied soldiers in German army camps were the limited amount and the quality of the food, medical attention, heating and infestations of lice. The German provision of food was supplemented by the International Red Cross supply of food parcels, on which the POWs depended.

A further grievance of British POWs was the long journeys to the camps which lasted many days in cattle trucks without adequate food, medical attention and a total lack of sanitation. Also, in the later stages of the war as Germany retreated, POWs were force marched, often many hundreds of kilometres in a malnourished state without adequate shelter or rations to sustain them.

By contrast, the German treatment of Soviet prisoners (Russian) was harsh and brutal. The Soviet Union had not signed the Geneva Convention and so Nazi Germany did not consider itself to be bound by the Convention in relation to Soviet prisoners. An estimated 2.7 to 3.3 million Soviet prisoners died in German POW camps. In 1941 6,000 Soviet POWs died of typhus in Stalag X1D adjacent to X1B in the Fallingbostel area.

Chapter 39

Fallingbostel, Germany – Stalag XIB

The Camp

Stalag XIB was situated outside Fallingbostel, near the village of Oerbke. Originally a civilian workers' hutment, it was converted into a prison camp to hold Polish prisoners after the defeat of their country in 1939. The original conversion was basically the fencing in of the original workmen's huts. As the war progressed, the camp was enlarged and became a substantial central holding camp. As it expanded, several sub-camps were built in the area to support it, Stalags XIC and XID.*

In addition to British POWs, Stalag XIB also held Poles, French, Dutch and later Italian forced labourers and some Canadians POWs. Americans also arrived after being taken prisoner at the Battle of the Bulge in the Ardennes (December 1944–January 1945). The name for POW in German is Kriegsgefangen, which was shortened to Kriegie by the POWs to describe themselves. Newly arrived POWs (1944 intakes) referred to the old hands as Kriegies. Some of these men had been taken prisoner as early as 1940 and had by this time been incarcerated for over four years and were instantly recognisable as they had a bold KG sewn in white lettering on both the leg of their trousers and the back of their jackets. These men were streetwise to camp life, methods of improvisation and survival in general.

By October 1944 the camp population had expanded to approximately 96,000, which was increased by 400 when Tom and his batch of airborne troops arrived from Arnhem. Conditions within Stalag XIB were poor and slowly deteriorating as the Germans struggled to manage the steadily increasing numbers.

*

Our guards were a mixture of regular German troops and older men who were outside the general call-up age for military service, many of them being recognisable by their insignia as veterans of the First World War. In addition to these, there were also troops that had been wounded and had not recovered sufficiently to undertake front-line duties. The older men belonged to the Landschutzen, which were the German home-guard battalions.

---

* Stalag is an abbreviation of the German word 'stammlager', meaning main camp.

Friday 7 October 1944

On arrival at Fallingbostel we were separated from our officers, who were taken to an offlag, or officers' camp, and we never saw them again during our imprisonment.

We marched into the camp as best we could with our shoulders back determined to show that we were not in any way cowed. In front of us were numerous compounds of huts surrounded by high strands of barbed wire. Once inside, we were allocated huts which were large, single-storey, bungalow-type buildings with windows all the way round. Inside were dozens of bunk beds in tiers of four. The larger lads were allocated the bottom bunks and the smaller lads such as me had to scramble to the top; I was so high that I was tucked into the angle of the wall and the ceiling. The logic of having the smaller lads at the top and the heavier ones at the bottom was to make the tiers more stable. All the bunks had wooden slats with a mattress of sacking which upon closer examination turned out to be bags that had previously held cement. Behind the huts were the latrines consisting of pits with the bough of a tree that voided a trench for support, and adjacent were several water taps. Our parachute smocks were taken off us.

Later that day we were watching large concentrations of aircraft passing over. It was a camp rule that in these situations we were not to look up and were required to return to our huts and to stay inside. We were new and hadn't been informed of these regulations and as the guards became agitated, we became more nonchalant, tending to shamble with a feigned disinterest when the guards tried to push us around. As we approached the hut, the guards were pushing us in to conform to the rule and were getting increasingly riled as we were not moving as quickly as they were demanding. At the back and also looking up was a glider pilot, previously wounded and limping he didn't get in fast enough and the guards shot him.

That first night has poignant memories. We were given a bowl of soup that tasted horrible.* We were still in the uniforms in which we had dropped, fought and been transported and to a man we stank. Blankets were issued and the huts were locked, lights out was 2100hr.

The Germans had searched me when I was moved out of the dressing station in Oosterbeek but had left me with a few items. That night I took stock of my remaining possessions, my beret, soap, razor, toothbrush, my empty wallet containing the pictures of a couple of girls and my Parker fountain pen. Surprisingly, they had failed to notice the pen which my father had bought me for my twenty-first birthday.

---

* The bowl of soup was known as 'skilly' and was to be regular issue. Skilly was a thin watery gruel usually consisting of oatmeal, scraps of vegetables and if lucky small particles of meat.

No. *C2/11M/83* 15¹ *(Parachute Squadron) (2. Troop)*   Army Form B. 104—83
(If replying, please quote above No.)

ROYAL ENGINEERS.

Record Office,

BRIGHTON.

7 - OCT 1944   19 .

SIR OR MADAM,

I regret to have to inform you that a report has been received from the War Office to the effect that (No.) *1898624* (Rank) *Captain* (Name) *Hicks Thomas* (Regiment) ROYAL ENGINEERS. *(151 Para. Squad)* was posted as " missing " on the *22ᵈ September 1944.* *North West Europe - believes Prisoner of War (wounded)*

The report that he is missing does not necessarily mean that he has been killed, as he may be a prisoner of war or temporarily separated from his regiment.

Official reports that men are prisoners of war take some time to reach this country, and if he has been captured by the enemy it is probable that unofficial news will reach you first. In that case I am to ask you to forward any postcard or letter received at once to this Office, and it will be returned to you as soon as possible.

Should any further official information be received it will be at once communicated to you.

I am,

SIR OR MADAM,

Your obedient Servant, .

Shields for

&Co. Col.

Officer in charge of Records.

IMPORTANT.

Any change of your address should be immediately notified to this Office.

Wt. 30051/1249 400,000 (16) 9/39 KJL/8812 Gp 698/3 Forms/B.104—83/9

On 7 October 1944 this impersonal letter was sent from the RE Record Office to Tom's parents informing them that he was missing, wounded and presumed to be a prisoner of war. This was the second letter that Tom's parents had received from the RE Record Office. An earlier communication had informed them that 'Terry' Hicks of the 1st Parachute Squadron was missing in action. This was an administrative error and on receipt Tom's father queried the Christian name and presumably the service number. Shortly afterwards this second letter arrived. In fact, the unrelated Terry Hicks (age 24) was a friend of Tom's and a member of B Troop. Killed at Arnhem, his date of death is recorded on the Groesbeek Memorial as 19 September 1944; he has no known grave.

As we settled down in our bunks after lights out the quiet became punctuated by 'ows' and 'oohs' as we found to our cost that the cement sacks were alive with red fleas from which were biting us. I sat up and pulled a layer of the bags back and thought, 'Bloody hell, look at these!' as they were jumping about 4in high. I started scooping them out and unfortunately quite a number fell through the gaps in my bed boards. Well, of course, the lad below me was having the same trouble resulting in the big lad at the bottom being knee deep in fleas. The language was ripe, but we eventually got used to fighting and living with them on a regular basis.

Sunday 8 October 1944

I have been here two days now and my wound has not been dressed for a week.

Thank God for Red Cross food parcels. We were issued one today and Mac and I shared one between us.* There are about twenty lads from our squadron here now and the only topic of conversation among us is food.

*

Red Cross Food Parcels

In 1939 the British Red Cross and Order of St John of Jerusalem set up the Joint War Organisation Council. The aim was to provide services to sick and wounded civilians and prisoners of war.

Prisoners of war were sent Red Cross parcels containing tinned food, soap and cigarettes in a box approximately 10in x 10in x 5in. The food items ranged from meats, sardines, cheese biscuits to chocolate, to name but a few examples. Items such as biscuits and chocolates had extra vitamins added to make up for the deficiencies in the camp diets. The cigarettes became the main currency for bartering in the camps. The parcels were not always standard in content and commodities like soap were often in short supply. The meats were also diverse and an example of this is the calves tongue from Argentina mentioned by Tom.

The aim of the Red Cross was to supply each prisoner of war with one box per week. In the event, however, the POWs received far fewer than this and towards the end of the war in late 1944 and 1945 they received very few or none at all, and the ones that got through were shared.

The parcels were trans-shipped under the Red Cross emblem from Britain in eight chartered ships delivering parcels to Marseille and Lisbon. From these

---

* Mac McBurnie became Tom's 'mucker', which was the term for the buddy system that was adopted within the camps. They shared food and 'mucked in' together and generally helped one another out. Mac McBurnie was a fellow C Troop Sapper from 1st Parachute Squadron RE, originally a Glaswegian but domiciled in Birmingham.

ports they were transhipped direct or through Geneva (Red Cross HQ) to the POW camps. In total 20 million were sent out between 1939 and 1945.

The parcels were eagerly awaited and appreciated by the prisoners who relied upon them for survival as the German rations were totally inadequate. Tom mentions them frequently and received parcels that had been packed in Canada, USA and Argentina as well as Britain.

*

A Day in Stalag XIB, Fallingbostel

Reveille was at 0600hr to enable us to be on parade by 0630hr for roll call, that is being counted by the guards, a procedure that could take anything from 10 minutes to 1 hour. We then cooked our breakfast outside before fatigues started at 0830hr. Fatigues were the cleaning of our dixies and our billets and the chopping of sticks for our cooking fires and stoves. At 1000hr we would walk around the compound until 1200hr, at which time we would be issued with our rations for the next 24-hour period. We were allowed to eat these rations as and when we liked.

The 24-hour rations were one teaspoon of jam, sugar or margarine and one-sixth of a loaf of black bread. In addition to this, we were issued with erzatz coffee, a substitute usually derived from ground acorns. We were also issued with skilly, which we started queuing for at 1300hr and sometimes took until 1430hr to arrive. It was always thin and watery, being made from various vegetables, peelings and anything to hand. The sauerkraut (cabbage) was particularly grim and went by the name of whispering grass as it passed straight through most of us. There were also five potatoes issued which we would save for supper to be eaten after the 1930hr roll call. These rations were issued by the Germans and the Red Cross parcels were in addition to this food and were greatly looked forward to.

After supper we prepared the following day's breakfast. At 2000hr I began shaking the fleas from my blanket in preparation for lights out at 2100hr, after which the fleas started to crawl back in again.

Monday 9 October 1944

The Red Cross parcel is working wonders. It's really funny watching the lads cooking over the outdoor fires and our compound looks like a red Indian camp.* We have been moved into the next laager with more of our own lads

---

* The Kriegies, that is the POWs who had been in the camp for several years, were highly organised with metal burners to heat their food. These burners were made from biscuit tins and had small wheels to increase the air flow from which they were able to generate

and the skilly is a little better, but we are still sharing a loaf of bread between six over 24 hours.

Tuesday 10 October 1944

Some more of our lads arrived. We have been issued with our first letter card to write home. I have written home and wished it Godspeed.

Wednesday 11 October 1944

We were walked 2 miles to another compound today for a hot shower, which was our first for three weeks. We also had our clothes deloused and have been issued with a small towel not much bigger than a handkerchief.

It was a little unnerving when we reached the compound where we were halted outside a large hut. Anything metal was taken off us and we thought they're going to shoot us, but instead we were ushered inside an empty room. Once we were in a gaseous mist came through ports in the ceiling making our clothes clammy and stinging our skin – it was a delousing. I had a toothbrush with me and it turned the bristles as black as a lamp brush, but fortunately I am still able to use it. Despite the indignity, the delousing must have worked because things were much more comfortable afterwards.

Thursday 12 October 1944

Today we have had a Roman Catholic mass and received communion. Our parachute smocks were inexplicably returned to us and dumped in a large heap, possibly because no alternative clothing was available. Mine was easily recognisable as it was bloodstained around the rent at the back where I had crudely sewn it up with string. Mac's was even more garish as he had a red devil painted on the back of his. This small oversight on behalf of the Germans was a morale booster to us as we were now in possession of both our smocks and berets.

800 Polish men, women and children have been brought in as forced labourers; we can hear them singing hymns. Also, twenty-five cigarettes were issued.*

---

considerable heat from little fuel. The new intake were the 'red Indians' with individual fires, and spent much of their time hunting for scraps of wood with which to heat their food, which was accomplished with much blowing and fanning within clouds of drifting smoke.

* Cigarettes were the currency within the camp and were used in most barter transactions. This was an advantage to Tom as he didn't smoke and was able to exchange them for food.

Friday 13 October 1944

Some more of the lads have arrived and we have had another Red Cross food parcel issued which will keep us going for a week. This parcel is from Argentina. I have also had a fresh dressing on the wound on my neck. The dressing of wounds is carried out by one of our medical officers who is also a prisoner. The dressings and bandages are all made from paper as cotton is unavailable. Fallingbostel has a makeshift POW medical hut in another compound which is reserved for the seriously ill and staffed by POW medical officers and orderlies.

Saturday 14 October 1944

Mac and I were detailed for a working party to collect firewood. On our march out we passed wire-fenced compounds holding thousands of Russian prisoners.* Up until now we thought that we had endured hardship but these poor souls were in a pitiful condition, emaciated and dressed in rags. We noticed that they were scraping about in the earth looking for roots to eat and wondered if we would be reduced to this. They had been given no shelter and had dug holes in the ground over which they had fashioned a bivouac of sorts. The German guards appeared to use their rifle butts freely on these prisoners.

Tuesday 17 October 1944

I am not sleeping very well and having bad dreams, and the fleas are also biting making the nights most uncomfortable. I have started walking fourteen times around the compound each morning but I find that I am soon tired. We were issued four cigarettes each today, but it is not enough for the lads who are smoking tea leaves.

Sunday 22 October 1944

Time is beginning to drag. Some of the lads are speculating that we might be home by Christmas but I don't share their optimism. I am sleeping better and have posted my second letter card home. I have been to mass and holy communion today.

The senior non-commissioned officer in the British section was the RSM of the 3rd Battalion, J.C. Lord, also referred to in camp parlance as the 'man of confidence'. If any POW had problems, he was the man to approach, and

---

* This camp was presumed to be Stalag XID.

if internal discipline were required, he was the man to deal with it. He was also the man the Germans would seek out if they had problems with us. J.C. approached the Germans for all sorts of things on our behalf, extra food, better bedding, medicine and anything else that would improve our conditions. The Germans, however, were not usually interested.

With us J.C. was every bit the professional soldier, insisting on the standard of discipline that he had carried through from his pre-paratroop regiment the Guards. He managed to keep himself as smart as possible. He had had his uniform off and had folded and pressed it as best he could, his shoes were greased and blackened while we were unkempt and scruffy. Shortly after our arrival, he spoke to us disdainfully, 'Soldiers, just because you're prisoners of war you need not be like this … I want to see a change tomorrow'. It was true, we were looking like tramps and many of us had not had the time or in some cases the inclination to reach J.C.'s standards. He would thunder, 'You man, there's a glasshouse at Aldershot when we get home', and even the German guards tiptoed around him such was the force of his personality. However, J.C.'s regime was to have little effect on me as I was to be moved on within sixteen days and all my energies were to be taken up with hard labour and trying to keep warm.

Fatigues within the Stalag consisted of barrack cleaning, collecting wood and the general tidiness of the camp area. Toilet fatigues were separate and as such were a job that had to be volunteered for, and once men had been accepted for this task the role became permanent and they were excused all other duties. Their responsibilities were the maintenance and provision of the open latrines.

Previously, following the death of the glider pilot, J.C .had requested and was granted the right to carry out a military funeral. However, the coffin provided was sub-standard and blacked with some form of dye resulting in the handling party becoming heavily stained. J.C. was furious at the lack of dignity and visited the camp commandant to complain.

During my sixteen days at Stalag XIB, we were continuously counted, fought battles with fleas and worked on arbeite kommandos (working parties) collecting wood. The arbeite kommando allocations were chosen on parade where we were required to stand in long rows five deep, the guards then walked along the front of the rows counting in fives. We always tried to stand in line with our mates so that when work was allocated or re-locations were sprung on us we would be unlikely to be separated.

On the sixteenth day at XIB we were paraded and counted in preparation to be moved away from Fallingbostel for various types of labour. The first 150 men were counted off and went to work in a sugar-beet factory, the next 150 to a city where we later learned that they were put to work digging out air-raid casualties and burying the dead. My particular arbeite was announced as 150 men for the eisenbarn, the railway, and I thought, I'll be all right there.

Monday 23 October 1944

My arbeite were moved today and marched through the camp to the showers where we were able to wash, and we were also subjected to a second delousing. Following this we were taken out of the camp and marched to the railway station to be moved once again in a cattle truck. A German family were watching from a wall as we marched past and a small girl of around 3 spat at us.

The arbeite commando that I am with are all from 1st Airborne and are made up of both glider and parachute troops. However, there are only two of us from our squadron.

Wednesday 25 October 1944

We spent two nights in the cattle van with many long halts. At one place there was an air raid and we could hear the bombing and flak guns outside. During the journey we were given a cup of water but no food and relied upon a Red Cross parcel that we had brought with us. Eventually, we arrived at our destination and the doors were unlocked and we were formed up in the station yard.

We had arrived at the village of Bad Grund in Lower Saxony. Bad Grund is situated south of Hanover among the foothills of the Harz Mountains and our journey had taken an uncomfortable 36 hours. My impressions were that the countryside was very picturesque with forest-covered hills.

Chapter 40

POW Lead Miner, Bad Grund, Lower Saxony

We were marched from the village station to what we learned on arrival to be a lead mine. We were not to be working on the railway, as I had first assumed, but were to be lead miners. There were, however, quite a few of the lads who had been moved with us that were to be detailed to work on the eisenbarn. Using Bad Grund as a base, they were taken out to work on the track and embankments of a nearby railway. Later during the winter, I was grateful not to have been selected for this work, as these lads returned to camp wet and blue with cold having had to work outdoors with inadequate clothing. At least it was warm and dry down the mine.

Already working at the mine were Russians, Ukranians, French and some Italians as forced labour, but they were not subjected to the same restrictions as ourselves and were allowed to leave the mine at night to walk to their quarters in the village. We were housed under guard in a wired off compound in an area covering several acres. Our new billets were large, two-roomed huts constructed of concrete which each held around seventy-five men. They were clean but cold. One room was used to live in and housed a large wood-burning stove for heating and cooking, while the other room was used for sleeping and was fitted with closely spaced three-tiered bunks. We were the first POWs to arrive at the mine to supplement the labour force.

Thursday 26 October 1944

The food on arrival was an improvement and appeared to be pretty plentiful after Fallingbostel. A loaf of black bread was now to be shared between four of us instead of the usual six. Fatigues were allotted similarly to those at Fallingbostel and were divided into general duties and latrine tasks. Those responsible for the latrines had to cart the soil away in tubs on a Chinese-style pole and scrub the toilet benches. Some men were content to undertake these duties on a permanent basis in preference to the general fatigues from which they were excused, following the same system as at Fallingbostel.

We elected a spokesman from among us to liaise with the Germans, as was the practice with prisoners of war. We selected a lance corporal, who then assumed the title of 'man of confidence'. Our shift patterns were morning, afternoon and evenings. The morning shift started work at 0500hr with reveille at 0430hr and finished after 9 hours work at 1400hr.

The new mine-camp hutments (our billets) didn't have any blankets on the bunks so we had no choice but to sleep in the clothes that we were standing in, that is the uniforms that we had left Britain in six weeks previously. I was still in my smock with the string-laced shoulder rip. We were issued with wooden clogs (one size) and a shirt made of a chenille-type material that stretched and lost its shape when washed. Both the clogs and shirts were to be worn at night when the Germans took away our boots and trousers to discourage escape attempts. We looked a right sight walking around our hut in these misshapen shirts which hung down to our ankles. We still managed to laugh.

Friday 27 October 1944

Today I started working down the mine on the day shift and it was not too bad. To find my way around I was issued with a hand-held carbide lamp. The carbide lamp was shaped like a normal lamp but with a naked flame which flared in front of a reflector. The flame was derived from acetylene gas which was released by a chemical reaction between calcium carbide crystals and water held in two chambers in the body of the lamp. The amount of water dripped onto the crystals was controlled by a valve that regulated the amount of gas and therefore the brightness of the flame. When working the lamps, which were our only source of light, were hung overhead on beams.

Passing into the mine I was led through a large shed where the civilian miners changed their clothes prior to starting work. We were all set to work in the clothes that we had arrived in. The shed had a high roof from which ropes were hanging down, the ends of which were secured to a rail by a padlock. The German miners secured their clothes to these ropes which were then hoisted up beyond reach to prevent them being stolen.

Beyond the shed were showers and an ultraviolet-light room which was for the sole use of the German miners. The UV light was believed to promote good health for the miners who were working underground and not gaining access to natural light. Its intention was to provide vitamin D and prevent skin disorders. It was difficult to steal the German miners' clothes but during the following months I was to sneak into the UV room whenever the opportunity arose.

The mine was quite deep with eleven levels underground. My job was to be at the rock face with the blasting kommando. I was joined by two German miners and several forced labourers, two Dutchmen, two Italians and a Ukrainian.

The blasting procedure started with ten holes being drilled into a 20ft face and then explosives were tamped in, and these were then fitted with a fuse. The fuse was lit from a carbide lamp after which we would retreat to take shelter. There was no danger of explosions from the naked flame of the carbide lamps as the mine was gas free.

The deep rumble of the explosion brought the lead–ore–bearing rock down creating clouds of thick dust. When the dust had settled we went forward and picked up the ore with our bare hands and a metal rake, manually handling it onto trays which we carried and emptied into tubs at chest height. We then pushed the tubs along the tunnels to be taken to the surface.

Working underground was hard, dangerous work and we had a common camaraderie with the other miners of the various nationalities sharing the same conditions. The German miners, who were older men, were mostly OK and hard working, although one or two were bullies. The main difference between us was that they ate better than we did and wore helmets, whereas we had to work without head protection and were often hungry during our shift.

Saturday 28 October 1944

Down the mine again. I rose at 0430hr and started work at 0500hr, finishing at 1400hr. The only food I have had is my bread ration and margarine during the 9–hour shift.

Sunday 29 October 1944

We had a change today, we were marched 5 miles to a steelworks where we spent the morning digging foundations before being marched back to camp at 1300hr.

Sunday would usually be the only day of rest that we had during the week, but it could not to be taken for granted as work parties that went under the guise of volunteering were often raised. We had no warnings of these selections, the compound gates would open and a 'You, you and you' would be commanded. A dozen men would then be marched into the forest to chop and gather wood, and although it was nice to be out, it was hard work after days down the mine. It was no use complaining that you had had a hard week. On this particular day we were marched out to dig foundations at a steelworks.

Tuesday 31 October 1944

We learned that Bad Grund is about 10 miles from Seeson. I was working the same shift as yesterday but the men woke me at 0430hr. The soup was like water and still there were no blankets. I had ersatz coffee (acorns I think) in bed and rose at 0630hr to sweep the billet. I had a slice of black bread for breakfast and then returned to bed.

We are still getting a quarter of a loaf of bread per day, a portion of margarine and two bowls of thin skilly. The lads have not had a cigarette issue since leaving Fallingbostel, which is almost two weeks ago and they are all browned off. No Red Cross parcels have been issued to date.

Wednesday 1 November 1944

Cheese has been issued, it tastes just like candle grease but I have still managed to eat it. We have been allowed to bring up the wooden offcuts from the props that are used down the mine to heat our stove in the billet. This additional fuel is supplementing the wood that is gathered from the surrounding hills by outside working parties.

Thursday 2 November 1944

The weather is getting colder and we still haven't been issued with a blanket. The French forced labour boys are saying that the town of Munster has fallen but we are doubtful. There are plenty of planes going over but we are unable to see them due to the low cloud. We know we are under the flight path of the bombers targeting Berlin and the white vapour trails that fill the sky have raised our morale and lowered that of the Germans.

The man of confidence has complained on our behalf to the German commandant and visiting Red Cross officials about the cold and our lack of blankets. Our clothes were thin and coming apart, we were still in the uniforms that we had fought in at Arnhem. We were also finding it hard to keep warm with the extremes of temperature, it was hot down the mine and very cold when we came out. Two Red Cross officials, a Swiss and a Swede, visited twice during our imprisonment, their visits were closely supervised by the Germans but we had little confidence in them.

Thursday 9 November 1944

Working at the face I was injured by a roof fall. I was partially covered in loose rock (erst) and injured my back, it was pretty painful and bleeding a little. I was taken to the surface and have had a dressing placed on it in the MI room.

I was allowed to rest on my bunk for the rest of the day and had a visit from the commandant, who spoke to me in monosyllabic English, 'Tomorrow doctor'. I had assumed a doctor was coming to see me! No such luck. The following morning a guard came to collect me with a stick and I hobbled using it, with him walking alongside, down to the local village to see the doctor. She took one look at me and said, 'On the Russian front we have hundreds of Germans worse than this ... go back to work!'. So back to the camp I hobbled with the guard alongside me, and on reaching my bunk I fell down onto it gratefully relieved to be back.

Later when rations were issued I was informed that as I was sick and unable to work I would receive only half rations. Full rations were five slices of bread and a bowl of soup, and you couldn't get much less than that. I was off sick (krank) for five days, during which time I had plenty of bed rest but very little food.

Friday 10 November 1944

Still sick with a very stiff back, and the snowfall continues. I have only had a cup of milk and two-and-a-half spoonfuls of sugar issued to last two days. I have had a new dressing applied and a pair of K.G. trousers and vest issued.*

Sunday 12 November 1944

It is still snowing. I heard rumours that rocket bombs were hitting London.

Tuesday 14 November 1944**

Yesterday Ginger Goode and another lad made an escape attempt. It was bitterly cold and snowing and they were caught within an hour. They were put into the cooler (solitary confinement) overnight and this morning they were gone, and we never saw them again. The possibility of escape was rarely discussed as a positive option, survival was our only concern. We were malnourished and too tired after our daily hard labour to contemplate it. The Allied front lines were approaching closer to us every day and liberation was a far safer prospect in our state of health. Officer camps, or offlags, were different, the officers didn't work and were better fed and had long, quiet days to plan. Schemes of escape kept them alert and helped to offset boredom and in some cases got them shot.

I have been to see the doctor in the village and have had the dressing changed again. I start back to work tomorrow. On my return down the mine I was detailed to work with an old German miner who was an infantry man during the First World War. He was known as old Willi and had a large white moustache and is a grand old fellow.

Wednesday 15 November 1944

I have been in the army for five years today and my pay will increase to 2s a day (plus parachute pay). The guards have started to lock our boots away at night to discourage any more escape attempts.

---

*   Kriegsgefangen. Both trousers and vest bore the bold K.G. lettering identifying the wearer as a POW.

**   Back in Britain, the chairmen of the LMS, Lord Royden, wrote a letter on this day from Euston station to Tom's father, Fred, expressing his sympathy for the worry that the family were experiencing at this time.

No. _b2|44.F_   _15. (PARACHU) Squadron_ Army Form B. 104 —83A.
(If replying, please quote above No.)   _(R. Troop)_

........ROYAL ENGINEERS.Record Office,

................_Brighton_................Station.

................_10 November_................19__44__

SIR ~OR MADAM~,

I have to inform you that a report has been received from the War Office to the effect that (No.)....._1898624_.......... (Rank)...._Sapper_.......... (Name)...._HICKS, Thomas S_.......... (Regiment) _ROYAL ENGINEERS (15' Parachute Sqn.)_.......... is a Prisoner of War..._in German hands_.......... ...._Stalag XI B POW No. 118259_..........

Should any other information be received concerning him, such information will be at once communicated to you.

Instructions as to the method of communicating with Prisoners of War can be obtained at any Post Office.

I am,
SIR ~OR MADAM~,
Your obedient Servant,

[signature] _RE_ _&c_ .

FoR CoL Officer in charge of Records.

IMPORTANT.—Any change of your address should be immediately notified to this Office. It should also be notified, if you receive information from the soldier above, that his address has been changed.

WT.30241/1250 500M. 9/39. KJL/8818 Gp.698/3 Forms/B.104—83A/6

On 10 November 1944 the RE Record Office wrote to inform Tom's parents that they had received confirmation that he was a prisoner of war, thirty-four days after they had been informed that he was missing.

Friday 17 November 1944

I have been paid 4 reichsmarks and 70 pfennigs by the Germans but have nowhere to spend it. Under the terms of the Geneva Convention prisoners of war that were required to carry out labour had to be paid and it was at Bad Grund that the Germans started to pay us. We were paid RM200 per month, and from this RM170 were deducted for our keep which left us with RM30.

If we broke the small porcelain burner in our carbide lamps, which was easily done, we had to pay for a replacement. When the billets were searched, as they frequently were, any cash found was confiscated as we were not allowed to save it. We also had to pay for the lorry that brought Red Cross parcels up to us from Fallingbostel, the money for which was collected in advance. If the lorry was cancelled, as it frequently was, the money was never refunded. I never had any spare money.

Saturday 18 November 1944

My bread ration was stolen today while I was asleep and boy was I hungry. Old Willi looked after me down the mine and gave me a sandwich.

By now Willi had befriended me and between us there was a degree of trust, so much so that he brought in for me a small hardback notebook and ink for my Parker pen. I in return gave him cigarettes. I was now able to copy my earlier notes from the loose paper sheets that I had been using to record my days since Arnhem. Fraternising with and providing any items for prisoners was strictly against regulations and Willi was taking a risk.

Willi's brother, Hans, was an inspector and an ardent Nazi who had a reputation for reporting any fraternisation. He was inclined to patrol the mine with an unlit lamp in order to 'snitch' on any indiscretions. Willi would often quietly say to me, 'Sshhhh … Hans' and then Hans would quietly appear out of the dark on his rounds.

Monday 20 November 1944

Today we were issued with a Canadian Red Cross parcel and have had a good feed. Mac and I are pooling our rations and making black bread and butter pudding. The recipe is black bread, ersatz margarine, raisins, sugar and coffee all fried in a pan, served with jam and dried milk reconstituted with water. It made our stomachs ache but has filled us both up.

There are rumours that a big Allied offensive has begun. Bombers are over every day now, both RAF and USAAF B17 Strato-fortresses.

The daylight bombing raids of the USAAF were to become a common sight as hundreds of bombers glinting high in the sky left white condensation trails on their route to pound targets around Berlin, Madgeberg and Hanover. By night the drone of the RAF raids steadily passed overhead flying in the same direction.

Tuesday 22 November 1944

We have been issued with two blankets and a mug. The blankets are of a thin cotton weave and give little warmth, they are also too short for our bunks, and

I am using my parachute smock at the end of my bunk to secure the blankets and keep out the draught.

For supper we made another good meal of chips, fried spam and fried bread followed by biscuits, jam and tea. The German guards are taking no chances with anyone escaping this evening, and we have had to hand in our boots and both pairs of trousers for 'safekeeping' until morning.

Saturday 25 November 1944

We were searched by the guards today and Mac had RM3 taken from him.

Monday 27 November 1944

I was working at 1400hr today. We had a real morale booster when far up in the distant sky we spotted dozens of fighter planes in a dog fight. Eventually, four were shot down and two pilots baled out. Although we had no way of telling which of the planes were ours, we hoped that it was a victory for us. The lads were milling around outside the air-raid shelter causing chaos in an attempt to delay entering so that they could watch the spiralling aircraft. The guards were going wild trying to get us in while the civilian workers were rapidly entering the other shelter, and they certainly move when the air-raid siren goes.

The RAF was over again tonight, a lovely moonlit night. There are rumours of a Red Cross parcel issue tomorrow.

Tuesday 28 November 1944

We have had quite a gala day as the rumoured Red Cross parcel has been issued, which Mac and I shared. We each had thirty-seven cigarettes and I have managed to exchange mine for a bar of chocolate. Included in our rations were jam, cheese and custard, so one of the rare days that we have had full stomachs.

Wednesday 29 November–Sunday 10 December 1944

We have been issued with a palliasse (straw mattress), made in Finland. Several fighters have passed over and one jettisoned its fuel tanks. Rations have improved but we have had no sugar for two weeks. The lads have decided that they will not be home for Christmas. Spring will see us on our way home I hope. Canadian Red Cross parcels issued, some were damp and the chocolate and raisins were bad. Big air raid has been taking place with hundreds of 'Forts' passing overhead. Slight snowfall. My boots are wearing out. Food parcels continue to arrive, some are shared and some are raffled and then shared.

Tuesday 12 December 1944

A towel has been issued. I am working on the construction of an air-raid shelter, and my hands are becoming a bit of a mess through handling the concrete. My boots are almost finished.

Wednesday 13 December 1944

An interpreter has arrived. We have been informed that we might get a parcel for Christmas. He has promised to send us letter cards from Fallingbostel so that we can write home.

Friday 15 December 1944

I have been paid RM27 and 90 pfennigs and then we were charged RM1 for a pint of Dunkle beer.* If old Ted served a pint like this in the Pack Horse at Royston, he would have been hung from his sign.

Sunday 17 December 1944

Nicht arbiete today, no work. We have been working hard down the mine recently. I have had a shower and my fortnightly shave, although my razor blade is getting blunt and my socks have little of the foot left. We had a decent meal tonight of roast meat, boiled potatoes, carrots and gravy and also managed a bread pudding and two pints of beer. I also borrowed a book from the camp library. This consists of a handful of well-worn books that have been read many times over; some were provided by the Red Cross and others by a local German lady.

Tuesday 19 December 1944

There are rumours today of a big German offensive with a parachute drop. The civilians are very elated but it has had the reverse effect on us and there are plenty of bad tempers around. Mac and I are saving two slices of bread a day in anticipation of making a Christmas pudding.

---

* Dunkle is the German word for dark and was used as a general description for dark beer.

Back Home

At about this time Tom's father, Fred, received a letter from Captain Eric Mackay RE, now back in Britain following his escape from Holland. The villagers of Donington had collected a sum of £130 when they became aware of the disaster that had befallen the 1st Parachute Squadron at Arnhem. The money was collected as a 'token of their regard and affection' for the sappers that had been based among them prior to the Arnhem operation. Captain Mackay stated that the squadron's survivors had asked that their portion of the money be given to those who were prisoners, and this numbered over a 100. He then gave suggestions of how this money could be spent and asked to be informed of any news that Tom's father might receive of the POWs, as the squadron survivors were eager to hear of their friends. News could come from a variety of sources, the Red Cross, Ministry of Defence, German radio or POW letters forwarded from Germany via the Red Cross.

*

This was first news that we had of the Ardennes offensive, which became known as the Battle of the Bulge. The Germans thrust into the US front line through the Ardennes region of Belgium, France and Luxembourg with several panzer armies. Following initial successes, the German miners were cock-a-hoop and believed that the tide had turned. There was much singing down the mine with the exuberant ringing of the mine-shaft bells, but of course it had the opposite effect on us.

Wednesday 20 December 1944

We have been issued with letter cards to write home. I have repaired my boots with belting. My neck keeps hurting, it must be the shrapnel that is still in there. Still no parcels but we have enough potatoes to see us over Christmas.

Christmas Eve 1944

The weather has turned bitterly cold over the past few days. We have not had a food parcel issued for two weeks and have given up hope of receiving one for Christmas, the lads are very disappointed. I have had a hot shower and have eaten fried bread and chips for breakfast. We all shared a couple of barrels of Dunkle beer which was very weak and tasted like shandy. Mac and I made two Christmas puddings from the bread ration that we have been saving. There was no use hanging up our stockings tonight so I lay in bed and ate raw turnip and read *Mein Kampf*.* Finally, I lay there and thought of home.

---

*   *Mein Kampf* (*My Struggle*) was written by Adolf Hitler in 1925 and is partly autobiographical and partly political theory, expounding Hitler's national socialist ideology.

Christmas Day 1944

I woke up at 0930hr and breakfasted on turnip. We had a short Roman Catholic service and then went for a stroll around the compound while some of the boys played football. For dinner we had potatoes, soup and a cup of beer. In the afternoon we watched the Italian and French play football followed by soup for tea. For supper we had two bread puddings and a few roast potatoes.

Tuesday 26 December 1944

The guards searched our billet while we were out and took Mac's knife. Fortunately, I had hidden my diary in the latrine. We try to bribe the guards when we have a surplus of cigarettes for the items that we need. Once they have accepted the cigarettes they are easier to persuade, however, most are reluctant as they are frightened of the repercussions of being found out. I have managed to obtain some ink.

Saturday 30 December 1944

A surprise today, we were issued with tinned milk, cheese, treacle and jam. It's snowing again. Rumours persist of a big offensive.*

Sunday 31 December 1944

No work today or tomorrow. It is still snowing and there must be about 6in outside. Fortresses were over today and the RAF is over tonight, and we could hear bombs detonating in the distance. I stayed up late for the new year and the lads sang 'Auld Lang Syne'. I wondered what the folks at home were doing and hoped that the new year would be a happy one.

Wednesday 3 January 1945

A total of seven letters arrived today but I'm out of luck. I haven't received one for four months. RAF were over again today. Washed my clothes without soap. It's snowing outside.

Monday 8 January 1945

Meat paste again. I wrote my fifth letter home. The guards patrol our compound outside the wire, pacing between the sentry boxes, and being older

---

* On 3 January 1945 the US counter offensive was to begin in the Ardennes salient.

men they are feeling the cold, shuffling and stamping around to keep warm. We have been having some sport by shouting out to them from the shelter of our billets, 'Come on in and get warm, you silly old buggers.'

Thursday 11 January–Saturday 20 January 1945

A Nazi general has inspected our billets. I have swapped two cigarettes for a new razor blade. Nazi officers have been at the camp trying to recruit the forced labour men into the SS. I have been paid RM30 and 30 pfennigs. Rumours around the camp are that the Russians are advancing in our direction. Jack was taken to Fallingbostel hospital today in a terrible state being unable to walk.

Monday 22 January 1945

The Lance Corporal has gone again to the station to collect the food parcels from Fallingbostel. We have been charged RM1 and two cigarettes each for the lorry but it is well worth it. A month's supply of parcels has arrived including an issue of twelve cigarettes each and everyone is in good spirits. I have traded my cigarettes for chocolate. This morning I have been down the mine at 0500hr, and I have also managed to wash my clothes. I am not going to bed hungry tonight thanks to the Red Cross.

Tuesday 23 January 1945

The lads were up at 0400hr this morning, eating! The Lance Corporal has been to the station again to collect the Fallingbostel supplies and has returned with overcoats and wooden slippers. The overcoats were from some theatre company's wardrobe and have been the cause of much hilarity, in fact we have been rolling around laughing. They must have been used for the 'Student Prince' or something and have great gaudy epaulettes in a variety of colours and sizes. Some were ankle length and one was bright blue, but we put them on and have been laughing ever since. The Germans, however, were indifferent to our humour as they are to most of the things that we find funny.

We had another good feed today and I managed to exchange some tobacco for a loaf of bread. The loaf was shared between four of us.

Wednesday 24 January 1945

Old Willi gave me some redcurrants and a piece of apple tart, which reminds me of home. The German miners' morale is now very low and many have been sullen and quiet.

News From the Rest of Europe

The German civilians and camp guards had every reason to be contemplating the future. Despite the Nazi propaganda promising the development of new super weapons, news of their army's reverses was filtering through. In the West the Americans had defeated what was to be the last German tank offensive in the Ardennes at the Battle of the Bulge. The 'bulge' had been squeezed out with the link-up of the US 1st and 3rd Armies on 16 January 1945. Preparations were now being made to enter Germany.

In the East the Russians were advancing on a broad front through Hungary and Poland. Budapest had been encircled by 19 December 1944, Russian troops had entered Warsaw on 11 January 1945 and Cracow had been taken on 19 January 1945. Fleeing civilians and wounded soldiers were bringing home to Germany alarming tales of the barbarity of the advancing Russians.

In the air the last major Luftwaffe attack on forward Allied airfields in Belgium and France had been made on 1 January. Since that date Allied aircraft had been moving over Germany with increasing freedom. German cities were being pounded by the heavy bombers of the USAAF by day and the RAF by night.

Life in the POW camps continued anxiously with both the prisoners and guards hungry for news as they tried to separate fact from rumour and propaganda, with both sides having very different interests.

*

Friday 26 January 1945

Another Red Cross parcel has been issued, this time from Canada. We will now be content for the rest of the week.

Sunday 28 January 1945

No work today. I had a mug of tea in bed and a lay in until 1000hr. We have developed a new dish, biscuits soaked in water and then fried in margarine and served hot with jam, they're just like flap jacks. All the boys are busy with hobbies, making aeroplanes, ships and badges. Several are entering the gin trade (from potato peelings) and are constructing a still. I have been making mugs from tin cans again. The most popular hobby has to be carving odd bits of metal. Knives if found were always confiscated by the guards. Badges were made by melting down pfennigs and pouring the molten metal into a sand mould to make a casting. The patterns were usually our cap badges.

I have sent a letter card to my friends the Yarringtons and also completed a second radio message card.*

---

*   Prisoners were allowed to complete a card with a short message for transmission over German radio. It was probably this message which was broadcast at 0200hr on 25 February.

Tuesday 30 January 1945

The snow is pretty thick outside. The Lance Corporal set out earlier for the Fallingbostel supplies but the lorry broke down, but they are going to try again later. I have been reading the *Camp and Signal*, Nazi propaganda.*

Wednesday 31 January 1945

Beer has been issued but this time they can't give it away it's so bad. One of the lads has gone sick and the doctor has given him herbs to make tea to relieve his kidneys, but the lads are smoking them.

Thursday 1 February 1945

The snow is thawing and beer has been issued again. We were searched by the guards as we came back from the mine today. One of the lads had his tins of food punctured by their bayonets.** I had my diary next to my stomach and it was nearly discovered.

Friday 2 February–Friday 9 February 1945

Canadian parcels have been issued. One of the lads found a Canadian girl's address in his parcel. The RAF are over again in great strength, and the lads are in good spirits and have been singing around the fire. Been under the UV ray again. On early mornings again and up at 0500hr. Three of our guards have been sent to the front and have been replaced with Home Guard soldiers (Landschutzen). Bread ration has been cut to five men sharing a loaf which is now to be issued every three days. A New Zealand Red Cross parcel has been issued, all the tins that were drawn have been punctured by the guards. We had to give RM10 each to pay for the lorry to bring in the parcels – I think we must own it by now!

Saturday 10 February 1945

I have had a good hot shower and managed to get under the UV ray again. Bombers have been over and the bombing shook our billets. I have exchanged eight cigarettes for a tin of coffee and a further six for a tin of sardines. It's a good job we have a parcel (and that I don't smoke).

Possibly the Germans did this as a propaganda exercise to undermine civilian morale at home.

* The *Camp and Signal* was a Nazi newspaper that was printed for POWs to read. The features were propaganda and mis-information. It was never taken seriously and was read as every other piece of print was read, solely to pass the time.

** Tins were routinely punctured by the guards to prevent the hoarding of food, which they considered would be necessary for any escape.

Sunday 11 February 1945

I have been working down the mine again at 0500hr. It's been a hard day and between us we have filled 103 tubs. I came up at 1200hr and had a good dinner of potatoes, turnips, peas and a tin of calf's tongue. The peas and tongue came from the parcel. It was the first time I have used a knife and fork since capture. I have written letter cards to the Lloyds and Talbots.* I had treacle and a kind of paste for supper, it was fish or meat, I couldn't tell which.

Monday 12 February 1945

I am on the same shift at 0500hr and was intending to have yesterday's paste again, however it smelled so bad that I have given it away, but only because we had some jam left.

Tuesday 13 February 1945

Our parcel is nearly finished now and we are down to sugar and paste. There are no cigarette papers available and the boys are making them out of cement bags. The RAF is going over.**

Wednesday 14 February 1945

There is a big air raid on tonight and all the lights are out in the billet. The naked flames of our miners' lamps are coming in useful and it looks like Dante's Inferno inside the hut with the flicker of the flames, the shadows and the smoke.

Saturday 17 February 1945

I have had a shave and a hot shower. We have music in the billet from our new acquisition, a gramophone, which has been donated by a German lady in a nearby village. We have had a whip round collecting any surplus money that we could find for her.

I have exchanged five cigarettes for half a loaf of bread but then I lost half of my pay playing cards. I managed to exchange twelve cigarettes for a bar of chocolate.

---

*   Friends, the Lloyds of Pertersfield and the Talbots of Widnes.

**   The RAF was also over Dresden. A force of over 800 RAF and US bombers created a firestorm in which many thousands of civilians died.

Sunday 18 February 1945

No work today and I was able to lie in. We have had a boxing match in the billet with Mac having three rounds with Col, using cigarettes as the prize. We had a good dinner of meat, potatoes, turnip, gravy and semolina, but it was our only meal today. This afternoon we had a football match and beat a combined Dutch and French team 5–0, then we played the next room and I sneaked one in as we won 3–1. There was a raised area of ground outside the camp upon which the forced labourers played football, and occasionally they played our POW team and we were allowed out under guard to watch. Also among the spectators were some of the forced labour families and the girls among them were of particular interest.

Monday 19 February 1945

On at 0500hr. Fortresses are knocking hell out of some place and they have been over in strength all day. I have been reading the *Camp and Signal* again.

Wednesday 21 February 1945

More mail has arrived but there is still none for me. I have been advanced ten cigarettes. I am getting a bit browned off with this gramophone playing the same old tunes. Read the camp newspaper, 'Woe is my comrades', poor propaganda.

Thursday 22 February 1945

A heavy air raid has been taking place at Seeson. Large formations of Liberator bombers have been going over with a fighter escort. The railway yards were the target and we could feel the vibration from the explosions. We were shepherded into the shelters. Our latest food parcel is almost finished. We have had a battledress blouse issued.

Friday 23 February 1945

More large formations of Fortresses have been going over again. We have been issued with the elusive Christmas food parcel, one for each of us and we have been eating like kings. Bill and Fred are sat at the table like a couple of pigs, full of Christmas cake.

Radio Messages

In the early hours at 0200hr German Radio Bremen broadcast brief messages from a long list of prisoners, and among them was one written by Tom. The broadcaster read from a previously completed radio card. The message was addressed to his parents and sister stating that he was in Stalag XIB and was well. In Britain the message was picked up by people that routinely tuned into the station listening for news of their loved ones and prisoners in general. Complete strangers, twelve of these people kindly wrote the same day to Tom's parents stating that they had heard his name mentioned, with several writing down the message verbatim.

*

Saturday 24 February 1945

Tiger has shaved his moustache off. We are living well off the parcel. I have sewn some wings on my blouse and exchanged a tin of pork stuffing for a tin of Nestlé milk. I have also managed to have a shave and shower and a few minutes under the UV ray.

Sunday 25 February 1945

There was no work today so I didn't get up until 0800hr. Mac cooked breakfast, a tin of beans, fried bread, honey, Christmas cake and tea. More football today and the lads inflicted a 5–1 defeat on a combined team of forced labour men that had been assembled from Dutch, Italians, French and Belgians. We paid more attention to the female spectators than the match. Dinner was good.

We had boxing this afternoon and some good fights. Mac fought Col dressed as a woman and we had a really good laugh, and even the German civilians were laughing for a change. We have had a supper of stewed steak, potatoes, Christmas pudding and custard. The Germans issued us with semolina and tea.

A rumour is going round that Turkey has declared war on Germany.*

Monday 26 February 1945

A new German unter-offizer has arrived and will be the new commandant at Bad Grund. He is disabled and is missing an arm and an eye having been wounded on the eastern front fighting the Russians.

---

* This information was both correct and recent. Turkey declared war on Germany on 23 February 1945, only two days before this diary entry. Turkey, however, had no intention of fighting on the Allied side and declared war only as a political expedient to allow it to join the proposed United Nations as a founder member following the now inevitable defeat of Germany.

Wednesday 28 February 1945

The billet is full of empty tins, a lovely sight together with the fog of cigarette smoke in the room. Tonight we will be having a sing-song with an accordion borrowed from the Germans.

Saturday 3 March 1945

It has been snowing for the last few days but it is very thick on the ground. Fortresses and Liberator bombers have been over again and it would be easier to say when they are not over. I have had a shave, shower and a few minutes under the UV. There is no work tomorrow so I have stayed up late and played dominoes. I have been getting browned off with the gramophone as there are now only two records left. Burberry took the locking ring off the spare spring and it shot across the room and nearly took Col's head off, which everyone found very funny apart from Col.

An interpreter has been reading to us from a German newspaper. He said that the Russians have been shooting prisoners of war when they have liberated a laager (prison compound). He also said that some English lads have been fighting for the Germans rather than be relieved by the Russians. They must

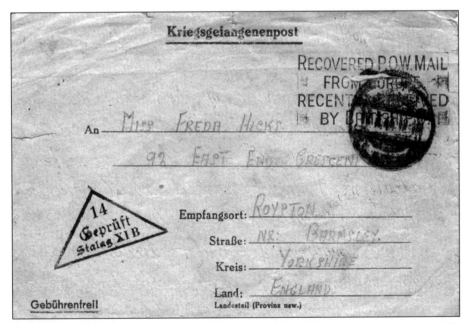

This was the eighth letter home to Tom's sister, Freda. Written in pencil, it still survives and is one of the two that reached home out of the many he sent. The letter although undated states, 'it is exactly 6 months since we dropped'.

think that we fall off Christmas trees if they think we would believe that. But forms were made available for any volunteers among us who wished to apply to join the SS to fight the Russians.

Sunday 4 March 1945

No work today. I had breakfast in bed which consisted of bacon and egg (powdered), fried black bread, syrup, margarine and tea. All we need now is the *Sunday Express*. I'm now using shaving soap to wash with.

Another letter card has been issued which will be the ninth one that I have sent home. It's snowing again outside so the football is 'kaput'. I'm getting a bit thin. We are having another sing-song tonight with the accordion. We have pinned up all the food-tin labels on the wall today and it has given us a real splash of colour. I have had my boots repaired and have also handed in my trousers for repair. The camp has its own cobbler and repair shops. Our socks have also disintegrated and the Germans have issued us with small square pieces of cloth to replace them. We were told that these were standard issue to the Russians and Germans. The idea was to place the foot in the centre of the cloth and to fold the ends in, the foot was then stuffed into your boot.

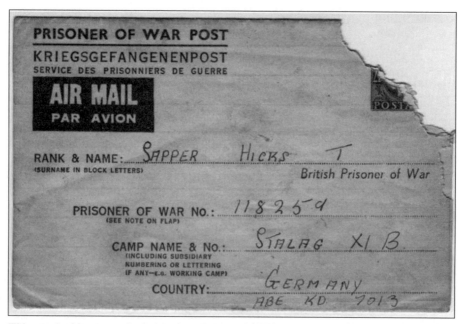

This standard letter was issued to the relatives of POWs by the Red Cross to enable them to write to the camps. Not all arrived. Unfortunately the corner of this letter and King George's head have been nibbled by a German mouse.

Monday 5–Thursday 8 March 1945

On at 0500hr as usual. Fortresses over again. I paid RM10 towards the cost of the lorry to collect our Red Cross parcels. I came up from the mine and found Jerry searching our beds and clothes. They punctured all the food tins that they could find but didn't unearth my diary. The RAF is over. Rumours floating around the camp but you cannot believe any of them. Snow is still hanging about on the surrounding hills. Fortresses have been going over for 2 hours. Crushed my finger at work.

Friday 9 March 1945

A Canadian food parcel has been issued between Mac and myself and it contains both soap and soap powder. I have been able to have my first good wash in days. Jerry has again punctured all the tins that have been issued, the rest we have left in the stores.

I have exchanged ten cigarettes for half a tin of dried milk, three for a tin of cheese and six for half a bar of chocolate. The loaf of bread issue is still being divided between five men every second night.

A propaganda leaflet has been issued telling how the Russians will overrun the world and it is asking for volunteers to fight them again, the Germans are becoming very concerned at the Russian advance.*

Saturday 10 March 1945

I have had a hot shower and a few minutes under the UV ray, Jerry will catch me at this shortly. We have had another sing-song with the accordion around the fire.

Sunday 11 March 1945

Working today until 1400hr. I have washed all my clothes in the wash house and have had a good dinner by camp standards, but we are only having one meal today. The Red Cross parcel has saved us again or we would have had nothing.

---

*   Advancing on a broad front through Poland, the Russians encircled Danzig (now Gdańsk) on 15 February 1945. This was followed by the capture of Poznan on 23 February and by 5 March they were approaching the German border at Stetin (now Szczecin). In the West the US 1st Army captured Cologne on 5 March and entered Bonn three days later on 8 March.

Two British prisoners have arrived in camp, having been marched from a camp in Poland to prevent them being liberated by the Russians. They have told us how their camp magazine (stores) of over 2,000 Red Cross parcels was looted by German refugees fleeing the Russians.

The two lads can't get a minute to themselves as our lads want all the 'gen' on the situation on the eastern front. I wrote a letter card to the Walls (family friends) today, I could just do with a letter from home.

Monday 12 March 1945

I'm working down on the eleventh floor. The mine is very hot and you sweat standing still. I came back up at 2200hr.

Five of the boys are going back to Fallingbostel tomorrow, two of them are sick. Frank is going the same way as Jack Wheeler with a kind of paralysis.* The other three lads are going back to the cooler because they have been caught 'doing a dodge'. They were going to work with the afternoon shift and then avoiding work by returning with the morning shift, a crafty dodge if you can swing it, but they have done it a bit too often.

Tuesday 13 March 1945

A great surprise, a large batch of mail has arrived and there is a letter for me from home postmarked 3 December. Dad has written that they haven't received any mail from me so far. Mac has received three letters, one of which is from his brother who has written that he has seen photographs in the newspaper of some of our lads who made it home from Arnhem. Lieutenant Simpson, Chick Weir and Johnny Humphries are mentioned.

Dad says in his letter that he sent me a parcel on 14 December, although I haven't received it. Also, that poor old Bill Yarrington was killed on 10 December.** Reg and some of the other lads have not received any mail and are very disappointed. The bread ration has been cut again, five men to a loaf for two nights and four men to a loaf for one night.

Wednesday 14 March 1945

It has been a beautiful clear day with lots of Fortresses flying over very high in the sky leaving their vapour trails. There is a raid on again tonight and I

---

* Jack Wheeler started suffering leg pains and was wasting away. His fellow prisoners made him a crutch but he became too weak to use it and he died in the makeshift hospital inside Fallingbostel.

** This was later found to be untrue.

can hear the RAF going over; outside there is plenty of silver paper floating down.*

Thursday 15 March 1945

Another nice day and I been have sat outside reading in the sun, I can do with a lot more of this weather. The nights are now getting shorter and this will suit our armies. I heard the RAF over again, when I came up out of the mine several searchlights were flashing around the sky, which is the first time I have seen searchlights around these parts. One of our planes circled around in flames and crashed but there was plenty of time for our boys to bail out, which I hope they did. Parcel 'fertig' roll on tomorrow.

Friday 16 March 1945

A Canadian parcel has been issued with fifteen German cigarettes. I have exchanged ten for half a tin of condensed milk and left a further two tins in the store. I have broken my badly battered toothbrush, and I will have to get a replacement quick.

There seems to be some doubt over what type of plane crashed last night, some say it had two engines and some say four. The local patter is that the crew bailed out and the German miners have brought some pieces of the wreckage to work.

Saturday 17 March 1945

There is a change in the weather today and it is raining. The Lance Corporal has returned from the station with six new men from Fallingbostel, conditions are reported to be pretty bad up there with eight men sharing a 1-kilo loaf of bread. They are also sleeping two to a bed and haven't any Red Cross parcels left.

Sunday 18 March 1945

No work. I made the breakfast of fried spam and bread, had a shave and a hot shower and a few minutes under the UV ray. One of the boys told me that Sam Dobbie and Bulham Brooks are in Fallingbostel camp hospital. The latest 'gen' is that Jerry Strachan, the 2nd Battalion's RSM, and fifty NCOs

---

*   This was dropped by the Allied bombers to confuse the German radar.

have escaped to the Russian lines and are now in Britain.* I wrote my tenth letter home.

Monday 19 March 1945

On at 0500hr again down on the eleventh floor. The German guards have now put an Alsatian dog on a chain outside the compound gate. Some of the boys are preparing billets for blind SS men down in the village and have stolen the guard dog's oats as they walked past. We are making oat cakes tonight.

Tuesday 20 March 1945

A nice day and the weather is improving. We heard the roar of aircraft engines after skilly and all dashed out to have a look. There were about twelve fighters circling around and we thought they were German until they dived and dropped bombs a short distance away. They then proceeded to fly very low strafing with cannon. Initially, we thought we saw German black-cross markings but they were in fact our own black and white invasion stripes. The US star stood out very plain but we haven't heard what their target was as yet. This will shake the locals. I expect our mine may get a bashing now that the light nights are coming. All the lads are eating oat cakes regularly now, woof woof!

Wednesday 21 March 1945

We have heard that yesterday's target was a train in the next village. The cannon fire destroyed the engine and several wagons, some of which were carrying ammunition. A bomb also fell in our village (Bad Grund) but did little damage.

The skilly was poor today but we noticed that the watch dog had a full bowl, but we shouldn't grumble as we have been having our fair share of his oats and biscuits.

The guards have been changed but we haven't seen them yet. A floodlight was put in the compound five months ago but they dare not switch it on in case it is seen by the RAF. We have no news of the war today.

Thursday 22 March 1945

---

* Rumours were constant and rife and not always true or accurate. Unfortunately, Bulham had been killed at Arnhem some eight months previously. The Jerry Strachan story was also untrue but nevertheless served to raise morale.

A beautiful day and I have spent the afternoon sitting outside in the sun watching vapour trails in the sky again. Some of the new guards have taken over and I have seen better specimens playing bowls in the park. The tobacco shortage is acute, and seven of the boys have been turning out their pockets and have succeeded in finding enough tobacco to make a flying kipper which provided one puff each.*

Friday 23 March 1945

The Lance Corporal has returned empty handed and the lads will be back to smoking tea leaves soon. It is another nice day and I am sitting out in the sun watching four fighters pass over high in the sky. A Canadian parcel has been issued but again we have no soap. I have just enough left to last to the weekend.

We have made some porridge from the dog oats and also some more oat cakes and they are very tasty. The latest recipe is one dog biscuit soaked in water for 48 hours, fried and served hot with margarine and jam. The RAF is over as usual.

Saturday 24 March 1945

We have summer weather again and some of the boys have been sunburned. I've had a shower with a tiny piece of shaving soap and also my weekly shave, with my razor blade lasting quite well.

A new feldwebel (German CSM) has arrived. The skilly was carrot again. The weather is still beautiful and should suit the progress of our armies. I played dominoes until midnight.

Sunday 25 March 1945

No work today. The weather is once again fine and as we sit outside talking in the sunshine we can hear bombs in the distance. After dinner we went up to the football field which is on high ground and commands a good view of the valley. The hills around are wooded and stretch for as far as the eye can see. A large cloud of smoke was hanging on the horizon marking the last US air raid. There was quite a crowd of us watching the game together with some French prisoners from another laager, forced labour men and some husky looking Russian girls. All of us are slightly sunburned, we returned to the laager at 1700hr.

---

* A flying kipper was a short stump of a cigarette made by the desperate method of emptying out pocket linings and gathering loose shreds of tobacco, which were then rolled and the resulting kipper was passed around.

It's very hot in the billet tonight so we have been up late playing dominoes as we will be able to lay in tomorrow. My bunk is shaking like a leaf as Bob is up above bug hunting again, and dead specimens are falling down on me.

Monday 26 March 1945

Up at 0900hr to a nice day and I have been able to read in the sunshine. Fred and Snowy have taken their bunks outside and have started a major offensive against the bugs and they're making a great slaughter. Six planes flew low over the camp this morning and we believed them to be USAAF Thunderbolts. Five of our divisions are rumoured to have been dropped near Essen and the lads are now giving the war a month.

Tuesday 27 March 1945

The parcel is getting low and I am now washing only once a day with scraps of soap and have taken to cleaning my teeth with a handkerchief and salt. I have only one pair of well-patched socks left.

Wednesday 28–Saturday 31 March 1945

The fine weather continues. Fortresses and Liberator bombers have been overhead all morning. Canadian parcel has been issued but there is no soap inside. Rumours are flying around, one of which is that our army is only 50 miles away. Rumours are coming in hourly and the latest is that Allied paratroops have been dropped near Hanover. Our army is reported to be advancing fast. A bottle of 'lemonade' has been issued. The lemonade was in fact a sparkling mineral water, but we called it lemonade because it was the only clear fizzy drink that we knew of. We had previously seen it before in a store down the mine. This occurred when we were working in a tunnel backfilling the spoil. The Germans did not move their spoil to the surface as we tend to do in Britain, they backfill old tunnels with it and then brick off the entrances. This particular day we were unsupervised and a side wall had collapsed revealing a store room entered from an adjacent tunnel. Peering into the store, we noticed stacked crates of this 'bottled lemonade'. It is extremely hot down the mine and we helped ourselves to this peculiar drink as we worked, but then fearing some sort of retribution if it was noticed that some of it was missing we peed in the bottles and replaced them in the crates. We then filled in the hole with rubble and backfilled past it. Maybe this was why the Germans started issuing it to us when they found that some of it didn't taste too good!

Sunday 1 April 1945

Easter Sunday. I was up at 0900hr as it was my turn to make breakfast, there was no fire lit so we forced a bit of cold spam down. I had a shower and shave using Snowy's soap powder. Dinner was not too bad but we are having only one meal today and are saving a few potatoes for tonight.

The weather has turned cold and is inclined to rain, but we all trooped up to the football field to watch our team play the Italians. The first half was not too good as our backs scored an own goal.

The second half was better and our boys did everything but score. Just 5 minutes from time their goalkeeper butted one of our forwards and the referee awarded us a penalty from which Woofe scored. Then the Ities played true to form and appealed to the ref but he remained firm, so they all walked off the field.

We played dominoes in the billet tonight and I wrote my eleventh letter home and I am hoping that I will be there before it arrives. We have no work tomorrow so I will stay up late and read *The Moon and Sixpence*.

Our armies are not here yet. The unter officer who lost his arm in Yugoslavia has been up with us nearly all evening, he is a good sport and has a rare sense of humour for a German. The bombers are over and all the lights are out.

Monday 2 April 1945

No work today, but we couldn't go to the football field due to the weather. Dinner was not too bad but we have had only one meal and are hungry once again. Mac and I have saved the potatoes for our supper. We were up at the football field after dinner but it was very cold with the wind and rain on and off. Our team beat the forced labour team 3–0.

The weather has cleared up and the clock has been put forward 1 hour so it is still pretty light even at 2000hr. All the boys are outside and we can hear the faint rumble of gunfire, I wonder.

Tuesday 3 April 1945

I heard gunfire again this morning at about 0300hr and a plane flying low. Several miners are noticeably away from the mine. The weather is rainy again, fighters are flying around and we have been issued with another bottle of mineral water!

Wednesday 4 April 1945

Nothing much doing today. I can't believe the rumours, the latest being that US troops are in Hanover.* I hope they don't move us from here.

The Germans have been reading out the news to us. They believe that their troops are hindering the Allied advance.

Our parcel is almost finished. There has been a heavy force of bombers over and we heard a stick of heavy bombs go down. Several fighters were flying low.

Thursday 5 April 1945

Rumours are still coming in, Reuters has nothing on this place. A big German convoy has been passing through Bad Grund heading East. Lorries are passing towing one or more trucks. There were 500 prisoners (not Allied soldiers) also marching in the same direction, and 42 local men have left the village for military training.

Friday 6 April 1945

A black day for some of us, but others had more luck as a batch of mail has arrived. There was none for me, but I can't complain as I received a letter from home a few weeks ago. Mac received one and Reg received his first.**

Parcels were also issued today. Mac, Curly, Snowy and I are sharing an English Invalide and a Canadian parcel, what a game we had dividing them between us. There are now no more parcels left in the stores. The Lance Corporal could not go to collect Fallingbostel-supplied parcels as the roads are full of transport, tanks and guns. The burning question is will we or won't we be relieved.†

---

*   The US 9th Army was not to take Hanover until 10 April, and this was some 40 miles north of Bad Grund. There was real concern at the time that the retreating and regrouping SS troops were moving at random and would be particularly vindictive to POWs due to the way that the war was progressing.

** Even at this late stage in the war with all the confusion and disruption in Germany mail was still arriving after many months in transit.

†   The Invalide Red Cross parcel was formulated for ill or wounded men and contained a small proportion of additional luxuries such as Horlicks, chocolate and condensed milk.

Chapter 41

The March to Liberation, 7 April 1945

Saturday 7 April 1945

There was great excitement down the mine when Jerry (German overseer) came dashing down and ordered everyone to stop work and leave immediately for the surface. The guards were rushing around in an agitated state with a great sense of urgency. When we emerged from below ground we didn't know what to think amid all the activity but everything pointed to a march. Our billet was in uproar as the lads began tearing up blankets with which to make haversacks to carry the scraps of food and what few possessions we had. I fashioned one out of my pillow and made a terrible mess as I dumped its filling onto the floor.

Outside the civilian miners were anxiously standing around and some were beginning to leave. The forced labour men were also standing by ready to move like us. But the command did not come, skilly was issued but for once I was not hungry being far too excited! Three Red Cross parcels were raffled off and Mac and I won a bar of chocolate and a tin of salmon. We packed them away in our haversack with our raw onions, carrots, potatoes and yesterday's dog-biscuit pie.

We were still standing to when several USAAF P38 fighters flew overhead and commenced strafing beyond the camp. We were ordered to the shelter for an hour before returning to the billet. There was still no sign that we were to move out. The billet floor was a real mess with all our unwanted kit, pillowcase contents and shredded blankets amid a sea of straw from shredded palliasse. We eventually sat down among it all and ate the sandwiches of black bread that we had cobbled together for our march.

We observed eight Mirauders fly over and drop their bombs nearby with no opposition; their fighter escorts were flying around strafing the nearby hillsides.

The excitement and urgency subsided – we are not moving tonight. I have remade my bed and unpacked. We will have to go steady with our rations with the uncertainty of a long march ahead. Outside it is a lovely clear night but rather quiet, after all the excitement I can't quite make it all out. Unable to sleep, we played dominoes until eventually going to bed.

Sunday 8 April 1945

Another day dawns, it's misty and will be warm later on. We stand around waiting for news. They say that there is still plenty of traffic on the road and that nearby Seeson is being evacuated. Our aircraft have been over all day. There is still no sign of a march.

Jerry says that we, along with thousands of other POWs, are to be marched to the US lines. I don't believe a word of it myself and it has probably been put around to maintain order, but some of our lads do.

A column of Allied POWs has arrived after being force marched from a camp in Poland ahead of the advancing Russians. Spurred on by their guards, they have been on the move for many days and walked several hundred miles. They have arrived in a very rundown state. There are many nationalities among them and all are dressed in rags and tatters. Among them are British, Canadian, Kiwi and Australian POWs. All are starving hungry. I have never seen our lads in such terrible condition, they were comparable to the Russian prisoners we had seen at Fallingbostel. They looked like walking skeletons, emaciated with prominent bones, I never thought I would see men like this, and I wish I had a camera to record the moment as no pen can capture the scene. The Germans have something to answer for.

We were so concerned at their state that we gave them the bits of bread that we had been saving to make bread puddings, together with any other scraps that we could find. They have even been scraping out the tins that we have thrown on the rubbish heap and we don't leave much.

This evening we have been looking after them, helping them out and washing their feet. We have also given them our beds. I am doubling up with Mac and most of the other lads are doing the same. All our lads have rallied to help and nearly all our rations have been unpacked and given over to them. We couldn't eat when these lads were so hungry.

The new lads have been washing and shaving and trying to catch up and get themselves clean. We have been trying to make them as comfortable as possible. The billet is a shambles and among the chaos we are cooking over our carbide lamps. The latest news is that the Americans are now 7 miles away. I hope so.

Monday 9 April 1945

We were up at 0600hr with our kit packed. The march was on, the weather was fine and had the makings of a nice day to start. The guards who came in yesterday with the new boys left this morning leaving them behind and they will be moving out with us. There are around 300 of us in total.

Our column marched out from the camp followed by three horse and carts which were to be used for picking up those who dropped out. We hadn't walked very far when some of our weaker lads began to fall by the wayside and were placed on the carts, but as the march progressed the carts began to fill up with guards.

The roads were very busy with a lot of the vehicles moving in our direction. We were occasionally forced off the road as a company of fast-moving troops headed in the opposite direction. Heads turned glaring at us as they passed by.

Back on the road, we were walking alongside SS troops on bicycles who were not looking very happy. There were also many young boys riding by with two anti-tank rockets tied to the cross bar of their cycles. All were dressed in new camafurers (fur-lined smocks) and they were laughing and shouting as if it were some sort of adventure. I thought that they would soon be changing their tune when they met the approaching Shermans.

There were still younger boys around who couldn't have been more than 10 or 11 years old in Hitler Youth uniforms, all wearing the bright-red Nazi armbands.

As the march progressed, the guards began hitting the lads with the butts of their rifles and more of them were falling out and sitting by the roadside. We passed by two stationary Tiger tanks, one with a broken track and the other with some sort of engine trouble but their crews paid no attention to us. Behind us there was the sound of heavy gunfire and bombing.

We were directed off the main roads and into the lanes. The countryside through which we were marching was still very hilly and wooded. The weather remained fine but there were no feelings of 'It's good to be out', only a pervading anxiety about how vulnerable we were, unarmed and malnourished among an unpredictable enemy. We eventually arrived at a barn where we stopped for the night.

Tuesday 10 April 1945

I had a good night's sleep in the barn before we moved out again on yet another beautiful day. The guards escorting us were increasingly edgy and uncertain, and several times we were halted to avoid meeting retreating columns of the German army. The very real fear was that they might open fire upon both us and our guards.

We were also concerned about our own roaming fighter planes that had been reported to be shooting up columns of troops on the road. They seemed unable to distinguish between German and POW columns from the air and both us and the guards were keeping our eyes on the sky.

As we arrived at the German town of Goslar, we heard two huge explosions behind us from where a pall of black smoke began rising into the air. The rumours in our column were that the Americans were close behind and we started to walk slower. The column was strung out over a mile and as we

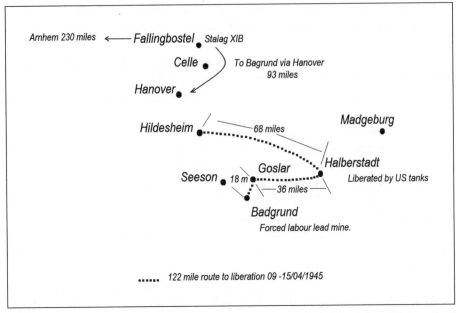

This map shows the location of Fallingbostel POW camp and Bad Grund forced Labour lead mine in Lower Saxony Germany. It also shows the route to liberation.

shambled into Goslar we were met by the sight of numerous Red Cross flags hanging from the windows and rooftops of the houses.*

There was still plenty of German transport on the roads that was moving in our direction, one truck towing three became a regular sight. Many of the retreating troops seemed to be on bicycles, including the officers, and it appeared that in order to have a car they needed to be at least a colonel. The young boys were still passing us on their bicycles with their anti–tank rockets and some of them were being organised to dig in at the side of the road.

Eventually, we entered a race track and were brought to a halt where the opportunity was taken to wash our feet and clean up. A siren had been sounding continuously and we presumed it to be a panzer warning of impending shellfire.

Back on the march again and the guards were as weary as we were, the sick wagons appeared to be full of them. We passed through another hospital town and some of the weaker lads and guards were left behind. The column straggled on and the few civilians that we saw looked extremely worried. Some of them gave us water but there were many who didn't. At every opportunity

---

* Towns that were draped in Red Cross flags and white sheets were indicating that they were sheltering the wounded and civilians.

we were trying to beg potatoes from the houses we were passing as we had not had any rations issued during the previous four days.

We were extremely hungry having given our rations away to the lads that had marched in from Poland. When we were called to a halt we would scavenge in the roadside fields, mostly potatoes and turnips, but we were eating anything that we could get our hands on including some rhubarb. Some of us began suffering with stomach cramps.

There were again USAAF Thunderbolts flying around and we were watching the sky anxiously, hoping that they would recognise our column as POW and not German infantry. A group of four Lancaster bombers flew over unescorted, but we didn't see any German aircraft and our aircraft seemed to be flying at will.

As night approached, we were directed into an open field where the grass was wet through, but we managed to settle down and make a brew, after which four of us huddled closely together to sleep. Our thoughts were of the new lads that had already marched from Poland, they had slept many times like this, so we didn't grumble.

We were disturbed by a huge explosion that went up about 6 miles away followed by a column of fire hundreds of feet in the air. I had never seen one as large as this an we surmised it must be the Germans carrying out demolitions as they retreated. We settled again to sleep.

Chapter 42

Liberation, 11 April 1945

We were roused at 0600hr and were issued a cup of thin soup. There was not as much transport on the road and we were still being marched eastwards away from the approaching Americans.

During the march we stopped for a break and watched several USAAF Thunderbolts that had returned and were circling in the sky around us. Our main concern was once again that they might drop their bombs on our column. We waved our berets and hoped that they would be able to see us.

The guards were now getting increasingly windy and they pushed us on again. Mac and I made up our minds that we would try to escape and hide up at the first opportunity. We were watching the guards and they did not appear to be as attentive. As our column approached the small town of Halberstadt, we slipped out of the column and hid in a surface shelter. Unfortunately, we were seen by a German woman who alerted the guards who came into the shelter after us. With bayonets attached to their rifles, we were cajoled back into the column.

We reached Halberstadt and observed the German civilians panicking and anxiously moving around cases of food on small wagons. Our guards appeared to have thinned out and the ones that we could see were more concerned with loading themselves up with provisions. The tables were turning. Discipline was breaking down and the lads in our column were beginning to scatter. We decided to slip away and hide up until the excitement had died down. We left the disintegrating column and hid in the back yard of a house where the occupants gave us a cup of tea.

As we sat in the yard, the gunfire seemed to be getting very close to us and half an hour later we heard tank engines so I went out to take a look, I couldn't believe my eyes because coming across a field was a Sherman tank with US troops advancing around it in open order. At the end of the main street there were two more, and each of these had a German soldier perched uncomfortably astride the gun barrels. These were German prisoners that had been placed there by the Americans to deter any anti-tank attacks on them. The length of the street suddenly changed its appearance as hundreds of white sheets were hung out of the house windows. More tanks appeared across the fields and many of us were overcome with emotion as we ran out towards them cheering and waving. I reached a sunburned American and nearly shook his hand off, and some of the older prisoners that had been in captivity for as long as five years wept. Emotions were running high and it was hard not to be overcome with the feelings of joy and relief that engulfed us.

The US tank crews threw us down food rations which were eagerly caught. One threw down an unopened parcel that he had been sent from home, casually asking that I throw the enclosed letter back on board. Those US tank crews received us with a kind and warm generosity.

Our German guards had melted away and the streets of Halberstadt were alive with cheering ex-POWs, some of whom with scores to settle were out looking for their ex-guards. Throughout the town every house had a white flag draped from a window and the civilians were keeping off the streets.

We ended up assembled in the town square where we were checked by a mobile team of US medics. The German mayor had been told to find us both food and accommodation in houses and schools. The accommodation was not to be a problem and many of the lads were already picking billets, but there wasn't enough food available and we had once again to rely on scavenging.

It was decided that we would sleep in the school and the civilians were ordered to bring in mattresses for us to sleep on. Others had been put to work sweeping the place and it was heartening for us to watch the master race at work after being their prisoners for so long. Prisoners were still coming in and the Americans could not believe that they were British as they arrived limping and dressed in wretchedly soiled clothing. Coffee and soup was provided by a US field kitchen and then we strolled around the streets enjoying our new-found freedom. There was now a large crowd of us mingling in the streets among the tanks and jeeps, prisoners were cheering. Up above I had never seen so many Persil-white sheets hanging out.

Out and about, the town was in flux. The forced labour men comprising Poles, Ukrainians, Russians, French and Ities were breaking into the shops and helping themselves – I had never seen such happy faces.

I later learned that the Americans knew where we were having spotted our column from their circling Thunderbolt aircraft. Our position had been reported back to their ground troops by radio.

*

Final Days of the War

The European war still had another three weeks to run before hostilities ceased on 2 May. Representatives of the German army were to sign the documents of unconditional surrender on 28 April, by which time the Allies were on the River Elbe, only 60 miles from Berlin. On 28 March the worst scenario for the Germans had taken place, an agreement between the Allies had been made to allow the Russians to take Berlin.

By evening I was feeling tired and could not remember such a happy and exciting day. That night I could not get to sleep on the spring mattress as I found it too soft after sleeping for so long on boards and straw-filled palliasses.

Thursday 12 April 1945

We were up at 0900hr. The school yard was full of US infantry and tanks and they seemed to be a fine lot of boys, very professional and we couldn't help noticing that every man had an automatic weapon. The firepower of a US platoon appeared awesome to us.*

At liberty, we walked around the town and chatted to the Americans. Tanks were parked everywhere with the crews snatching a few hours sleep while they were still able. These boys had advanced so fast that sleep had been well nigh impossible for them. Another American gave me a personal parcel in yet another demonstration of generosity. We also managed to obtain a few pounds of sugar from a shop on our wanderings. The town was now under curfew and the German civilians were not allowed onto the streets after 1200hr.

Impatient to be off, some of our lads had already left the town after having taken civilian cars in an attempt to start the long journey home.

It had been reported that some fanatical Hitler Youth were still fighting and holding out on a hill some 4 miles away from Halberstadt and were being engaged by tanks. Later, a few German prisoners and wounded were brought in.

I had some white bread today. I couldn't believe my eyes that bread could be so white after living on black bread for so long. I still couldn't believe we were free.

Friday 13 April 1945

Up early again and we once again walked around the town trying to get some milk and eggs, the civilians always said the same thing 'fertig'. We came across an empty shop with a cellar full of French clothes and picked up a few things to take home; I found a smashing fur coat. We also managed to obtain a few bottles of preserved black cherries which tasted wonderful with some milk that we eventually managed to get hold of. Unfortunately, we scoffed the lot and felt sick afterwards, finding they were too rich for our malnourished stomachs.

---

* Only the NCOs carried a light machine gun (Sten) in the parachute battalions, the rest of the men in the rifle companies carried a .303 rifle.

A US patrol with tanks returned loaded with loot, and they had been throwing cigarettes and cigars down to our lads who were smoking well these days.

The young Germans were still reportedly holding out on the hillside beyond the town and prisoners are still trickling in, many of whom appear to be around 15 or 16 years old. I obtained a small pack to replace my improvised haversack and a dagger and a belt for souvenirs. The belt had 'blood and honour' embossed around the buckle.

We were informed that the nearest airfield from which the RAF was operating was at a place named Hildesheim and that eventually trucks would be sent out to collect us. We had now been in the town for a week and were getting impatient to be off, so a group of us decided that we would start to walk if we were not collected soon.

Saturday 14 April 1945

We lay in. There is still no sign of the trucks that are coming to move us out. Reg and Snowy have repaired a DKW car which seems to be running OK and we intend to push off on our own tomorrow.

Sunday 15 April 1945

We were up at 0600hr and loaded up the car with our kit. Unarmed, we set off with another load of lads in a second borrowed car following behind, we must have looked like a travelling circus. We did not have much luck with our purloined transport as it kept breaking down, and by the time we had travelled about 12 miles we must have pushed it for half the distance. The battery seemed to be 'fertig' so we pushed it into a ditch.

Now on foot, we came across an old fire engine that we spent time trying to get started but without success. Several of the lads found two horses in a stable and they departed down the road with two of them astride each horse. Shortly afterwards we came across a field with several sleek race horses cantering around, and Mac set off to catch one for us but it was a futile task as he could not get anywhere near them.

Chastened, Mac and Curly decided to head for Goslar while Snowy, Reg and I started back to the school in Halberstadt. We had barely walked a mile or so when we met a diesel truck heading for Kassel, so we jumped on the back picking up Mac and Curly on the way.

The roads were now full of US trucks, all moving fast. Slave-labour people were also making their way home on anything that would move, bicycles, cars and trucks. Walking among them were Russians, mostly peasant people that appeared bewildered by so much movement around them but they all waved and smiled. They had massive journeys ahead of them.

We stopped for water at a large house where several Eastern European forced labour families had taken up residence. They welcomed us, but we couldn't get out quick enough when we saw that the bath was filled with excrement.

The whole area was in flux with bands of displaced people of many nationalities on the move, all with the sole objective of getting home. It was every man for himself as there was no law and order. The roads were still dangerous and we were constantly on the lookout for any German troops that were still armed.

Most of the villages that we passed through had white flags hanging from the house windows and a few had been damaged by shell fire. We stopped at one village cafe and had a glass of beer and were surprised to hear the British news before we moved on again. It was then that I saw some concentration-camp prisoners for the first time. They were on an old truck that came slowly grinding along with two wheels at the front and a double axle at the back, and two of the rear wheels were locked and dragging. There was a large group of men aboard and they were dressed in a type of striped pyjama. They were stick thin, so thin that their emaciated heads were large and out of all proportion to their bodies. 'We are Dutch', they shouted, 'and we are going to Holland'. We scrounged a lift and climbed onto the tailgate but we hadn't gone more than a mile before it broke down and we had to start walking again.

We stopped another old truck that was plastered with French and Belgian flags and carrying forced labour men. However, as we arrived in Hildesheim this truck, our third, also broke down, so we began to walk through the town. As we made our way through, we observed what a mess it was, the bomber boys had really had a go at it and hardly a building was left standing.* Strangely, I did not see one crater in the road as it twisted through the shattered buildings. A lasting memory is the skeleton of a church spire standing alone above the ruins. We were finally picked up in Hildesheim by a US truck that took us to the nearby ex-Luftwaffe airfield.

As we approached the airfield we could see Dakotas landing and on arrival we found that it was now under the control of the Americans. A large canteen had been set up and was feeding the POWs the best that it could. There were many hundreds of POWs collecting there and more coming in all the time. We had to queue around the perimeter of a football field ten deep for 2 hours waiting our turn to be served, and on reaching the counter we were given doughnuts and coffee.

---

* Hildesheim was attacked by 280 Lancaster bombers on 23 March 1945. In a little over 15 minutes the centre of the town was completely destroyed. It was captured by the 2nd US Armoured Division on 8 April, a week before Tom walked in.

There were huge queues for everything but the latrines as nobody seemed to want to go, and the lack of food was the perceived reason for that. Eventually, we found a mattress in the roof of the barracks and turned in with five of us sharing one big bed.

Monday 16 April 1945*

We were up at 0700hr and queued for the next 4 hours to be registered and inspected by a medical officer – that is he asked us if we had lice, we said no and he said pass! When we returned to the barracks we found that our kit had been rifled, Reg's looted spoons and my looted fur coat were gone. On the airfield the Dakotas had been landing and taking off all day.

We were moved into a different barrack and our situation was a little better now that we had been organised into companies and were drawing 'K' rations.** Men were being called forward for repatriation and we were all crowded around a US captain who was calling out plane loads of names over a microphone. Our names were not called so I compensated for the disappointment by writing a letter home. We were each given a blanket and then we once again turned in.

Tuesday 17 April 1945

We were paraded at 0800hr and a colonel informed us that we were to get six weeks' leave on our repatriation, double food rations and single-ration money. Names for departure were being called out all day, and in between the calls we were each given doughnuts, chewing gum, coffee and twenty cigarettes by the Americans. I wrote to the Talbots and Bells and after tea a US dance band played for us

During our first two days on the airfield there were Dakotas flying in and out repatriating POWs back to Britain. Dying to get away, we watched a group of about a hundred officers arrive and they were flown out ahead of us, so you can imagine the comments from the ranks looking on.

That night there was a big storm with rolls of thunder and great flashes of lightning. Mac and I nearly jumped out of the bed at the first of the thunder claps as our nerves were a bit fragile.

---

*   On this day Arnhem was taken by the Canadians.

** This was an individual combat food pack introduced by the USA in the Second World War. The pack contained around 3,000 calories and was designed to be light in weight and to be consumed when no other food was available. It contained three basic meals of biscuits, cereal, tinned meat, dried fruit, chocolate bars, chewing gum and cigarettes. Most of the troops found that the packs were lacking in bulk and left them feeling unfed.

Wednesday 18 April 1945*

The weather was not too bad today and the aircraft kept landing and departing, but the organisation appears to be getting into a muddle with men leaving this morning that had only arrived last night, while others such as ourselves that came in on Sunday were still here. Everyone was anxious to get home.

Things are being straightened out, and a new system has been introduced and we have all been numbered off into groups of twenty-six (one plane load) and have been marched to the airstrip. We couldn't wait to fly out.

At last, throwing our blankets away, we climbed aboard the old DC and took off. As we gained height I could see the ruined tower of the church in Hildeshiem fading away below. We had not been airborne for long when a problem arose, and our pilot informed us that the starboard engine had gremlins and that we were to return to Hildeshiem. The disappointment was palpable. However, all was organised when we landed and we were issued with two new blankets, rations and another billet, and despite our let down we found that the Americans were very efficient.

Friday 21 April 1945

Down on the airfield again on another beautiful day. I had not seen so many Dakotas together for a long time, the Americans were flying their boys out in their hundreds, but there were very few British aircraft around. Dakotas were also flying overhead from another airfield and the skies looked pretty busy. A Dakota landed with a few high-ranking RAF officers on board and we were told that we should be away today. One of the officers asked Reg if we were from the 1st Airborne and commented that we had put up a good show.

A Red Cross van arrived and served us with coffee and doughnuts. We spent our time sunbathing on the edge of the airstrip and scrounging around the wrecked aircraft hangars that were full of damaged German planes. One RAF aircraft landed and took out twenty sick. All our boys are sunburned but browned off, our luck was out for another day and again we were returned to the billet.

Saturday 22 April 1945

Today it is raining like hell, there are low clouds and I don't expect to see many aircraft arriving in this. We have been issued with a new razor, comb and toothbrush by the US Red Cross. A new club has been opened for us and

---

* On this day the Russians began the final offensive towards Berlin.

we are able to write, read and listen to the African–American dance band. We are being given bags of comfort but no aircraft.

Things have begun to move, a few RAF planes and a lot of US Dakotas have arrived. This looked like the real thing, and shortly afterwards and although the weather was pretty rough, we were swiftly loaded and took off. Flying low, the aircraft was bouncing around and we were informed that we were heading for Brussels.

We flew over several airfields with all the hangars and barracks burnt out and derelict, but the fields away from the buildings appeared to be full of US Thunderbolts. As we approached the Rhine, I noticed that both banks were pitted with shell holes and further on there were two wrecked Dakotas.

As we flew over Brussels, a lot of the boys were air sick after the turbulent low-level flight out of Germany. We landed in Brussels at around 1800hr and were offloaded and had to take an impatient stroll around the airfield perimeter while our aircraft was refuelled. Away again and this time we climbed high above the clouds. It was pretty cold but we were flying along nice and steady and it wouldn't be long before we were home. Everyone was crowded by the cabin windows, we were not all paratroopers and it was the first time that many of the boys had been in the air which for them made the flight doubly exciting.

As we flew over the French coast we could see the barbed wire and wrecked coastal defences, it all looked very peaceful after all the fighting that had taken place. Leaving the coast of France, we flew out over the English Channel, and far below a small convoy of ships was pitching and ploughing through the swell. Someone shouted, 'There they are … the old white cliffs, lads' and there they were in all their glory, a snaking ribbon of white. There was a lump in my throat and I noticed that mine were not the only eyes that were misting up.

Looking down over Britain, there were the small churches and silvery twisting streams, this really was the old country as we had left it. Over the aerodrome we circled and then came down with the tyres bumping once, twice and then we were home and I said a little prayer.

We were the first POW flight of the day when we touched down in the evening at Hurn (near Bournemouth). The aerodrome was ablaze with lights and all the buildings were illuminated which was strange to me after all those years of blackouts. I was the first one out and stood on the step and stared, there were swarms of WAAFS with red, white and blue ribbons in their hair, and again I felt the lump in my throat.

I jumped down the last few feet onto our own soil again and picked up a handful of earth and squeezed, repeating the gesture that I had made last September when I had left for Arnhem. Down among the crowd, I had never been kissed and slapped so much, everyone was talking and laughing.

We were taken to a huge hangar which was decorated out with our Union flag and streams of red, white and blue bunting. A band was playing and inside small tables were set out with a light tea. Several of the RAF medics were taking no chances and before we were allowed in they went over us with a delousing gun. A Red Cross nurse was standing by just in case we needed the extra support. The wonderful Red Cross that had sustained us

From Hurn we were loaded into a truck and driven through the countryside which struck me as so English and verdant. There were flags and bunting everywhere along our route and it was so good to be home. A chap threw a bottle of beer into the lorry which we caught and passed round. The old POWs that had been imprisoned for four or five years were amazed and could not get over all the girls in uniform.

On reaching the transit camp everything was well in hand. We were given a Red Cross bag containing a shaving kit and then we had supper with real eggs, after which we were registered once again. A personal telegram was issued to confirm to our next of kin that we had returned. All our particulars were taken for our pending leave and then we went to bed. That night after all the excitement it was like a dream, I lay in bed and relaxed in the thought that I would not be waking up to the 7013 Arbeit Kommando.

Sunday 23 April 1945

I was up like a lark with no one shouting, 'Rouse, rouse', only, 'Wakey, wakey'. I momentarily thought of poor Allan Wake who we had left behind in Arnhem. It was to be a busy day for us and everything had been arranged so that we had no trouble at all with our processing. New uniforms were issued and I finally threw away my old smock and jumping trousers that had served me so well.

Thousands of men were being repatriated from POW camps, and many had been years away from home but future choices had to be made quickly. I was given a choice of going with the 6th Airborne Division to the Far East or returning to my original RE unit at Longmoor.

The 1st Airborne had been decimated at Arnhem and in a much-reduced state was currently preparing to leave for Norway to participate in the disarming of the German garrison. 1st Parachute Squadron RE had also been decimated and although still in existence, it would have had few of the lads remaining with whom I had soldiered in C Troop.* I had to make a decision before going on leave.

I had always intended to return to the railways and was keen to resume my progress through the grades to become an engine driver after demobilisation. My pre-war position and grade were being kept open for me at Royston, so by returning to my old RE unit at Longmoor I reasoned that I would be able to get some refresher training. The war in Europe was over and I had just

---

* See Appendix 2 for a brief finale.

emerged from a period of hardship. Given the uncertainty of the future and my desire to return home, I made the decision to go back to Longmoor.

By lunch we had been issued with rail warrants to make our way home on leave. We had been paid and it was good to have some real money once again and be able to spend it. I was feeling quite well off as I had all my accumulated back pay from my seven months as a prisoner.

My warrant routed me via London to Doncaster. We said our goodbyes to the staff that had been so good to us and were driven to the station in a truck that carried the divisional sign of Drakes Drum (Wessex Division). When our train reached Waterloo, our small group split up and we went our separate ways. I said goodbye and shook hands with Mac, Reg and Tubby with whom I had been through so much. Snowy and I changed stations and boarded a north-bound train from King's Cross. We looked at each other and shook hands and grinned. We were almost home.

We arrived in Doncaster at midnight and everywhere looked deserted, but everything was arranged and private cars were waiting outside the station to take Snowy to Wath and me to Royston. We left each other with a promise to meet again soon. The Royal Association of Motorists organised volunteers using their private cars to collect POWs from the various stations and take them home. I was driven the 18 miles home to Royston where I arrived at East End Crescent well after 1. The houses in the crescent were draped in Union flags in celebration of our victory. I remember thinking, thank goodness it was dark, how I would have hated to walk through the crescent in daylight with all the attention that this would have caused.

The house was in darkness, they didn't expect me to be home so soon. I pushed open the gate to the front path of dear old 92, the catch was still broken – the times I have said that I would repair it. The lump was back in my throat again and I was once again feeling emotional. I knocked on the wall in the old 'knocker-up' style and could hear the scamper as they came tearing down the stairs. There was Dad with his hair as white as ever, he looked a little tired and my younger sister, Freda, how she'd grown. There was so much to say. I learned that my mother was ill in Leeds General Hospital which dampened our celebrations, but I was home alive and well. 'He knows not England, him who only England knows.'

'He Knows Not England, Him Who Only England Knows'

This is the last line in Tom's battered old POW diary and shows his depth of feeling for the England that he knew and had been longing to return to. Sadly, he found out that his mother, Anastasia, was terminally ill, and in fact she was so ill that she was not conscious of his home coming and died shortly afterwards. His younger brother, Bob, was still with RAF Coastal Command in Ceylon, serving in Catalina Flying Boats with 205 Squadron in the dual role of wireless operator/air gunner. The war with the Japanese in the Far East was still being fought.

Chapter 43

Returning to Longmoor, June 1945

My leave pass on repatriation was initially authorised for six weeks, but this was extended by letter to eight weeks. After this period I was required to return to Longmoor. Following my repatriation leave I was not to be demobilised from the army for further year.* The army system was not working on a first in, first out basis but one of age plus years' service, so older men were being demobbed first. For example, I had joined up at the age of 20 and by the end of the war I had served for over five years. I therefore had twenty-five 'points' counting towards my demobilisation. A man aged 30 with the same number or less years' service would be demobbed before me. The reason for this system was because a lot of the older men had families and this was seen as the fairest way to demobilise men from the armed forces, the personnel of which still numbered in the millions. Once a man's points had been calculated, he was placed into a numbered group consisting of thousands, mine was Group 27 with a demobilisation date of May/June 1946.

On returning to my old camp at Longmoor after eight weeks' leave I was surprised to meet men who had spent the entire war there, and as staff they were now all SNCOs. Nothing seemed to have changed very much except that the stock of locomotives had increased, and in particular I recall a 2–10–0 Austerity carrying the name of *Major General McMullen* resplendent in Longmoor blue.

I had not been back at Longmoor for very long before I was once again on the footplate resuming my former job as a locomotive driver second class. My red beret and battledress with my parachute wings and campaign ribbons were now in my locker. I was once again dressed in the workaday denims and cap of a RE footplate-man.

By coincidence, I was the driver of the locomotive at the head of the train meeting one of the RE railway companies (I think it was 190) returning from the Middle East in November 1945. A troop train had brought them on the Southern main line to Bordon where they were transferred to our train to take them on the last leg of their journey into Longmoor Camp.

---

* Demobilisation was the process of formally returning conscripted soldiers, sailors and airmen to civilian life. Between June 1945 and January 1947 4,337,100 men from the armed forces were demobilised.

As I hung out of the cab in my railway fatigues watching the mass of khaki-clad figures on the platform, I was recognised by several, who exclaimed, 'Look, it's Hicksy ... he's still here while we've been away winning the bloody war!', and similar banter. That night there was a welcome-home party for 190 in the Weavers Club. After my shift, I scrubbed up and put on my walking out uniform which was the one with the red beret and parachute wings of which I was immensely proud. Later that evening, I went down to the Weavers and entered as casually as I could manage. I sauntered in and was delighted to see quite a few jaws drop. Needless to say, we all had a good laugh and had many stories to tell.

A further red-beret encounter took place at Longmoor. The RSM was not sure which colour beret I should be wearing now that I was back in the RE, and I was fearful he might stop me wearing the red one. Fortunately, an inspection came to my rescue. I was on parade for the visit of the Chief Royal Engineer, Brigadier Henniker, and was still wearing my red beret. As 'Honkers' walked down the line with the RSM in close attendance, he stopped by me and looking intently he recollected and after a pause said, 'Hicks, C Troop', and he chatted quite amiably with me for several minutes. The Brigadier had been with us in Sicily where he had been wounded, allegedly by his second in command who threw a grenade into the trench that he was in! The last time I had seen him was at Donington when he came to say goodbye to the squadron prior to us leaving for Arnhem. As he passed on down the line I thought my red beret must be safe from the RSM now.

Shortly before my demobilisation in 1946, I had a surprise visitor one morning when I was attending a technical lecture in one of the Longmoor classrooms. A captain came in through the door and the sergeant instructor brought the class to attention, as was the custom when an officer entered a room. I was surprised to see Curly Clayton half in and half out of the door asking the sergeant if he could speak to Sapper Hicks. I was excused and the class had the view of an over enthusiastic officer hugging and shaking the hand of a ranker through the windows. On returning from Tunisia, Curly had been successful in his application for a commission and had then been posted outside the airborne division into a field company. None of us had seen him for over two years.

So Curly had me out of the classroom and away for a pub lunch in a car that he had borrowed (without permission) from his Major. We had a good afternoon followed by a spot of bother on the way back when the car seized up due to Curly forgetting to check the oil, so it had to be abandoned within the sprawl of Longmoor camp.

I also met Captain Eric Mackay once again at Longmoor, where he was giving a series of lectures.* We met by chance and he was kind enough to ask

---

* Captain Mackay was an Arnhem escapee and later Major General.

me if I would like to be his batman as he was shortly going out to Africa, but I declined. I still wasn't keen on this role and was now intent on returning to Royston. I had also met a local girl back home in Barnsley.

I stayed at Longmoor for almost a year where in addition to engine driving I attended the trade school and was able to refresh and update myself on locomotive practice and theory. This was fortuitous as I would require this instruction to take my LMS driving exams when I returned to Royston.

In June 1946 I was finally called forward to York, which was the centre dealing with the demobilisation of Group 27. I travelled from Longmoor to York with Tom Featherstone who was one of the lads that I had originally joined up with from Royston shed in 1939. Tom's war had taken a completely different course to mine but our demobilisation points were the same and so was our demobilisation date. On arrival, we were administratively demobilised and our uniforms were exchanged for civilian suits and a trilby, but I retained my red beret.

Part Four

Life Continues

Chapter 44

Demobilisation – Returning to Royston Shed, July 1946

ollowing demobilisation, in June 1946 I returned to my reserved occupation as a fireman at Royston engine shed, where I started work several weeks later in July. With the war years included, I now had twelve years' seniority. I had passed my examinations for driving at Longmoor and was now able to pass the LMS driving examination within four months of my return. The driving of the various locomotive types was to be no problem for me as the theoretical training at Longmoor and instructors had been excellent. However, I found the road-learning process was both difficult and tedious.

Little had changed at Royston during the war years, although the engines were dirtier than I remembered and many were in a rundown condition due to the heavy workload to which they had been subjected. Maintenance schedules had also been stretched because of the manpower shortage during the war. But the conditions of service remained the same, a 48-hour week was still being worked followed by the solitary rest day, and our paid holidays were still only seven days per year and there was still no paid sick leave.

I could have used a few days sick shortly after returning home when I started experiencing short bouts of recurrent malaria, but I couldn't afford to lose any pay and mostly just 'soldiered' on. Fortunately, it was on its way out of my system and the symptoms completely faded away within a couple of years.

The year 1946 was memorable for me, and was both difficult, happy and sad. I was adjusting back into civilian life and was fortunate to marry Sadie McCullough, the daughter of a Barnsley miner, who I brought back to East End Crescent. Sadie, aged 20, immediately took over the running of the house in those austere days of rationing. My father, who was now chronically ill and at home, required nursing and my younger teenage sister, Freda, was still dependent on the household budget. It was quite a hard introduction to married life for a young bride, but coming from a mining family my mother-in-law, Margaret McCullough, had seen to it that all of her three daughters were well schooled in the running of a working man's house. Later that year, my father died on Christmas Eve, aged 59.

I was now a substantive passed fireman and qualified to take out trains as a driver when the opportunities arose. However, these chances only came up when the shed had more work than could be covered by the existing available drivers. Before a driver could take a train out on the LMS he had to learn and be familiar with all aspects of the route, or road as the routes were known. Before the war, a passed fireman would learn these roads gradually over a period of time as he went along and this allowed him to drive only the routes he was familiar with. However, when I returned to Royston the policy had changed and the four most senior passed firemen had to know all the roads that they were liable to drive over, which covered many hundreds of miles of track. I hadn't been working at Royston for almost seven years and Tom Featherstone and I were put at an immediate disadvantage as we had dozens of roads to learn.

At the end of the road-learning process the passed fireman or driver had to sign a Board of Trade document confirming that he was cognisant with the route before he was allowed to take a train over it. If a driver had a new road allocated or he moved into another link, he was again allowed time to learn the new road.

I spent much of that hard winter of 1946/47 road learning, riding as third man in the cab memorising gradients, speed restrictions, signalling and water points as I travelled the routes. Some days I would walk around sidings in freezing fog and snow committing to memory track layouts, points and yet more signals. Eventually, after a period of around three months, I was satisfied that I understood the roads that I was to drive over and I signed the Board of Trade document recording my competency while also acknowledging my responsibility.

Chapter 45

Engine Driver, January 1947

Early in 1947, a vacancy occurred and I was registered as a full-time driver and admitted onto the drivers' roster. Having recently completed several months' road-learning, I began picking up relief work. My entry onto the roster was not all plain sailing as difficult situations occasionally arose with some of the other passed firemen. Many of these men were older and had greater route experience than me, albeit obtained while working through the war years.

Sometimes I would be rostered with one of these chaps and one instance in particular springs to mind. A fireman would usually assist the driver in reading the signals and maintaining his route orientation, but not on this occasion when I was in charge of a fast freight belting down to Nottingham in fog. I could feel that my fireman was brooding and sensed his disinclination to help me out. It was obvious that he was miffed at being 'nobbed' back into firing. On this journey I spent much of my time hanging out of the cab so as not to miss a signal, knowing all too well that it could take up to a mile to stop if we met a red light on a greasy rail. On these occasions, you felt very much alone and a steely concentration was required on the job in hand, never would you show a weakness regardless of how difficult the situation appeared.

On runs such as these experience was gained and hopefully a grudging respect as the train was brought in with a total indifference towards a sulking fireman. Fortunately, this attitude was the exception to the rule and most of my firemen were relaxed and both helpful and supportive. As the months passed by, I was able to find my feet.

We had quite a number of young drivers and fireman at Royston that were in their late twenties and early thirties. This was quite unusual in our area as drivers from other sheds tended to be quite a lot older, with many well into their fifties, and this did not go unnoticed. Several times, for instance, when we had brought a through coal train into Mirfield our older relief crew would often remark within earshot, 'It's them baby drivers from Royston', which would make us grin at one another gleefully. I believed it gave us an edge similar to those of my old squadron days. This also related to our engines as we were still one of the few sheds in our area to have been allocated the 8F engines.

Driving in the 1950s and 1960s

Having settled once more into a driving routine at Royston shed, Tom worked the links throughout the 1950s and 1960s. The final pages of this memoir describe the various 'turns', as the jobs were called, and some of the routes that he experienced. This period was, like the decades before, dominated by coal and smoke; every house, school, hospital, factory and power station was mostly heated by coal and coke. The railways were the major carriers, transporting it countrywide from the mines and coking plants. There were also some passenger turns and fast freight relief work, but the movement of coal remained the mainstay of Royston shed.

*

I was fortunate to become a driver before nationalisation as many passed firemen were to be pushed down the seniority scale after it. Just ¾ of a mile away from our shed ran the ex-Hull and Barnsley Railway which had an engine shed at Cudworth (opened in 1885). The H&B was part of the LNER and a separate company from us in the LMS. After the 1948 nationalisation of railways, the new British Railways began to rationalise its engine sheds. This resulted in the small H&B shed closing and most of its staff being transferred to Royston in July 1951.

Many of the H&B drivers were older men that were inexperienced in our wider range of routes. However, through the time-honoured system of seniority they entered our links and 'nobbed' many of the Royston men, knocking them back down the ladder on the driving rosters. But there were also advantages for us in the amalgamation. We took over the H&B work to Goole and Hull and in the longer term the elderly drivers retired creating more driving opportunities for the younger men at Royston. The road to Goole and on to Hull docks was a pleasant country amble taking out coal and returning with trains of Scandinavian timber for building and pit props (used as coal-mine tunnel supports). Most of the route was through flat, quiet country well away from the main line and our industrialised area. So rural was the transition that we had to slow down on the approach to level crossings and sometimes draw to a halt, only waking up the crossing keeper by giving crows (short blasts) of impatience on our whistle. At one particular crossing an old lady would come out to open the gates, and one late evening she came out in her nightgown!

The only memories I have of anything that unduly disturbed these saunters east were of occasional hot axle boxes on the coal wagons, something we were likely to encounter on the H&B because of the age of the wagons, the laden weight on their axles and duration of the journey. The axle boxes on these early wagons were lubricated with fat and were prone to overheat, resulting in the need for the guard and driver to keep looking along the train for anything amiss. The first signs of a hot box were either smoke or a red glow which became apparent in the depths of a tunnel or in the dark, and nearly always at the end of the journey on the approach into Hull. The only remedy was to slow down, identify the wagon and then shunt it out into a siding as soon as possible, for a hot box could set the wooden wagon alight if left unattended. Fortunately, the H&B was not a busy line and we were usually able to do this without too much difficulty.

Chapter 46

Coal Trains and Passenger Turns

Coal was the reason for the existence of Royston engine shed, moving coal and coke from the south Yorkshire coalfield and in particular from the coking plants and mines around Barnsley. We moved it to the Midlands, across into Lancashire, east to the docks of Goole and Hull and to the numerous power stations.

South Yorkshire was cross-hatched with numerous mineral lines and coal was on the move 24 hours a day. The trains taking coal into Lancashire left Carlton sidings heading north down the Midland main line where they forked left at Royston Junction. We then went through Mirfield and up over Copy Pit summit and down towards Burnley.

Our southerly routes took us up the Midland main line as far as Rotherham where we were routed down the old Midland main line to Chesterfield, bypassing Sheffield by way of Canklow and Stavely. Running up this route at night was quite spectacular as the track was hemmed in by South Yorkshire's heavy industry. Several steelworks and the huge coke ovens at Manvers would be glowing red, throwing sparks and flames into the night as we passed by. But if we were taking a train through Sheffield up to Chinley we were into the hills of the Peak District and the echoes of our engine were the only sounds that disturbed the peace. The pre-war coal trains to Garston docks had ended with the introduction of diesel-powered banana boats shortly after the war, which left our runs down to Toton (Nottingham) and up to Carnforth as our only long-distance lodge turns.

We did have a few passenger turns. Royston shed was responsible for the pull and push workings from Cudworth to Barnsley using our small 2–6–2 mixed traffic tank engines. We also had the Cudworth to Leeds all stations and Cudworth to Sheffield and all stations to Edale in the Peak District. Summer-only 'hikers' specials' were also worked from Normanton to Edale. The Edale working required us to take a 5-hour break at Sheffield Millhouses shed before going back to Edale for the return working; it was a popular and well-paid turn. A variety of engines could be rostered for these turns ranging from a 2P 4–4–0, 4F 0–6–0 or a Stanier Black 5 4–6–0.

The Edale workings south-west of Sheffield required us to pass through the Dore and Totley tunnel (3 miles 950yd), and once inside when our smoke completely enveloped the engine we were completely in the dark; our steam engines did not carry cab lighting. With handkerchiefs held over our mouths, we would listen for a change in the exhaust beat which occurred when we passed the overhead air vent, and on hearing this we would know that we were halfway through the tunnel.

When entering the tunnel at Dore and Totley there is a gradient for about three-quarters of its length before it dips downgrade for the remaining quarter. Inside, water constantly drips down from the roof making the rails extremely greasy and many an engine slipped furiously on this uphill climb. I have slipped so badly in the Dore and Totley that the train has almost reversed out of the tunnel without us knowing it due to the density of the smoke and the darkness.

Once the gradient had been climbed and we began the descent out of the tunnel care had to be taken not to let the euphoria of the climb distract us. The train could pick up speed and end up travelling so fast that the station at Grindleford, which was the next stop after emerging into the daylight, could be overshot! The train would then have to carry out an ignominious reverse back into the station.

They say that you can fly an aeroplane by the seat of your pants, well you can do the same with a steam engine and can feel a wheel slip coming from the change in vibrations. When slipping occurs the driving technique is to shut off the regulator and then to open it at the end of the slip, that is to reduce power to stop the driving wheels spinning and then to open it again momentarily to increase power as the spin recedes to enable the wheels to grip onto the rails. The opening and shutting down of the regulator becomes a two-handed job and on some slips my arms have almost been dropping off as I have slowly nursed a heavy train up a long greasy gradient.

It was always essential to have the sanders working efficiently to lessen the slips that we encountered on the climbs and descents and in the numerous tunnels on our hilly routes. Occasionally, we would work Manchester-bound coal trains through Chapeltown and then down through Sheffield Midland and on via the tunnel to Chinley, where we were relieved. Descending on the brakes down into Sheffield, on occasion we had to come to a stand outside Millhouses engine shed to have our depleted sand boxes replenished. When this occurred the cleaners would bring sand across to you in a wheelbarrow to be manhandled up to the sanders in buckets before we could proceed.

Occasionally our passenger turns would extend to handling the Paignton to Leeds and Bradford 'Devonian Express' from Cudworth through to Leeds. When this train was running late the express would sometimes be brought to a halt at Cudworth where we would relieve the crew that had brought it down from Birmingham. Usually, we would have a good run through to Leeds as all the signals would be set to enable us to recover lost time. It was a handsome train with the coaches liveried in chocolate and cream with a green 5XP 4–6–0 engine in charge. On arrival at Leeds city, the train would be reversed with another engine taking it on the final leg of its journey to Bradford.

The next major reorganisation that affected us at Royston happened in 1958 when the sheds in our area were transferred to the North Eastern Region. Royston lost its 20C shed code to become 55D under the new administration. We now began a system of work that to us appeared to be extremely inefficient. Where previously we had taken trains such as the 'Barrow Babies' on return trips to Carnforth, we were now stopped by inter-regional demarcation lines. This resulted in us having to be relieved at Skipton by London Midland men. We would then as often as not have to make our way back to Royston as passengers having only been driving an engine for half a shift. It was even more wasteful if we were driving to York where Eastern Region men would relieve us after we had only been driving for an hour and a half, and again we would make our way home as passengers. Although these new shift patterns often resulted in paid idleness, we still had plenty of coal coming out of the mines that required plenty of work to keep it moving.

Chapter 47

Coal Over Copy Pit Summit

Our 8Fs were now extremely hard worked and to assist in the toil we had around a dozen or so 2–8–0 WD Austerities transferred into Royston during the 1950s. These were ponderous, rough-riding engines that lacked the finesse of an 8F and I was always grateful to avoid being rostered on one, especially for the run over Copy Pit.

When hauling a coal train over Copy Pit to Rose Grove (Burnley) we still required a banking engine to ensure that our train would crest the summit. This was achieved by coming to a stand at Todmorden Stansfield Junction where another engine would be attached to our rear. Several crows on our whistle would signal the start of an all-out effort to get the train over the hill. Once at the summit, the banker would drop off and return to assist the next train up.

Well that was the plan, but sometimes the banker took it a little too easy which made our job a great deal harder at the front of the train. We could always recognise a slacker by the beat of his exhaust at our rear, our engine would be working flat out with its exhaust thundering up through the blast pipe while his would be a whisper. To show our displeasure, I'm ashamed to say, we would occasionally pee on the firing shovel and throw it into the firebox as we entered Holme or the Kitson Wood Tunnels – it's amazing how such a small drop of water can cause such a vile stench. This draught of displeasure was quickly carried out of our chimney and back along the roof of the tunnel where the crew of the banking engine would get the full benefit. Incidently, you didn't get many Royston men frying bacon and eggs on their shovels!

The 'Lanky' into Manchester was always a busy line on which passenger trains had the priority over our heavy coal trains. We were often diverted into a passing loop to clear the main line, allowing the Liverpool–Manchester–York expresses to pass by.

At the summit of Copy Pit the line of the passing loop is on a downward slope and our coal train would often pull into this. There we would stand just short of the points waiting to be switched back onto the main line. If the rails were greasy we would sometimes be unable to stop and the weight of our wagons would push us over the points (which were set for safety) onto a set of buffers beyond them. Due to the greasy rails, we would then be unable to reverse out and would have to wait for an engine to come up behind to drag us back up past the overshot points. Our only problem of course was that we hoped that it wasn't on the same day that we had shown our displeasure to a slacking banker, as we could be stuck there for quite a while!

Chapter 48

Trippers and the Scramble into Carlton Yards

The local link at Royston was mostly concerned with bringing wagons of coal from the local colliery sidings along the main line to the large freight yard at Carlton. These wagons would start their journey within the colliery and be brought along a single-track route by the colliery's own shunt engines to a siding, from where they would be collected by our engines. These short journeys were termed trippers due to the numerous trips back and forth that would be made during the working day. The work tended to start and finish in daylight hours and was a very popular turn with some drivers, even though the crews were often required to prepare their own engines before leaving the shed. The engines used on these turns were a mixture of the shed's allocation of 8Fs, Austerity 2–8–0s, 0–6–0 4Fs and 3Fs.

The yards at Carlton were often so busy that coal trains were backed up the line as far as Walton some 4 miles to the north, all waiting for their turn to move in. The signalman at Walton box would bring us to a stand and then hold up a handful of fingers indicating how many trains were in front of us. Sometimes at night a green light would be waived allowing us to move along slowly. On foggy nights, of which there were many in the days of coal, we would hang out of the cab just inching along as we looked for the red tail light of the train in front.

It could be a similar situation from the south when trains of over thirty full or empty wagons from Carlton Colliery were trying to move into the yards. Here we had to cross the four main lines and if you were caught after 2100hr you could stand for over 3 hours waiting to get across due to the volume of main-line traffic. On these occasions we would stand simmering as the steady procession of fast freights thundered north to Leeds and Carlisle and south to London and the Midlands. From his elevated position in Carlton box, the signalman would be looking across at us anxiously trying to judge when he could find a space get us across into the yard. We on our side of the track would be looking across just as apprehensively, keeping our engine in trim for a lumbering sprint.

When our opening came we would hear the points change followed by the raised peg of the solitary signal. Opening the regulator, there was no time to lose as we set our heavy train into motion from a standing start. The signalman would often hang out of his box waving frantically and shouting, 'Come on, come on' as a dim view was taken if a fast freight was slowed for a mineral working. Timings were so tight that any delay in the system could slow all the fast trains down the line. When we got cracking our long train would snake across the main tracks and enter the marshalling yard. Once in, it would be broken down to join several more trains being assembled. However, from the signalman urging us across with all haste we then met the shunters who were waiting to dissemble our train in the yard. They too had been waiting for us to come across, often for hours and would be anxious to get their work moving as soon as we entered the yard. Invariably, we were moving too fast. So as we rattled in we were greeted by gesticulations and shouts of, 'Slow down ... slow down ... slow down' from the shunters.

The shunters were skilful men, strong and fleet of foot, who would uncouple and begin to dissemble the train with their poles as the first wagons entered the yard. Running alongside, they risked life and limb as they jumped the intersecting rails calling out the destinations from the tickets on the moving wagons, 'Five for Derby' they would shout as they stuck in their poles to uncouple the heavy steel links, followed by another call of 'Six for Leeds' and so on. As many as five men would be hard at it. The faster we were moving the faster they ran alongside and all the time yelling for us to 'Slow down'. What a game! When we were finally in, the signalman would quickly duck back into his box to re-throw the points and raise the main-line signals to give the next fast freight the all clear.*

Now very much older, we still managed a prank or two. I recall a tortoise pie I left for Jimmy Guthrie, an amiable scot and fellow driver who was on the shed link one day. Our pet tortoise had failed to survive the winter and as the ground was frost hard an internment in the garden was out of the question, especially as I was due to sign on. I, therefore, took it to work with the intention of placing it in the firebox, but then another opportunity arose, there was a change of engine and Jimmy Guthrie was to take over. I wrapped the deceased in the greaseproof paper that held my snap (sandwiches) and placed it on a warm ledge above the firebox. As Jim climbed aboard and I swung down the other side, I casually said, 'I've left a pie on the front for you Jimmy ... it should be nice and warm soon.' 'Thanks, Tommy,' he replied in his broad Perthshire accent, 'I'll hae it later'! When our paths crossed again he said to me, 'You know that bloody pie, Tommy, I should have known something was wrong before it began to stink ... and I was quite looking forward to it ... I'll be looking to repay the favour shortly'. I had to keep my wits about me from then on when Jimmy was around.

---

* The Midland main line was extremely busy up until the early 1960s with records showing that over seventy passenger trains a day were passing through Royston. These were a mixture of all-stations trains between Leeds and Sheffield, mail and parcels and the London to Glasgow and Edinburgh expresses and overnight sleepers. In addition to these, there were over twenty express freights and numerous local mineral workings.

Chapter 49

Final Days at Royston

By 1964 the planned demise of the steam engine was becoming a reality, and all over the country diesel-electric locomotives were replacing the steamers. The drivers at Royston were being sent on conversion courses which many of the older men (and some of the younger ones) who had been brought up on steam found extremely difficult.

Diesel locomotives were introduced into Royston and the last fires in the steam engines were dropped in November 1967, following which they were shunted into lifeless rows to await being towed away for their final disposal as scrap. The coal hopper that had rattled for thirty-seven years became silent and was replaced by a clutch of cylindrical tank wagons from which diesel fuel was to be pumped. Royston was the last shed to use steam engines in the West Riding of Yorkshire.

The sheds that had once been alive with drifting smoke and numerous men was now to be used as a diesel stabling point and became little more than a huge garage. Many of the older men decided to retire and those that were left were transferred to the new regional diesel depot at Healey Mills near Ossett. In September 1971, the shed finally closed and the tracks were lifted. Shortly afterwards it was demolished and the site levelled. A small wood of birch, hawthorn and brambles now hides the memories.

I 'soldiered' on for a further eleven years at Healey Mills, driving diesel-electrics among men from all over the West Riding who had been displaced from the other steam sheds. I had now to commute the 12 miles to Healey Mills instead of walking down the lane as I had done for so many years. I retired in 1982.

Since then the railway estate of East End Crescent has been sold to the council, which in turn has sold houses to the sitting tenants. The Crescent that was full of railwaymen has gradually lost its identity as men have moved out to other jobs and many of the older ones have passed away. The many neat front gardens that were tended by the shift-working railwaymen have now been paved over to accommodate cars.

Behind the Crescent the busy four-track section of the Midland main line that was constructed by an army of navvies in 1840 has gone, as has Royston & Notton station with its four platforms and waiting rooms. The rails in the huge yards at Carlton have been lifted and the foundations of ash have been excavated and taken to be recycled into building blocks.

The local collieries have also gone, their stacks levelled into smooth hills of rough grass and scrub. The demise of coal has transformed the whole landscape. Most of the families that are now living on the one-time LMS railwayman's estate are probably unaware of the railway heritage that has preceded them.

Chapter 50

Parachuting Again

Following my retirement in 1982, I decided that I would like to experience parachuting once again. So away I went to the Para Jump Club at Bridlington to join a course. On arrival, I found that my jump mates were mostly young lads, first-timers and very nervous. Not dissimilar to the queue for the balloon jump at Tatton.

The morning was spent in the classroom and I was impressed with the theoretical instruction. We were then suspended from the roof and were taught the skydivers' 'star-position' to be adopted on leaving the aircraft. Our instructor seemed very young with his long hair and jeans but nevertheless very efficient. With no shouting, he purposely stressed the required landing position of feet and knees together. It was strange to experience parachute training without any yelling! Then came the field work, forward and back rolls, similar to Hardwick and Ringway but very condensed. We were going to jump from a Cessna 85. I had passed the aircraft on the field and due to its size thought it was a static model.

We were fitted with our parachutes, emergency 'chute on the chest. I always thought that when the steel handle of the emergency 'chute was pulled (in case of main-chute malfunction), the 'chute would pop out and open unaided. How wrong I was, the handle is discarded and the canopy has to be manually thrown out. Well I reasoned, I never needed one before so why should I worry now. With my very quiet jump mates we walked to the Cessna, me in my gardening boots (ex–army from Millets) carrying the two parachutes. As I walked out, I was reminiscing about my last walk out to an aircraft, much the same age as these lads, and loaded down with so much kit that I had to be helped aboard.

Our pilot was jean clad, long haired and similar to our instructor, who had now donned a red and yellow jump suit and goggles. The scene was set. My jump mates had not been quiet all the time, they had had a meeting and voted me No. 1, the first to jump, giving way to age they said. It dawned on me then that I had been No. 1 before on the lip of a barrage balloon. I had to give a good impression for the old red beret, so with a steely grin I climbed aboard.

It took the small Cessna an age to climb up to 2,000ft. As No. 1, I shuffled across to the door and took my place on the threshold with my legs dangling outside. The hard floor pressing into my backside was very similar to the old Whitley, and the noise and the wind took me back forty years.

The engine throttled back, a tap on the shoulder and I was out shouting as instructed, 1,000 and 1, 1,000 and 2, 1,000 and 3, check the canopy. With a heart-warming crack and a jerk the best part of parachuting began. It was quite a shock to look up to see several panels missing, I thought there would have been a few wet 'drawers cellular' in the old days at seeing the sun shining through gaps in the canopy.

Coming down was great and I wished it had been from 6,000ft. By pulling my steering toggles, I could run, hold and tack, it was great stuff. Then came the crunch, mother earth was still as hard as ever. My landing was pure RE 'arse over head' and a spider's web of rigging lines around my feet and knees. There was no one to give me the last rites, so I nonchalantly daisy chained my rigging lines and humped the 'chute back to the packing room.

My report: groundwork good, parachute control good; this pupil (me) forgot all about his star position and left the aircraft with his knees and feet together! Old Sergeant Baker at Ringway would have been proud of me, for we had different style in the old days.

Another Tennis Racket

Tom enjoyed his working life as he progressed through the grades on the pre-war LMS and his postwar driving on the new British Rail. He found his war years adventurous and exciting, and despite the tragedy, he experienced both comradeship and humour, the memories of which he has carried forward and still cherishes. Along the way I was born in 1948, followed by my brother Chris in 1952. Sadly, our mother died prematurely in 1976. Dad encountered further sadness when Patricia Moore, his partner and companion of over twenty years, died in 2009.

Following his renewed interest in parachuting in 1983, he continued to make the occasional parachute jump over the following ten years. Later, when the opportunity arose to join a proposed Arnhem veterans' parachute team, he became a founder member. In 1994, the group of veterans began jumping onto Ginkel Heath outside Arnhem as part of the annual remembrance celebrations. His last jump was made in September 2007, when at the age of 88 a depleted team of five veterans jumped in tandem with the display team of the Parachute Regiment the Red Devils.

The 'lads' from the 1st Parachute Squadron RE have met every September since 1946 when one of their officers wrote to reunite the then mostly civilian squadron. Age and infirmity has now taken its toll and it was decided at their 2012 reunion that it would have to be their last. In remembrance the remaining five sappers placed a memorial to the squadron under the Arnhem Oak in Donington churchyard.

Every year Tom still travels to Arnhem to be present on 17 September when the remaining survivors of the battle come together with their Dutch hosts for the remembrance service at Oosterbeek Airborne Cemetery.

Tom is still very active and plays tennis several times a week, but if asked he is quick to reply 'but only doubles'. He rambles every Saturday morning with his friends from Notton Tennis Club, maintaining that 'he just manages to keep pace thanks to the gel on his ankles and a liberal intake of cod-liver oil'. At home every spare hour is spent in his garden where flowers and vegetables are grown in profusion, as they have been every year since he left the army. A new interest has recently emerged: Monday night is jazz-club night, where he now enjoys a dance and a pint!

Tom is now 93 and still full of life, and it therefore seems fitting to bring his story to a close with his own words, 'There goes Tom … into his nineties and he has just bought another tennis racket'. He also invariably wears a small paratrooper's badge! .

Norman Hicks
April 2013

Appendix 1

Royston Locomotive Depot

The shed, as it was known to the local railwaymen, was opened in March 1932, with the primary task of moving coal from the developing South Yorkshire coalfield. The shed was part of the London, Midland and Scottish Railway (LMS) and was designated as shed number 20C. It employed around 500 men in the mid-1930s when it had an allocation of approximately 70 steam engines. It closed to steam in November 1967.

Appendix 2

Demise of the 1st Parachute Squadron RE, 1941–5

The 1st Parachute Squadron RE was devastated at Arnhem, and only 13 of the 143 men that jumped were evacuated (4 men escaped shortly after the evacuation and they may have been included in the number of evacuees).[1] There were also 28 members of the squadron in the sea party that travelled overland and did not parachute into or reach Arnhem.[2] After September 1944 there were probably between 43 and 47 men remaining in the squadron, and of these very few had seen any action.

After Arnhem the remnants of the squadron regrouped at Nijmegen on 27 September 1944 and were flown out to RAF Conningsby on the 29th before once again returning to Donington. In the months that followed Arnhem, the squadron began taking in replacements from other airborne squadrons and newly volunteered sappers who had recently completed parachute training. In February 1945, the reforming 1st Parachute Squadron was renamed the 1st Airborne Squadron RE with the addition of the survivors from the 4th Parachute Squadron RE.

None of the officers and men that were taken prisoner at Arnhem returned to the squadron following their liberation from the German POW camps in April 1945.[3] Malnourished and with many of them weakened by wounds, they were considered unfit for further airborne duties. Many more were awaiting demobilisation and either chose to return to their original pre-parachute units or were posted back to them due to their poor physical condition. The original 1st Parachute Squadron RE had in reality ceased to exist after Arnhem.

Over the next three years the 1st Airborne Squadron RE continued to evolve. It had already taken in the remaining parachutists from the disbanded 4th Parachute Squadron and was to undergo several more changes as the postwar army was reduced in size. This reformed and mostly inexperienced squadron flew out to Norway and Denmark on VE day (8 May 1945) with the depleted 1st Airborne Division to assist in the disarming of the German forces.

Following this deployment and the disbanding of the 1st Airborne Division in November 1945, the 1st Airborne Squadron RE was attached to the 6th Airborne Division in Palestine. In April 1948 the 6th Airborne Division was also disbanded when it was downsized to brigade strength and became 16 Independent Parachute Brigade. The numbers 1 and 6 were kept in the title of the new brigade to honour their predecessors, the 1st and 6th Airborne Divisions.

Prior to the disbanding of the 6th Airborne Division, it had been decided that only one parachute engineer squadron would be required to support the new brigade. The 1st Airborne Squadron RE and the 3rd Parachute Squadron RE were to be reformed into one unit. This new parachute engineer squadron was to be named the 9th Independent Parachute Squadron, the number 9 being chosen in honour of the 9th Field Company which was the senior RE Field Company and originated in the eighteenth century.

In anticipation of this decision, the 1st Airborne Squadron RE was disbanded in July 1948 when it left Palestine. However, the name of the squadron remained with the rear guard party of twenty that returned later in August. At its demise there were only three soldiers within its ranks who were regulars.[4] Its final CO and acting CRE in Palestine was Major Eric O'Callaghan.

In November 1948 selected regular soldiers from the airborne squadrons were posted to Hameln in Germany and 9th Independent Parachute Squadron was created, becoming the first airborne squadron to be formed from regular soldiers.

Notes

1. See Martin Middlebrook, *Arnhem 1944, The Airborne Battle* (1995).
2. Via Sapper Jack Hobbs, a member of the sea party.
3. Lance Sergeant Paddy Padfield (B Troop veteran) recalled that some men did eventually rejoin the 1st Airborne Squadron RE after recuperating. He himself returned in February 1946 after almost a year with 20 Bomb Disposal Squadron.
4. Via Lance Sergeant Paddy Padfield, one of the remaining three.

Appendix 3

Tragino – Operation Colossus

This raid by parachute troops was an attack on an aqueduct in southern Italy by men of No. 11 Special Air Service Battalion, shortly before they were converted into the 1st Parachute Battalion. The raid on 10 February 1941 had only limited success and all thirty-eight men on the raid were taken prisoner. Among the raiding party were a number of RE and as a result it was realised that the developing parachute battalions needed to be supported by specialist engineers. Subsequently, an Air Troop was formed which was expanded into the 1st Parachute Squadron RE. The three troops were at full strength by June 1942.

Three Songs of the Paratroops, 1942

These three songs are the ones that Tom and his mates sang most often during their training at Ringway and on the numerous journeys by truck.

Oh Come Sit By My Side If You Love Me
(sung to the tune of *Red River Valley*)

Oh, come sit by my side if you love me
Do not hasten to bid me adieu,
But remember the poor paratrooper,
And the job he is trying to do.

When the red light goes on we are ready
For the Sergeant to shout 'No. One',
Though we sit in the plane close together,
We all tumble out one by one.

When we're coming in for a landing,
Just remember the Sergeant's advice,
Keep your feet and your knees close together,
And you'll reach mother earth very nice.

When we land in a certain country,
There's a job we will do very well.
We will fire old Goering and Adolph,
And all of those blighters as well.

So stand by your glass and be ready,
And remember the men of the sky.
Here's a toast to the men dead already,
And a toast for the next man to die.

Bless 'Em All
(parachute version)

They say there's a Whitley just leaving Ringway,
Bound for old Tatton Park,
Heavily laden with parachute troops,
Bound for the jump they adore,
There's many a soldier that's jumped once before,
There's many a one had a fall,
But you get no promotion this side of the ocean,
So cheer up my lads, bless 'em all.

Bless 'em all, Bless 'em all.
Bless all the sergeants and their paratroops,
Bless all the packers and their statichutes,
'Cos we're saying goodbye to them all,
As out of the Whitleys we fall,
You'll get no promotion if your 'chute doesn't open,
So cheer up my lads, bless 'em all.

And I Ain't Going To Jump No More
(sung to the tune of *John Brown's Body*)

'Is everybody happy?' said the Sergeant, looking up,
Our hero feebly answered, 'Yes' and then they hooked him up,
He jumped into the slip stream and he twisted twenty times,
And he ain't going to jump no more.

Chorus: Glory, glory what a hell of a way to die,
(repeated three times)
And he ain't going to jump no more.

He counted loud, he counted long and waited for the shock,
He felt the wind, he felt the air, he felt the awful drop,
He pulled the lines, the silk came down and wrapped around his legs,
And he ain't going to jump no more.

Chorus

The days he loved, and loved, and laughed kept running through his mind,
He thought about the medicos and wondered what they'd find,
He thought about the girl back home, the one he'd left behind,
And he ain't going to jump no more.

Chorus

The lines all wrapped around his neck, the 'D' rings broke his dome,
The lift webs wrapped themselves in knots around each skinny bone,
The canopy became his shroud as he hurtled to the ground.
And he ain't going to jump no more.

Chorus

The ambulance was on the spot, the jeeps were running wild,
The medicos they clapped their hands and rolled their sleeves and smiled,
For it had been a week or so since a 'chute had failed,
And he ain't going to jump no more.

Chorus

He hit the ground, the sound was 'splatt', the blood was spurting high,
His pals were heard to say, 'Oh, what a pretty way to die',
They rolled him up still in his 'chute, and poured him from his boots,
And he ain't going to jump no more.

Chorus

There was blood upon the lift webs, there was blood upon his 'chute,
Blood that came a' trickling from his paratrooper's boots,
And there he lay like jelly in the welter of his gore,
And he ain't going to jump no more.

Appendix 5

Roll of Honour of the 1st Parachute Squadron Royal Engineers

The following list contains the names of the fifty-nine men of the 1st Parachute Squadron who died between 1942 and 1945, many of whom were known to Tom and were comrades of his.

M represents a memorial for those with no known grave (NKG) and C represents cemetery.

First Casualty

Name	Rank	Age	Date of Death	Troop	Interred/Memorial
Strachan, Ian*	Cpl	–	07/05/42	–	Brookwood, Surrey (M)

Tunisia, 1942–3

Name	Rank	Age	Date of Death	Troop	Interred/Memorial
Dorman, Stephen	Maj	26	18/12/42	CO	Medjez-el-Bab (M)
Geary, Patrick	Capt	23	29/11/42	A	Medjez-el-Bab (M)
Hewitt, Anthony	Capt	23	21/07/43	C	Brookwood, Surrey (M)
Brown, James	Lt	31	26/02/43	A	Massicault (C)
Holland, John	Lt	22	29/11/42	A	Medjez-el-Bab (M)
Mothersill, Allan	Lt	21	10/03/43	C	Tabarka Ras Rajel
White, George	Lt	21	24/11/42	A	Medjez-el-Bab (M)
Muir, William	Sgt	25	24/11/42	A	Medjez-el-Bab (M)
Sayer, Lawrence	L/Sgt	23	24/11/42	A	Medjez-el-Bab (M)
Alexander, Robert	L/Cpl	22	28/02/43	–	Medjez-el-Bab (C)

---

* It is not known why this sapper has a memorial and no known grave as there were no operations at this time in 1942.

Name	Rank	Age	Date of Death	Troop	Interred/Memorial
Greenwood, Sam	L/Cpl	25	30/11/42	A	Massicault (C)
Harris , Harold	L/Cpl	25	28/05/43	A	Medjez-el-Bab (C)
Hill, Fred	L/Cpl	24	24/11/42	A	Medjez-el-Bab (C)
Hornby, Francis	L/Cpl	21	24/11/42	A	Medjez-el-Bab (M)
Mercer, Reg	Cpl	22	24/11/42	A	Medjez-el-Bab (M)
Calcott, Albert	Spr	22	24/11/42	A	Medjez-el-Bab (M)
Craighan, Harry	Spr	21	28/11/42	A	Massicault (C)
Hepple, George	Spr	27	26/12/42	C	Medjez-el-Bab (C)
Hillings, Jack	Spr	23	24/11/42	A	Medjez-el-Bab (M)
Huck, Edward	Spr	29	08/02/43	–	Medjez-el-Bab (C)
Elvidge, Jack	Spr	25	24/11/42	A	Medjez-el-Bab (M)
Manning, Norman	T. L/Cpl	29	24/11/42	A	Medjez-el-Bab (M)
Mitchell, John W.	Spr	22	24/11/42	A	Medjez-el-Bab (M)
Mitchell, Victor J.	Spr	23	24/11/42	A	Medjez-el-Bab (M)
Moat, Leslie W.	Spr	25	24/11/42	A	Medjez-el-Bab (M)
Nelson, Lionel D.	Spr	22	27/02/43	A	Medjez-el-Bab (C)
Parfitt, Alfred E.	Spr	28	22/04/43	–	Bone (C)*
Rickleton, John A.	Spr	21	24/11/42	A	Medjez-el-Bab (M)
Ritchie, Duncan H.	Spr	32	27/02/43	A	Medjez-el-Bab (C)
Stanmore, Frank	Spr	22	24/11/42	A	Medjez-el-Bab (M)

Sicily

Name	Rank	Age	Date of Death	Troop	Interred/Memorial
Pratt, Ramsay	L/Cpl	26	14/07/43	C	Catania War Cem.
Brown, Reginald	Spr	–	14/08/43	–	Catania War Cem.

Algeria

Name	Rank	Age	Date of Death	Troop	Interred/Memorial
McManus, Patrick	Cpl	29	28/08/43	–	Le Petit Lac (C)

---

* This entry is unusual as the squadron (only C Troop) were only in Bone during November 1942 and January 1943.

Arnhem, September 1944

Name	Rank	Age	Date of Death	Troop	Interred/Memorial
Robertson, Richard	Lt	–	21/09/44	–	Groesbeek (M)
Sankey, Peter	Lt	21	23/09/44	HQ	Oosterbeek (C)
Hoath, Fred	Sgt	27	20/09/44	C	Oosterbeek (C)
Hazelwood, William	Cpl	25	20/09/44	B	Groesbeek (M)
Simpson, William	Cpl	29	20/09/44	B	Oosterbeek (C)
Adams, William	Spr	24	25/09/44	C	Oosterbeek (C)
Bretherton, John	Spr	27	20/09/44	A	Oosterbeek (C)
Brooks, Thomas	Spr	24	21/09/44	C	Groesbeek (M)
Butterworth, Norman	Spr	27	27/02/45	–	Oosterbeek(C)
Campbell, John	Spr	24	22/09/44	C	Oosterbeek(C)
Gillham, Henry	Spr	28	19/09/44	–	Oosterbeek (C)
Gray, David	Spr	22	19/09/44	B	Groesbeek (M)
Gueran, Sidney	Spr	27	18/09/44	B	Groesbeek (M)
Hemmings, Kenneth	Spr	21	19/09/44	C	Oosterbeek(C)
Hicks, Terry	Spr	24	19/09/44	B	Groesbeek (M)
Hughes, Rowland	Spr	22	02/04/45	C	Groesbeek (M)
Kill, William	Spr	29	28/09/44	B	Oosterbeek (C)
Madden, William	Spr	27	17/09/44	B	Groesbeek (M)
Morrison, Wallace	Drv	20	18/09/44	C	Oosterbeek (C)
Neville, Daniel	L/Cpl	29	20/09/44	B	Groesbeek (M)
Sherwood, Henry	Spr	26	20/09/44	C	Oosterbeek (C)
Taylor, Gilbert	Spr	24	21/09/44	C	Groesbeek (M)
Wake, Allan	Spr	19	22/12/44	C	Oosterbeek (C)

Unknown

Name	Rank	Age	Date of Death	Troop	Interred/Memorial
Birket, William D.*	Lt	24	13/08/44	C	Rome (C)
Wheatley, Alfred A.	L/Cpl	26	23/11/44	–	Hendon, London (C)
Snelling, Harold**	Spr	–	–	–	–

---

* This officer was with Tom in Tunisia but then left the squadron either on a detachment or posting.

** This sapper's name is listed on the squadron re-union remembrance list but his death is not recorded on the War Graves Commission Roll of Honour. Harry Snelling 1919918 flew with B Troop to Sicily in 1943.

Bibliography

Frost, John. *A Drop Too Many*, Pen & Sword, 1992

James, Julian. *A Fierce Quality – The Fighting Life of Alastair Pearson DSO &
Three Bars, MC*, Leo Cooper, 1989

Liddell Hart, Sir Basil. *History of the Second World War*, MacDonald & Co.
(Publishers) Ltd, 1989 edn

Middlebrook, Martin. *Arnhem 1944, The Airborne Battle*, Penguin, 1995

Ministry of Information. *By Air to Battle*, HMSO, 1945

Ronald, D.W. and Carter, R.W. *Longmoor Military Railway*, David & Charles,
1974

Ryan, Cornelius. *A Bridge Too Far*, Hamish Hamilton, 1974

Saunders, Hilary St George. *The Red Beret*, Michael Joseph, 1950

Stainforth, Peter, *Wings of the Wind*, Falcon Press, 1952

Urquhart, RE Major General C.B., DSO. *Arnhem*, Cassel & Co., 1958

Additional Sources
Pegasus Archive
Tom Hicks' POW diary and personal papers

Index